PSYCHOLOGICAL ISSUES IN BIBLICAL LORE

Albert I. Rabin, PhD, is professor emeritus of psychology at Michigan State University. He is founder and former director of the psychological clinic at Michigan State University. Dr. Rabin also served as lecturer at Boston University Graduate School, professor at the City University of New York, visiting professor at the Hebrew and Bar-Ilan universities (Israel) and Fulbright Lecturer at the University of Aarhus (Denmark).

Since retirement, he was a Visiting Scholar at the Hebrew University in Jerusalem, Visiting Professor at the U.S. International University, and Distinguished Professor of psychology at the Wright Institute at Berkeley, California.

Dr. Rabin published more than 150 articles and reviews in different professional and scientific journals, contributed chapters to more than thirty edited books, and authored, coauthored, edited and co-edited seventeen books in the areas of assessment, personality development, and kibbutz child rearing.

Dr. Rabin served on the Board of Consulting Editors of the *Journal of Consulting and Clinical Psychology,* and the *Journal of Personality Assessment* and of the *Israel Annals of Psychiatry and Related Disciplines.* He was the recipient of the *Distinguished Contribution Award* of the Society for Personality Assessment, and the *Distinguished Faculty Award* of Michigan State University.

PSYCHOLOGICAL ISSUES IN BIBLICAL LORE

EXPLORATIONS IN THE OLD TESTAMENT

A. I. RABIN, PhD

Springer Publishing Company

Springer Publishing Company, Inc.
536 Broadway
New York, NY   10012-3955

Cover design: Scala/Art Resource, NY; S000734; K104969; color transparency. Masaccio (1401–1428). Expulsion from Paradise. Post-restoration. Brancacci Chapel, S. Mariadel Carmine, Florence, Italy.

Acquisitions Editor: Ursula Springer
Production Editor: T. Orrantia

98 99 00 01 02 / 5 4 3 2 1

Library of Congress Cataloging-in-Publication Data

Rabin, Albert I.
    Psychological Issues in Biblical Lore : explorations in the Old
Testament / Albert I. Rabin.
        p.   cm.
    Includes bibliographical references and index.
    ISBN 0-8261-1212-9 (hardcover)
    1. Judaism—Psychological aspects.   2. Judaism and psychology.
I. Title. II. Series.
BF51.R33 1998
221.6'01'9—dc21   98-17874
                                                                        CIP

Contents

Preface   *vii*

1 The Bible and Psychology   1

2 The Life Course: Childhood to Senescence   10

3 Sexuality   45

4 Aspects of the Biblical Family   77

5 Building the Family   97

6 Male and Female   112

7 Special States of Consciousness   144

8 Biblical Psychological Themes   193

References   *203*

Appendix A   *207*

Appendix B   *209*

Appendix C   *211*

Index   *213*

Preface

Several years ago I set myself the task of exploring psychological themes in the Hebrew Bible, I consider this ancient anthology of literary, ethnographic, historical, and religious work to have had a significant influence upon Western society that spawned the discipline of psychology. The focus of the textual examination is on the *Hebrew* Bible, also known as the Old Testament or the "Original Bible."

In his introduction to the book *Understanding Genesis* (1966), N. M. Sarna points out that the collection of books representing the Hebrew Bible is but a small portion of the texts that survived after many years and were canonized about 2,000 years ago. He further states that "... this relatively tiny collection of Israel's literature, known as the Hebrew Bible, ultimately succeeded in capturing the hearts, minds and loyalties of so many diverse people, totally removed racially, geographically, and culturally from its Israelite source" (p. xix). It is this influence of the ancient texts upon our society which became concerned with the issues of psychology that is, broadly speaking, the subject matter of this work. The present effort is in a tradition of biblical study that was originated in the 17th century by Benedict Spinoza, who viewed biblical studies as a scientific enterprise involving a methodology based on rationalism and critical textual examination.

The Hebrew Bible, despite its being "a small portion" of the texts that might have been included, is in actuality a vast literary collection, authored and edited over a period of many centuries. It consists of some 39 "books," ranging in length from a single chapter of 21 verses of the Book of Obadiah to the 150 chapters and 2,257 verses of the Book of Psalms. My reading of the texts started with the Hebrew version of the Bible. Then it moved to the several English translations, starting with the time-honored King James Translation followed by several modern renditions such as the Oxford edition, the Jerusalem Bible, and the Tanakh (Torah, Neviim, and Kethuvim). A list of the texts most often consulted appears in Appendix A.

Invariably, in my readings, the Hebrew text was my final authority. I attempted to stick to the literal Hebrew meaning as closely as possible (Alcalay, 1965). In that respect I am in agreement with the procedure recently demonstrated in the translation of the book of *The Five Books of Moses* (E. Fox, 1995).

Many modern writers on the Bible have dispensed with the use of such terms as Jehovah, or Yahweh, for the name of the Hebrew deity. The name used in the present text is that of *YHWH,* which conforms most closely to the original Hebrew (based on the verb "Hayo," "to be").

A number of different methods of referral to textual materials have been adopted over the years. Following quotations that are literal rendering of biblical text, the abbreviated version of the relevant book title appears in parentheses. The abbreviation is marked by a dot, followed by the chapter number, marked by a comma, then followed by the verse number(s). Occasionally there will not be close correspondence between my numbering, which is based on the Hebrew text, and some of the translations that use a somewhat different system in the division of chapters and verses. However, these are only slight textual variations. An example of the notations used for biblical references follows. If the quotation is from the Book of Genesis, chapter 7, verses 6 to 15, the reference in our book will appear as: (Gen. 7.6–15). A list of the 39 books and the corresponding abbreviations appears in Appendix B.

The ancient works of the Bible and the extensive literature of modern psychology represent vast areas of intellectual achievement. Psychology as a discipline concerns a large array of issues and topics, many of them not dreamed of by scriptural writers and redactors. My task, therefore, was to select, according to personal predilection, a limited number of psychological issues, factors, and variables which are dealt with in the Bible. My concern is not with the historical sequence of the literary productions, for I am attempting to deal with some of the psychological themes of the total Bible that were passed on over the many years since its canonization, and with the modern attempts to address those perennial problems and issues. It is a sort of circular enterprise: how the theistic ancient world has defined its culture, and how the developments of this culture interpret the phenomena that were, at least in part, its progenitors.

A. I. Rabin

CHAPTER 1

The Bible and Psychology

THE BIBLICAL ANTHOLOGY

Over the centuries, the Bible has been "all things to all people," for everybody found in it what they were looking for, and sometimes the unexpected as well. The 39 books that constitute the canonized Hebrew Bible differ in size and in the extent that they contribute material of relevance to psychology. Most useful in this respect is the Torah (the five books of Moses), or the Pentateuch, as it is known in the vernacular. It consists of five major books: Genesis, Exodus, Leviticus, Numbers, and Deuteronomy.

Much narrative concerning human behavior and relationships fills the pages of the Pentateuch. However, the remaining books vary greatly in this respect. For example, there is very little that is relevant to the theme of biblical psychology in the work of the twelve "minor prophets" (Hosea, Joel, Amos, etc.), while the works that are classified under the rubric of "major prophets," Joshua, Judges, Kings, Samuel, Isaiah, Jeremiah, and Ezekiel contain much rich material that can be drawn for our purposes. The last category of the works in the Hebrew Bible, that of "Kethuvim" (writings) represents a miscellany varying in the degree to which it offers descriptions and contains issues that are akin to modern psychology. There are the so-called "wisdom books" (such as Proverbs, Koheleth-Ecclesiastes), the poetry of the Psalms and the Song of Songs, the stories of Ruth,

Esther, and Daniel, and other works which are quite intriguing and contain much material that is pertinent in our context.

In this extensive anthology of the books of the Hebrew Bible (Hebrew with the exception of the books of Ezra and Daniel, which are partly written in Aramaic), a very large variety of themes may be discerned. First, and foremost, it is a moral code of the ancient Israelites. It concerns the principles of monotheism and the rules which govern interpersonal relationships as the foundation of the social life and as the conditions under which the family, tribe, and national entity may thrive and develop. These "rules" are mainly enunciated in the book of Deuteronomy but also in the other books of the Pentateuch (the "five books of Moses"). The decalogue, or the "Ten Commandments," may be seen as the centerpiece of the ancient code of behavior.

Second, the Bible represents a sort of "ethnography" and descriptive cultural anthropology of a small Semitic people chiefly during the two millennia prior to the Common Era (B.C.E.). The lives and struggles of persons, families, tribes, and nations is narrated and depicted in considerable detail in the totality of the 39 books of the Hebrew Bible.

Third, we find a vast array of literary works, of prose and poetry, that served as models for creative writing over the centuries. The "Song of Deborah" (in the book of Judges) celebrating a military victory; the book of *Psalms,* expressing the joy and anguish of tortured human souls; the *Song of Songs,* with its celebration of love and eroticism; and so on and so on, are prime examples of the great achievement of the human spirit, its imagination and creativity. The poetical prose of many of the prophets, minor and major, further enhances the greatness of the overall literary contribution.

Fourth, the Bible is a *historical* document, or rather, a collection of many such documents garnered over many centuries and edited and canonized for the most part at the end of the pre-Christian period. Of course, not all the books are clearly historical, just as they are not poetical or ethnographic or mythological, as are many of the narratives in the book of Genesis and others, under the influence of the prevalent traditions in the ancient Middle East more than three thousand years ago. There are the purely literary works, mentioned earlier, that are largely works of the creative imagination, such as the Song of Songs, the book of Job, and others. But the vast majority of the work is historical, although many critics, in the absence of much archeological support, have questioned the historical basis of the Bible. According to some authors, the critics have adopted a "minimalist" approach to the Bible (Halpern, 1955; Shanks, 1997). Yet historical it is to a considerable extent. As Shanks says; "Some parts of the Bible are historically more reliable than others," but he admits that the "historicity of the Bible has taken some severe hits" (p. 34). Most of the books of the Prophets, Kings, and Chronicles are definitely historical, presenting events of internal and external strife and conflict of the Israelite nation over more than a millennium prior to the common era.

In his review of "Three Thousand Years of Biblical Study," Speiser (1960) avers that "for all this great spread of time and the number of writers involved, the Bible shows a consistent underlying unity that stems from a single central theme ... a history of a society embarked on a specific quest, the quest for a way of life. A way possessing universal validity. Everything else is subordinated to that main theme" (p. 202).

Speiser perceives a unity in the great diversity of the 39 books of the biblical anthology: the historical, literary, ethnographic and ethical. It was achieved most likely in the process of redaction of the various texts, whose final canonization took place early in the Christian era (Bratton, 1967; Golb, 1995). Yet according to the documentary hypothesis of the Bible the diversity is retained by tracing four major textual traditions. This hypothesis regarding the authorship of the Bible is based largely on the linguistic and stylistic analyses of the texts, and especially of the terms applied to the deity. According to this hypothesis, four major patterns were discerned by biblical scholars. First, is the J. documents in which the name of God is given as YHWH, though the letter *J* refers to the Yahwistic tradition (or Jehovah). The *E* refers to God as Elohim, while *P* refers to the priestly tradition of authorship and *D* to the kind of material found mainly in the book of Deuteronomy. These subdivisions, as mentioned above, are mainly based on linguistic and historical analysis of the textual material.

However, the so-called "documentary hypothesis" does not remain unchallenged. In his well-reasoned monograph, Kassuto

(1983) presents some persuasive arguments that lead him to conclude that the documentary hypothesis is "null and void." For our purposes it is not essential to subscribe to the views of either one of the adversaries in this debate. Ours, as stated, is not a historical approach to the Bible. I am concerned with it as a compendium of literary works that have been passed on to Western society some 2 millennia ago as a religious testament and as a guide for all generations. And as such, it is regarded here as one piece which trumps, or bypasses, the temporal dimension. Thus, for example, for our purposes it is irrelevant whether the narrative of Genesis preceded those in the book of Joshua, etc. or whether a particular episode was the work of J, E, P, or D.

In his work *Actual Minds, Possible Worlds* (1986), Jerome Bruner tells us that "Nicholas of Lyra proposed many centuries ago ... that biblical texts are amenable to four levels of interpretation: *Litera, moralis, allegoria,* and *anagoria,* the literal, the ethical, the historical and the mystical. Literary and general linguists have insisted that no story, no text can be understood at a single level" (p. 5). The attempt to be made in the present work has little concern with the historical or mystical levels of interpretation of biblical texts; I am concerned for the most part with the literal and the ethical aspects of the biblical writings and their relevance to issues defined as modern psychology.

Of course psychology as such is a relatively recent invention, and cannot be directly considered as a part of the biblical opus. But my focus is upon episodes of behavior and upon the description of different states of awareness and action that reflect psychological issues and principles; essentially, how the "literal" interpretation fits into modern psychological theory and, possibly, how psychology's concerns in turn have been influenced by those biblical parameters that define Western civilization and culture. I am not concerned with the exegetic approach of the religious interpreters, nor with the symbolism and metaphors that are of such interest to those writers interested in the examination of the scriptures as literary works—the prose and poetry, the texture of the sundry narratives and the rhetoric of prophetic oration. The "Book of J." (Bloom & Rosenberg, 1990) and Alter's *The World of Biblical Literature* come to mind (1992). Our effort concentrates on the literal narratives of the textual material and the examination of the ethnographic descriptions, presented especially in the Pentateuch, but in many of the "historical" texts as well, of a developing and struggling Israelite nation moving toward its evolving destiny. Perhaps, it is true, as Bloom avers in the "Book of J" that the Bible is essentially a literary work that became a religious text over the years. My concern is chiefly with those accounts of human behavior and interaction that demonstrate psychological principles seen from the vantage point of a modern systematic discipline. Hence, for example, the interaction between siblings as described in the Cain and Abel or the Esau and Jacob stories are grist for the analytic observations informed by modern psychology. A less direct interpretation of the differences between the genders, as reflected in their differential status and behavior within the ancient society, is another example of psychological material relevant to present-day psychology.

Some additional specific evidence of the influence of the "original" Bible upon everyday Western, and more specifically, American culture may be obtained in the various terms and expressions found in American and English literature as well as in ordinary social interaction. For example, such expressions as "Am I my brother's keeper?", the "Tower of Babel," the "golden calf," "a land flowing with milk and honey," and "the ten commandments" are some of the standard biblical references that are a part of our written as well as oral communication traditions and that directly involve Hebrew Bible textual material. Some of these expressions are listed by Hirsch (1987) under the rubric of "cultural literacy," the list of words and terms that he uses to define "literacy" in the American culture. Some of Hirsch's items, as well as others of equal popularity, but probably not viewed by him as essential, appear in Appendix B of this volume. According to him, his list contains "what every American needs to know" and, in part, it also reflects the importance of the Bible's penetration in the language and thought patterns of American society and civilization.

Nearly a century earlier, Ralph Waldo Emerson, as quoted by Sivan in his book on *The Bible and Civilization* (1973), commented that "Our Jewish Bible has implanted itself in the table talk and household life of every man and woman in the European and American nations" (p. 193). Sivan also details the impact of the Scriptures on various other aspects of civilization, such as law, politics, and the arts. The present work is an attempt to extend the list of recipients of this influence to psychology as well. As is the case generally, the input of the scriptures is acknowledged, but our effort is to be marked by greater detail and specificity.

PSYCHOLOGY'S BRIEF HISTORY

In the preface to the first edition (1929) of his classic *History of Experimental Psychology,* E. G. Boring quotes Ebinghaus' famous phrase regarding the science of psychology: "Psychology has a long past, but only a short history" (p. vii). The past of psychology is coincident to and can be traced to the ancient documents recording human existence. The records present accounts of emotion and thought, behavior and perception, and imagination and creativity, as well as the interpersonal and group and family relations of human beings in their communities. One such document (or collection of documents) with a long trajectory, extending into modern life, is the Hebrew Bible.

More than a century ago, the father of American psychology wrestled with the problem of defining his subject matter. In his epoch-making *The Principles of Psychology* (1890/1950), William James defined psychology as "… the science of mental life, both of its phenomena and conditions. The phenomena are such things as we call feelings, desires, cognitions, reasonings, decisions, and the like; and superficially considered, their variety and complexity is such as to leave a chaotic impression on the observer" (Vol. 1, p. 1). In most of his work, James attempts to conceptualize and reduce the "chaotic impression" by discussing such abstractions as faculties and especially the "condition" under which they operate.

The range of psychology's concerns has not diminished during the past century. If anything, the number of topics and interests embraced by psychology has expanded remarkably. Witness the valiant attempts of elementary psychology textbook authors to define that subject matter. Certainly the field is no less chaotic than in the times of William James. As a young student of psychology some decades ago, I often heard the "impertinent" question: "What is psychology?" to which the operational but facetious response would be "What psychologists study!" It is justifiably argued that psychology is not a unitary discipline in the traditional academic sense, but a *field of study* consisting of a wide array of subdisciplines or subareas that are loosely related. The "chaotic impression" is not "superficial," as James would have it, but remains central to the enterprise of psychology.

Some years ago, Bruner (1979) lamented and pointed in the same direction: "The disturbing symptom of our discipline has been its steady loss of conceptual unity. It increasingly consists of a collection of topics-cum-procedures, between which it is even more difficult to discern workable conceptual connections" (p. 170). He further bemoans psychology's abandonment of mentalistic and teleological issues on the altar of objectivisms and positivism (Bruner, 1990).

Essentially, what we find is an involvement with a wide range of phenomena: human thought and behavior subjected to scientific study and method, the product of 19th-century rationalism. The concern with the phenomena—"feelings, desires, cognitions" and so on—dates back to the earliest writings of our civilization. However, the "conditions," to use James' phrase, under which such phenomena are controlled and modified, or the scientific approach to psychology, is of much recent origin; the *past* of psychology is long, but the *history* is relatively short. The Bible represents, in part, the *past* of psychology—status and states of persons and their interactions presented in narrative and various literary forms whose impact served to determine the parameters of society's concerns. These, in turn, became the focus of the scientific endeavor that began to create the "short" history of what came to be known as scientific psychology, or the discipline of psychology.

In his *Actual Minds, Possible Worlds* (1986) Bruner points out that "We all know by now that many scientific and mathematical hypotheses start their lives as little stories or metaphors, but they reach their scientific maturity by a process of conversion into verifiability, formal or empirical, and this power of maturity does not rest upon their dramatic origins. Hypothesis' creation ... remains a tantalizing mystery" (p. 12). It is this relationship between "little stories and metaphors" and the scientific endeavor, between biblical past and psychology's brief history, that is the major thrust of our undertaking.

Fundamentally, I join Bakan (1966) who states that "I shall attempt to read the Bible as a 'psychological document' in which important problems of ultimate concern are reflected" (p. 201). At the level of psychological analyses we observe the frequent conflict between the real and ideal, between prescribed and proscribed behavior, between ethical principles and actual life as it is lived. And herein lies the greatness of the biblical texts. They present narratives and descriptions of the vicissitudes of human existence, unvarnished and without beautification of life as it is. In Bloom's phrasing (Bloom & Rosenberg, 1990), "the Bible is not primarily a religious document," but a human document concerned with everyday behavior and thought and interaction among human beings and the possible trajectories of such processes into the future.

The sheer quantity of material in the 39 books or texts makes selection of themes an inevitable strategy. Only a small portion of the biblical psychological documentation is being addressed in the pages that follow. The several chapters that follow this introductory statement take a developmental and ethnopsychological approach in the discussion and interpretation of the material, including its relevance to our present-day society, culture, and modern (also "postmodern") civilization.

THE CHAPTERS THAT FOLLOW

Chapter 2 is an examination of the *life course* as experienced and viewed by the ancient Israelites. Next is a series of issues concerned with *sex and sexuality,* laws and behavior, comparing ancient Mosaic and Judaic law with current cultural mores, especially those in American society at the close of the 20th century (chapter 3). The next chapter (4) deals with the aspects of structure and dynamics of the interrelationships within the *biblical family.* A relatively novel set of concerns with the need and motivation for bearing and having children as the beginning process in *building the family* is the focus of the next brief chapter (5). Our next concern is the issue of *gender* and gender differences reflected in the ancient era and in the light of some current psychological research and sociopolitical experience in the so-called postmodern society (chapter 6). Chapter 7 is a fairly extensive treatment of what I call *"special states."* A number of unusual emotional and cognitive experiences are the center of attention in this chapter. Chapter 8 provides a *summary and concluding remarks* and comments regarding the entire excursion of psychology into an ancient culture.

CHAPTER 2

The Life Course: Childhood to Senescence

STAGES OF DEVELOPMENT

In modern times in particular, but to some extent in ancient times as well, the life span has been subdivided into different periods or stages of development. In modern parlance, we speak of infancy, toddlerhood, the preschool period, and of school age and preadolescence, followed by adolescence, young adulthood, adulthood, middle age, old age, and senescence. Even the last stage is being further subdivided into "young-old age," "old age," and "old-old age." This penchant for greater and more detailed differentiation and discrimination has marked the scientific era in general and psychology in particular.

Different developmental and stage schedules have been explored extensively by a variety of theorists and investigators of mental life. Some have been concerned with the fundamental effects of early childhood and infantile experience upon later development of the adult personality. They have concentrated upon the early period of life in great detail, while cavalierly conceding that there are other, later periods that are also important in a person's life. From the viewpoint of psychoanalytic theory, for example, by the time the child is 3 years old, several distinct stages of development have been passed (oral, anal, etc.) in the normal course of development. Later, the so-called genital stage kicks in, according to Freud, and the human being is left with the struggle of integrating these earlier phases of development that stem from the libidocentric theory of psychoanalysis. Disciple Erik Erikson (1950/1963) extended the Freudian theorizing, *cum* a combination with cultural and social factors, well into adulthood and old age. Erikson went beyond the period of childhood and the Freudian, primarily psychobiological stages into a consideration of young adulthood (intimacy vs. self-absorption); later adulthood (generativity vs. stagnation); and old age, in which the polarities were described as "ego integrity vs. despair" (p. 268).

A more recent effort at distinguishing stages of adulthood in contemporary American society is represented by the work of Levinson set forth in *The Seasons of a Man's Life* (1978). This work subdivides the period encompassed by the adult years into three main "seasons"—early, middle, and late adult eras. The basis for this particular classification is not so much the personality characteristics of the adult as is the "person's relationships with various aspects of the external world." The criterion for the classification in this instance is the social-psychological rather than the primarily biological and psychological factors.

These examples of different categorizations and divisions of a person's life are informed by the varying theoretical stances assumed by their originators. Thus, Freud concentrates on the effects of the biological-libidinal development on the organism's attempt to navigate in its life space, while others are more cognizant of interaction with the environment, society and culture, and their normative demands and expectations of the individual.

The efforts of analysis and differentiation in the life course are not entirely new in the history of humanity. Many reflective individuals, saints and scholars, philosophers and scientists, have observed the various twists and turns in the life course. This trend, however, became especially salient at the end of the 19th and throughout the present century, with the advent of systematic psychology and its various ramifications.

Although the biblical literature does not demonstrate a specific concern with "stages," "eras," or "seasons" in the course of a person's life, nevertheless, one may discern some implicit division and categorization. Basically, three broad categories which even present-day "common sense" dictates, are distinguished in the biblical narratives; these are the periods of *childhood, adulthood,* and *old age.* A precise delineation in terms of age (number of years) is no more discernible in the Bible than in our common, everyday language. But then, modern scientific procedures of mensuration and number in human thought and behavior have not been embarked upon until the last two centuries. Even now, the number of years that define or demarcate certain periods, stages, or seasons in a person's life are approximate and imprecise, and the various subdivisions shade into one another.

THE EARLY YEARS: CHILDHOOD

Most of the writings of the Bible give accounts of active men and women in the second category—that of adulthood. Childhood and old age are much less frequently mentioned, and receive much more limited treatment in the text. The scarcity of mention and concern with childhood is not only characteristic of ancient times, of the period covered by the Bible, more than two millennia ago. Childhood was actually "discovered" only recently, as reflected in the art and writings of the Western world.

In his book on *Centuries of Childhood* (1962), the cultural historian Aries does not have much to say about the treatment of childhood even through the Middle Ages and the Renaissance. There was nothing that distinguished children from adults in graphic and artistic portrayals, except for size. Children have been viewed as miniature adults; the depiction of children *as* children in paintings and portraiture does not seem to have evolved until the 17th century. As a distinct phase of life, then childhood was not recognized until the last 2 centuries, or so. It also seems that until the close of the Middle Ages the child was not much differentiated from adult society once it was weaned. The situation did not differ, in this respect, in the earlier millennia of recorded human history.

In the biblical writings, no special attention to childhood as a particular stage of development is readily noted. There was no clear definition of the period of childhood at the time of the ancient Hebrews discussed in the Bible, any more than in the centuries of the Christian era discussed by Aries. Children, when they are mentioned, are considered primarily as objects, not as actors; as beings in need of protection and nurturance, but not so much as behaving and thinking organisms. Once the infant was weaned, it appears that the community at large took over.

Although the biblical literature does not propose a stage theory of child development, some clear landmarks are to be discerned. It seems that weaning was such a landmark. In the account of Isaac, the long-awaited son of Abraham and Sarah, we are told that "the child grew and was weaned; and Abraham made a great feast the same day that Isaac was weaned" (Gen. 21.8). Of course, weaning meant that the child no longer was dependent on his mother's or nurse's milk; it also seemed to be an indication of reaching a certain level of greater maturity and autonomy. It must have been an indication that the child would survive at a time when infant mortality must have been very high. This view may be further reinforced in the story of Hannah, who had been childless and prayed for a son. In her prayer she made a solemn promise to the high priest Eli, that if she were to bear a son she will dedicate him to the work of the Lord by making him a "Nazarite." God remembered Hannah and she gave birth to a son, whom she and her husband Elkanah gratefully welcomed. Then, "Elkanah, with his entire household went up to make the annual sacrifice to the Lord ... Hannah did not go with them for she said to her husband—'When the child is weaned I will come up with him and we'll be before the Lord, and then he will stay there forever.' Elkanah said, 'Do as you see fit, stay until he is weaned. Only may the Lord see your vow fulfilled'." (1 Sam. 1.21–23). Subsequently, Hannah did bring young Samuel to the priest Eli, where he served and, later, became one of the prophets who exerted great influence in the establishment of the Israelite monarchy.

Again, weaning was an important landmark and stage of development attesting to a point of relinquishment of the early dependent state and a capacity for physical and psychological survival in the adult world. As is the case of adulthood and senescence, no specific age at which weaning took place is reported.

The frequent reference to children, mostly infants, was in the terms *taff* or *olalim;* neither word is indicative of the gender of the children; they are generic terms, and sex or gender are indeterminate. Age was also indeterminate; the primary implication was that they were not quite complete persons and in need of care and protection. In the King James version of the Old Testament, the Hebrew word *taff* is variously translated as "children" or "little ones." Thus, when members of the tribe of Reuben were commanded to wage war on the Canaanites, they were told that "Your wives, little ones, and your cattle shall remain ... on this side of the Jordan" (Jos. 1.14). All noncombatants, women and children, were to be left in relative security, behind the battle lines. Similarly, in an earlier passage, "Our little ones, our wives, our flocks and all our cattle shall be there in cities of Gilead" (Nu 32.26). Again, "the little ones" was a fairly broad class of young persons of an indeterminate age, who were not yet ready to join the ranks of the adults in battle against their enemies, in the conquest of the promised land. In these, and numerous other passages, the collective noun *taff* stood for immature children of both sexes and of varying ages.

In the Hebrew language, nouns are either masculine or feminine. The term for the male child is *yeled* and for the female *yalda*. The use of these terms in biblical literature is similar to their use in English—boy, girl—for they do not denote a specific age range and are frequently extended in use from infancy to maturity. For example, "Schechem said to his father: ... get me this girl (*yalda*) for a wife" (Gen. 34.4). Here the word for a female child is employed, although the reference here is to a nubile young woman. Or, let's take another example of a male child. "Reuben said: did I not tell you not to do the boy (*yeled*) wrong: But, you would not listen and his blood is on our hands" (Gen. 42.22). In this context, Joseph is called "boy," when his brothers sell him into slavery; but he actually was a young man, if we consider the context of the story. The words for male or female children were employed rather loosely, much as they are today in everyday language. The terms "boy" or "girl" were applied to persons of a wide range in age, as in English, from infancy to adulthood, and sometimes, even beyond.

LAD-LASS ADOLESCENTS

In addition to the word *yeled,* the Hebrew word *naar* also covers a fairly wide age range (*Naara,* for girl). Absalom, the son of King David, was killed following the unsuccessful rebellious uprising against his father. The king, who had not yet received the news about the death, addresses the following question to the Cushite messenger: "Is the young lad, Absalom safe?" (1 Sam. 18.32). Here the word lad (*naar*) was used in part because of David's affection for his son, although Absalom was old enough to mount an insurrection and threaten his father's kingdom. On the other hand, when Manoah and his wife were expecting the birth of a son, he begged: "Oh my Lord, let the man of God you sent come here again and teach us what we shall do to the child to be born" (Jud. 13.8). In this context, the word for "child" is actually the same as for boy or young man (*naar*) and the same word that David used in inquiring about the welfare of his traitorous adult son, Absalom.

Since the Bible is not a scientific document, but a mythical and historical narrative, the employment of such terms as infant, baby, child, lad, boy, young man, is not precise as to age. The same is true with the parallel terms for women (girl, virgin, young woman, etc.). This is similar to common usage in everyday speech and fictional narratives. Moreover, the word "child" was, and is, used in the sense of "*offspring*" as well as in the sense of young immature persons, much as we speak of "adult children."

It may be concluded, therefore, that there is little semantic precision with respect to the possible stages of childhood to which our current psychologically minded century is very sensitive. But, then, as was previously noted the Bible does not register much concern with children as actors; they are viewed primarily as objects as being acted upon. The commandment "Honor thy father and mother" applies to children of all ages; it is not addressed to young children only, but stresses the expected behavior of children. Children are to be taught the principles and practices of the religious doctrine, but again, no age specification is spelled out. Once a child was weaned and was no longer dependent on mother or nurse for survival, he or she joined the rest of the community. They remained part of the mass that needed protection, especially in times of war—the "women, children, cattle, and flocks." Once the male children reached the middle teens, they joined the ranks of farm workers, herders and warriors, or protectors of the women, children, and the domestic animals of the extended family. Although, again, ages are not specified, young women, upon reaching puberty, were considered nubile, married early, raised a family, and became engulfed by a multitude of household duties and some agricultural pursuits, in addition to taking care of the children.

LITTLE FOCUS ON CHILDREN: THEIR VICISSITUDES AND PARENTAL AUTHORITY

The behavior of individual men and their characteristics is the subject of many biblical narratives. Similarly, some women are described in considerable detail. But the behavior of individual children and their characteristics is rarely the focus of biblical works. To be sure, some children do appear in the biblical limelight, but not as initiators of action, but as passive, obedient, and submissive victims of circumstances and of adult discipline or ministration. For example, young Isaac is nearly sacrificed by his father Abraham (Gen. 22). Ishmael nearly succumbs to hunger and the desert heat after he and his mother Hagar are evicted from the patriarchal household by mistress Sarah (Gen. 16). Infant Moses, placed in a box on the river after the Pharaonic command that all Hebrew male newborns be eliminated, barely escapes with his life when accidentally spotted and rescued by the Egyptian princess (Ex. 2).

Children were under the absolute control of their parents, especially the father, the undisputed head of the household. In a sense, the father represented the deity, since he was instructed in the rules and laws that defined the religion. The ancient religious practice of sacrificing children, especially the firstborn male children, was not unknown in the biblical period. Sacrificing children to the "Moloch" was occasionally practiced. Israelite monotheism denounced the practice of child sacrifice, but occasional deviations from that prohibition are recorded in the Bible. Certainly, some of the neighboring tribes not subject to the God of the Hebrews continued the practice well into the millennium prior to the common era. Mesha, the king of the Moabites, mounted an unsuccessful rebellion and upon his defeat, "He took his firstborn son, who was to succeed him to the throne, and offered him up on the wall as a burnt offering" (2 Kings 3.26–27).

A similar sacrifice was reported in the case of the Judean king Ahaz who "... did not do what was right in the sight of YHWH as his ancestor David has done. ... He even consigned his son to the fire, in the abhorrent fashion of the nations which the Lord dispossessed before the Israelites" (2 Kings 16.2–3).

These episodes recorded in the Bible are interesting examples of deviations in the ordinary behavior of the Israelites, especially in the case of king Ahaz. It probably represented a sliding back, a regression, away from monotheism to the religious practices which still obtained in the surrounding cultures. The religious injunction of the Mosaic faith involves compensatory acts in lieu of giving the firstborn to God. Compensation, or more precisely "redemption," was (and is) a procedure whereby some monetary payments are made to the priests, this releases the father of the child from the obligation to dedicate him to God. Thus, we find in the book of Exodus, the following: "And you must redeem every firstborn male among your children" (13.3). Interestingly enough, in a later section of the book of Exodus, the Lord admonishes: "And you shall give me the firstborn among your sons" (22.29). These are no longer references to the act of sacrifice, but to the dedication of the eldest son to the service in the temple of Yahweh. The story of the prophet Samuel is a case in point. The story of Abraham, on the verge of sacrificing Isaac, is illustrative of a transitional period in the history and development of Israelite monotheism.

In this connection, it is appropriate to consider a related issue concerning the relationship of children to their parents. Following is a quotation from the book of Leviticus which can be interpreted as a modification of the Fifth Commandment, "Honor your father and your mother." This quotation is from the King James version of the Bible which is closest in meaning to the Hebrew Bible: "Ye shall fear, every man, his mother and his father, and keep my Sabbaths; I am the Lord your God" (Lev. 19.3). Other translations of the text seem to soften the injunction by using the words "revere" or "respect," but the precise translation is actually "fear." Perhaps the latter word was more suggestive of the great authority over life and death that was held by the father of yore.

This near-digression demonstrated the absolute power, control, and undisputed ownership of children by their fathers. But, then, wives were in a similar position to that of their children in this radically patriarchal society—a matter to be dealt with chapter 4.

A broader historical review of the care of children through the ages may also be of interest in the present context. In the opening paragraph of the chapter on the evolution of childhood, DeMausse, author of the *Foundations of Psychohistory* (1982) paints a grim picture: "The history of childhood is a nightmare from which we have not really begun to awaken. The further back in history one goes, the lower the level of child care, and the more likely children are to be killed, abandoned, beaten, terrorized, and sexually abused" (p. 1). In antiquity, including the period covered by the Old Testament, child sacrifice was quite common. The description of Abraham preparing to sacrifice his son Isaac upon the Lord's command was apparently a throwback to the time when child sacrifice was common practice. Also, the Egyptian Pharaoh's decree to throw the Hebrew male children into the river, is another instance of an ancient attempt at "ethnic cleansing" in which newborn children were the innocent victims. We are told that it was not until 374 CE that killing of an infant became classified as murder (DeMausse, 1982). Thus, when we view the ubiquity of unpunishable infanticide as an index of attitudes towards a young child, we can understand that there was little concern about the thoughts, feelings and of course, the lives of young children. Hence, the era covered by the Hebrew Bible, the two millennia prior to the advent of Christianity, reflects the paucity of material and interest in the earliest stages of human development.

With the exception of their recognized state of dependency, behavior and thought of young children was of little concern. The recognition of the qualitative and quantitative difference between childhood and adulthood, and childhood as a developmental state, did not become part of society's concerns until many centuries after the biblical opus had been canonized, sealed, and delivered.

ADOLESCENCE

A rather recent concept in the area of developmental psychology and in the social sciences, in general, is that of adolescence, designated as the transitional period of life between childhood and adulthood. It is that span of years—14 to 25 for males, and 12 to 21 for females—that separates the earliest era of dependency from the point of recognition and acceptance of full membership in the adult society. There is no evidence that such a distinct period or stage in a person's development was recognized in biblical times, nor for many subsequent centuries in the history of humanity. This transitional period between childhood and adulthood, as it is defined at present, was not considered in those times. Somehow, the child turned into an adult when his biological and physiological maturation and his life skills qualified him for the adult role defined by the society. In this context, I am using the masculine "him" because the foregoing was true for the male of the species.

Certain markers of achievement of adult status were present in the Israelite societal tradition. For example, it was not until the age of 20 that men qualified for membership in the armed units of the tribe and the nation (Nu. 1.3); a higher age qualification applied to members of the tribe of Levi, who were designated to serve in the sanctuary.

Similar age markers are unavailable for women in the biblical literature. Apparently, the female's passing into adulthood corresponded with the level of maturity, physical and sexual, that made her nubile, i.e., ready and ripe for marriage. As we well know, that age could have ordinarily been from 13 years and upward, if not earlier. The main qualification for the female to enter into adulthood was the capacity to bear children. One may speculate that the lack of clarity of criteria for readiness for marriage may have been the reason for the frequent mention of the state of "barrenness" in the Bible. It may well have been that many young brides were not sufficiently developed and physically mature to have born children early in the marriage. Of course, as I will discuss in a different context, the idea of infertility of men, of husbands, as a cause for not having children was not entertained in biblical times. The fact is that many of these very young women, who would have been classified as barely adolescents in the present era, did get pregnant and bore children after some years of married life. But, of course, supernatural explanations, rather than the achievement of greater sexual maturity, were given for the change in their fertility status. Thus, in biblical terms, "YHWH had closed the womb," which was then opened upon appeal and petition.

It is not surprising that our information in this area is so meager. It was not until the beginning of the 20th century that G. Stanley Hall introduced "adolescence" as a separate stage of human development. However, the word "adolescence" first appeared in the 15th century, indicating that historically, adolescence was subordinated to theoretical considerations of human development (Muuss, 1988).

The inevitable conclusion is that the Bible has little to offer us regarding this stage of human development. As noted earlier, adolescence is primarily a concept of 20th-century developmental psychology.

The references made earlier to the terms *yeled-yalda* (male-female, boy-child, and girl-child) and to *naar-naara* (male youth and female youth), are indications that a rough distinction was made between these periods of pre-adulthood. However, very little delineation of psychological differences between these two periods is presented or even hinted at in the biblical text. It is possible that the distinction was actually elaborated in the usage of the language in post-biblical times. It maybe that later development of the language refined the semantics and meanings of these terms.

BRINGING UP THE YOUNGER GENERATION

Acquisition of wisdom was the foremost goal of parents for their offspring. Wisdom was precious, and was to be obtained from learning at the feet of the older generation. Respect for the older generation, learning from them, and the perpetuation of their code and principles of good behavior was the foremost goal and objective for the growing children. The reference seems to be mainly to the male children, for the upbringing of the female children is hardly considered in the text.

"Honor your father and mother" is one of the commandments that sets the tone of the relationship between the generations. The Fifth Commandment does not especially stress an affectionate relationship, but instead conveys an attitude of deference, respect, and submissiveness to the absolute parental authority.

In the book of Proverbs, which is attributed to the wise king Solomon who followed King David on the throne of ancient Israel, many chapters begin with the words "My son," follow such-and-such a path, and observe such-and-such rules in relation to God and men. Among the numerous admonitions that make up the book of Proverbs, there are statements and bits of advice regarding the guidance and discipline of the younger generation. A few brief selections from that book follow.

Chasten your son while there is hope, and do not be concerned for his moaning (19.18).

Train a child in the way he should go, and when he is old he will not depart from it (22.6).

Do not withhold correction from the lad, for if you beat him with a rod, he shall not die. (23.13)

Foolishness is bound in the heart of the child, but the rod of correction will drive it from him. (22.5)

The rod and reproof give wisdom, but a child left to himself brings his mother shame. (29.15)

Correct your son and he shall give you rest and shall be a delight to your soul. (29.17)

These are but a few of the aphorisms about childrearing and discipline of children that we find in the book of Proverbs. We can now attempt to glean several principles which underlie this proffered guidance of the new generation. Some of them are clearly at odds with the notions developed in modern psychology.

First, we note the stress on punishment—physical punishment, what Skinnerian behaviorists would call "negative reinforcement" (Skinner, 1938).

Second is the idea that punishment effectively establishes a pattern of desirable behavior which lasts into adulthood and brings gratification and satisfaction to the parents of the offspring.

Third, the absence of discipline and the failure to acquire socially desirable habits as a result of neglect ("a child left to himself") brings shame to his father and mother.

Fourth, in the case of the impulse-ridden child, "foolishness is bound in the heart of the child," a condition which apparently occurs naturally; this child is in need of definite and strict guidance.

The recognition of the need to guide the upcoming generation and socialize its members is virtually universal. It has been clear since the dawn of civilization that the guidance and socialization of the new generation is essential and the *sine qua non* for the perpetuation of the existence of all societies. The dictum "spare the rod and spoil the child" is not palatable or acceptable to most members of modern society, nor recognized as an effective teaching mode by modern experimental, educational, and dynamic psychology. Yet, although the principle of negative reinforcement has lost the glamour it held in the days of classical behaviorism, it is retained in the educational and childrearing practices of many societies around the globe.

Another, somewhat related issue in the upbringing of the new generations is the issue of impulsivity versus self-control. Take, for example, the following quotes from the book of Proverbs:

The impatient acts stupidly. (14.17)

Patience is wisdom. (14.29)

He who is slow in anger is better than the hero; and he who controls his spirit than one who conquers a city. (16.32)

In these and many other examples we note the importance attached to impulse control—an admirable quality to be instilled in the upcoming members who are to make up the fabric of the society. Those who exhibit self-control show wisdom and heroism, but those who do not are stupid. This is related to the natural foolishness of children who have to be taught to curb their impulse expression. These aphoristic admonitions are neither finely tuned, analytical, qualified, or conditional; they are unqualified, simple, and direct. There is in the biblical text a constant dichotomizing and juxtaposition of good versus evil, wisdom versus stupidity, and patience versus impulsivity. There is little, if any, of the relativism and contextualism which characterize modern psychology and psychiatry in the judgment of behavior, morality, and the capacity of the growing person to adapt to his society and become a productive member of that society.

In classical psychoanalysis, the concept of ego is most relevant in the present context. In the structure of the psyche, Freud refers to the ego as that structure designated to serve "three harsh masters"—the id (instinctual needs and drives), the superego (conscience—the moral imperative), and external reality (Fenichel, 1945). The ego is viewed as the mediator between these masters, and successful mediation determines a person's adaptation and efficacy in their environment. In the process of this coordination, according to Freudian theory, need gratification is important, but only under appropriate circumstances. To satisfy the necessary conditions imposed by reality demands and one's conscience, it is imperative to control the expression of the drives; to suppress some of them, albeit temporarily; and to postpone gratification. This self-control is stressed frequently in the biblical texts concerned with the upbringing of the young.

ADULTHOOD

At the end of the previous section on adolescence, I referred to the point of achievement of adult status in the ancient Israelite society. This point becomes clear in the description of census-taking in the books of Exodus and Numbers. Some time after leaving the land of Egypt, the rag-tag assembly of various extended families and tribes had to be organized in preparation for the takeover of the promised land of Canaan: "And the Lord spoke to Moses at the Tent of the Presence in the wilderness of Sinai in these words: 'Number the whole community of Israel by families in the father's line, recording the name of every male aged twenty years and upward, fit for military service'." (Num. 11.1–3).

For the first time, a clear line of demarcation between childhood and adulthood is drawn in the Bible. The census is concerned with men, capable of fighting in the upcoming battles and wars of conquest of what was to become the land of Israel. Capacity for participation in warfare seems to be the only criterion; no upper age limit is spelled out. Women, obviously, did not count. As I indicated earlier, in terms of our present understanding of duties and responsibilities, women probably started their adult careers as wives and mothers at a much earlier age. In terms of work and family responsibilities, adult tasks were assigned to male youths at a much earlier age as well. But, when it came to battles of conquest, the age of 20 appeared paramount.

The tribe of Levi, whose male members were assigned a variety of ritual and administrative tasks related to the sanctuary, did not participate in the general census. Members of this tribe were not to be assigned to military duty, and were dedicated to the service of YHWH. In the case of this tribe, a separate counting of the adult members took place. This census required the numbering of all members between the ages of 20 and 50 who were assigned to the service of the Lord, at the tabernacle. Again, the age of adulthood, that of trust and responsibility, is marked by the 20th birthday. However, in this selection process, the upper age limit is also designated. Apparently, 50 was the upper limit for men assigned to many of the demanding tasks involved in the frequent transportation and maintenance of the tabernacle. Considering the shorter life expectancy of that era, it is safe to assume that "retirement" took place at age 50, which then marked the beginning of senescence. Of course, in most instances covered by the historic period, the leaders of the people whose ages were recorded pointed to much longer lives. However, when preparing for the construction of the temple, the permanent sanctuary of the Israelites in Jerusalem, King David organized the work force of the Levites by using age 30 as the lower limit. The census yielded 38 thousand men who were assigned to four major categories of employment. More than half of that number was assigned to work on the construction of the building; another group consisted of officers and judges; and two smaller groups of four thousand each were porters and musicians (1 Chron. 23).

During the time of Moses, when the tabernacle was transported from one battle zone to the other, a younger contingent of the Levites was apparently more useful (20 years of age). A more skilled and older work force for the construction of a permanent sanctuary in Jerusalem was apparently preferable many years later. It is fairly clear that age 20 was an important point in time that separated the children from the adults. Warriors, priests, judges, officers, construction workers and artisans, musicians, and others employed in maintaining an organized society were adults. Even the royalty followed this principle. With very few exceptions, the beginning of ascension to the throne was marked after the 20th birthday. Most of the kings were given their power when they were in the twenties or thirties, with very few older or younger exceptions.

References to ages of women are practically nonexistent in the Bible. There seems to be no mention of women in the census-taking procedure. The transition of women from the status of childhood to that of adulthood was most likely very gradual, unmarked by turning points of general social and cultural significance. They were not expected to serve on the battlefield, nor in the sanctuary; there were no military or ritual demands made upon them. Their function as mothers, wives, and workers in some domestic industries defined the vast majority of their roles.

Only the last three stages of Erikson's (1950/1963) epigenetic schema concern the period of adulthood. The relevant dichotomies are as follows: intimacy vs. isolation, generativity vs. stagnation, and ego integrity vs. despair. The first two are dealt with during the years of active adulthood, from the post-adolescent twenties to the period of senescence or old age. Intimacy is viewed by Erikson (1950/1963) as "the capacity to commit himself to concrete affiliation and partnerships and to develop the ethical strength to abide by such commitments, even though they may call for significant sacrifices and compromises" (p. 263). The obverse of this position is that of distantiation from other persons and isolation. Next is the stage of generativity vs. stagnation. Generativity refers to "The primary concern in establishing and guiding the next generation ... [it] is meant to include such more popular synonyms as *productivity* and *creativity* which, however, cannot replace it" (p. 267). Failure to achieve generativity involves a regression to "pseudo-intimacy" and frequently, a "sense of stagnation and personal impoverishment" (p. 267).

The Bible does not enter into this level of microanalysis of the human psyche. There are numerous examples that would demonstrate the latter dichotomy in the lives of some prominent figures in the ancient biblical document. One may speculate as to the meaning of intimacy in a basically polygynous society. What does "commitment" mean when several wives are involved? How does intimacy fare under such circumstances? Introspection about close relationships is at a minimum, and there is little we can glean from this information. Generativity, on the other hand, is often demonstrated in the functioning of the charismatic judges and other leaders, including the prophets, in the Old Testament. There are specific directions by the religious leaders for teaching instruction and the development of the younger generation. There is, however, no normative statement or indication of the period of life specifically involved.

Levinson's (1981) concern with the life course involves an examination of the changes in what he calls the "life structure" through adulthood. "The primary components of the life structure are the person's relationships with various aspects of the external world. The nature of the life structure, and the forces that lead to stability and change, have their sources conjointly in personality, biology, and the sociocultural world" (p. 77). Levinson divides the adulthood period into the early and middle adulthood "eras," on which he reports in detail in his work based on the autobiographies of a selected sample of adult, middle-aged men (1978). He also postulates a "late adulthood era" which was not dealt with in his original research report (1978). Essentially, this global and biographical approach has limited application to biblical life course description. The work is much too closely tied to the current American cultural scene, and is not of great relevance to our concern. Little generalization can evolve from this timebound and culture-bound evaluative analysis.

Adulthood throughout history was, and remains, the period of maximum capacity and energy in the achievement of society's valued goals. Those personalities most written about in the Hebrew Bible—Joseph, Moses, and David—as well as all the prophets made their mark during the adult period of their lives.

AGING, SENESCENCE, AND WISDOM

In his *History of Old Age,* the French cultural historian G. Minois (1989) refers to a report by Henry Valois on the examination of the 187 prehistoric skulls of human beings. Of these, only *three* were judged to have belonged to persons over the age of *50.* If we were to assume that this was a random sample, it would indicate the relative infrequency, or rarity, of people of an age that would now qualify to have reached the stage of "late adulthood."

The reference here is to the *prehistorical* period; most likely, the situation with respect to human longevity had improved, during the early *historical* period, reported in most of the books of the Bible and extending beyond the age of 50. But we have no way of knowing the average, or modal, life expectancy even in those times, beginning with the period of the judges (in the books of Joshua and Judges) through the era of the monarchy (the books of Kings 1 & 2, and the several books of the prophets), and later. What we do have are the fragmentary reports and descriptions of prominent personages (mythological figure, charismatic leaders, prophets, royalty), their careers, and in many instances their ages at the time of death. It is in this connection that Minois (1989) comments referring to the Bible, that "These are legal, historical, prophetic, poetic and philosophical writings, giving us a fairly precise picture of the role of the old, within a small Semitic people in the Near East" (p. 25).

It should be mentioned, parenthetically, that although some of the descriptions of old age are very informative, the writings of the "prehistoric" or mythological period, represented by the book of Genesis in particular, apparently refer to a time scale which differed markedly from the one adopted in the later books of the Bible. The term "year" obviously involved different temporal periods than did the same term assumed during the later "historical" era. The obvious example, of course, is the age of Methuselah who was reported to have lived 969 years (Gen.

5.27), or Noah, who lived 350 years after the flood (Gen. 9.28), or Sarah who was to become a mother at the age of 90 (Gen. 17.17). Most likely, the years represented different durations; but the exact ratio between those prehistoric years to the later or current historic years is not known. It is also, interesting to note that this state of affairs existed about the time that neighboring Egypt had introduced the lunar year, which was apparently adopted later by the Israelites (Witrow, 1988).

Old age and aging, its infirmities, and its limitations are described with varying degrees of detail throughout the several books of the Bible. We may end up with a compendium of characteristics of the failing organism, physical and psychological decline, with which we are quite familiar in modern life and which has served and continues as a fertile area of gerontological investigation (Poon, 1980).

BIBLICAL OLDSTERS

An interesting example of self-observation and reflection upon the condition of old age can be obtained from the following excerpt of the second book of Samuel. Many years after Barzilai had shown kindness to King David when he was on the run, escaping rebellious pursuit by his traitorous son, Barzilai was invited by the king to join him as his long-term guest in the capital of Jerusalem. Barzilai gratefully declined the invitation by saying—"I am today four score years old and can I distinguish between good and evil? Can your servant taste what I eat or drink? Can I hear any more the voice of singing men and singing women? Why, then, should I be a burden to my Lord the king?" (2 Sam. 19.35).

Here we note the resignation of the aged Barzilai to the fate and ravages of old age. He stresses the sensory deficits that are interfering with his enjoyment of life; he cannot hear, taste, enjoy food or music, or make reasonable judgments. It seems that this insightful self-description contains both the elements of anhedonia due to sensory deficits, and recognition of the cognitive deficits.

An analogous, but much earlier, document by an Egyptian

scribe of 4500 years ago expresses similar sentiments regarding the limitations of old age, accompanied by much anguish and wretchedness: "O sovereign my Lord. Oldness has come; old age has descended. Feebleness has arrived; dotage is here anew. The heart sleeps wearily every day. The eyes are weak, the ears are deaf, the strength is disappearing because of weariness of heart, and the mouth is silent and cannot speak. The heart is forgetful and cannot recall yesterday. The bone suffers old age. God has become evil. All taste is gone. What old age does to men is evil in every respect" (Pritchard, 1955, p. 412).

It may be of interest to note that the description of the condition of this ancient scribe refers to two main kinds of weaknesses. First are the physical symptoms of deafness, inability to speak, weak eyes, etc. Second is the reference to something more central—the heart. The heart is the center of what may be later called the seat of the *mind* and of the *self.* The heart is seen as weary, lacking in energy and motivation; it is also forgetful, "cannot recall yesterday." It is an interesting example of self-observation and description of the general deterioration process as the inevitable end of the human condition.

At the very beginning of the first book of Kings, we are told about the aging King David. "Now King David was old and well on in years; they covered him with clothes, but he did not get warm. Then his servants said: 'let there be brought to our lord the king a young virgin and she will stand before the king, and serve him and lie in his bosom and the king will be warm.' So they sought … and found and brought Avishag the Shunamite to the king. And the girl was very beautiful, she took care of the king and served him; but the king knew her not" (1 Kings 1.1–4).

Considering King David's history as a ladies' man, it is of special interest that "he knew her not," despite the proximity of Avishag, who served him and warmed him. There is loss of interest in sex and the loss of sexual prowess. So, in addition to the strictly physical deficit as far as temperature (and circulation) is concerned, there is another incapacity and loss of interest, of a more psychosomatic nature, akin to the anhedonia present in the case of Barzilai.

Numerous references to "dimmed vision" can be found scattered through many of the biblical works. Isaac, for, instance, "grew old and his eyes became so dim, he could not see" (Gen.

27.1). Similarly, "Eli was ninety and eight years old; and his eyes were dim that he could not see" (1 Sam. 4.15). However, failure of eyesight, or other sensory capacities, was not universally noted in old age. Moses, for example, not only retained his vision, but also showed no evidence of deficit at the time of his death. The text tells us—"and Moses was a hundred and twenty years old when he died; his eye was not dim and his vigor had not failed" (Deut. 34.7). It seems that failing health and sensory deterioration was not inevitably or universally noted in old age. In some instances, vigor and vitality were retained until the end. Such individual differences in the well-being of the aged are consistent with observations and studies in the expanding field of modern gerontology.

Modern psychology stresses the negative aspects and deleterious effects of aging upon sensory acuity, physical endurance, speed of response, and cognitive capacities of the elderly. As noted, there is little that is new about these observations, which are detailed in some of the anecdotal material and the descriptions contained in the biblical narratives. However, one particular characteristic attributed to the aging person by ancient Israelite lore and scriptures has been relatively rarely mentioned in modern systematic psychology. The term *"wisdom"* hardly ever appears in the pages of current psychology texts. Yet, this is a highly valued trait which is often mentioned, in the biblical texts, to characterize—not by virtuosity, but by pragmatism, good sense and good judgement—the aged and the elderly. Thus, motor and sensory deficits are seen to coexist with the elusive virtue of wisdom or good judgement, allegedly the province of the old.

WISDOM

Not infrequently do we come across, in the Bible, the juxtaposition of youthful, immoderate judgment with the wise counsel and deliberation reflected in the proffered advice and guidance of older individuals. In contrasting the two, it is usually the younger men who appear less seasoned and less successful advisors. Although at times they may succeed in having their advice accepted and followed, it is invalidated by subsequent results and consequences.

When King Solomon died (circa 930 BCE) and his son, Rehoboam, took over the kingdom, the people complained to the new king about the oppression they had suffered under the rule of his father. They requested, and in a sense it was an ultimatum, that he lighten the yoke which was placed upon them via conscripted hard labor and various other royal service demands. They addressed Rehoboam by saying: "if you lighten the heavy yoke he (father Solomon) laid upon us, we will serve you" (1 Kings 12.4).

King Rehoboam then consulted

> the elders who had been in attendance before his father Solomon when he was alive. "What answer do you advise I give these people?" And they said: "if you serve these people today, work for them and speak kindly to them, they will serve you forever." But he rejected the advice given to him by the elders and consulted the young men with whom he grew up, who were standing before him. He said to them: "what do you advise I should tell the people who said to me that I lighten the yoke which your father put upon us?" And the young men ... said, "tell the people as follows and say: my little finger is thicker than my father's loins. Now, my father put a heavy yoke on you and I will add to that burden; my father smote you with whips, and I will chastise you with scorpions." (1 Kings 12.3–11).

This bit of advice was unfortunate, nay, destructive, to the health and survival of the Israelite kingdom. Following Rehoboam's adoption of the young men's advice, the revolt that had been brewing for quite some time broke out in the open and a split in the kingdom resulted. Jeroboam, the opposition leader representing the northern part of the kingdom, was waiting for just such an opportunity. The vast majority of the people followed Jeroboham and founded the kingdom of Israel; a minority remained loyal to the house of David, whose dynasty was perpetuated by Solomon's son, Rehoboam, via the establishment of the kingdom of Judah (Judea).

Thus we have seen that the less moderate and less wise advice did not serve Solomon's heir well. The kingdom would have probably remained intact and united had Rehoboam heeded the advice and wisdom of the elders, the advisers of the older generation. They were, apparently, more perceptive and sensitive to the plight of the people who suffered much under Solomon's regime, lightening the burden or at least a promise of this course of action would have helped to preserve and consolidate the kingdom. An interesting sidelight may be cast on Rehoboam's motive. As noted above, he said that his "finger is thicker than his father's loins." He apparently needed to establish his superiority over his late father and, possibly, surpass him by maintaining his independence. The results, as we noted, were disastrous and divisive.

There are other examples of the operation of wisdom in human affairs. The admonition in the book of Proverbs spells out the advantages of wisdom which is viewed as an acquired virtue allotted by the deity. The mentor in the book of Proverbs says: "My son, eat honey because it is good … sweet to your taste. So shall knowledge and wisdom be to your soul" (Prov. 24.13–14).

The term "elders" is employed in various contexts in the Bible. They were a sort of institution who served in an advisory capacity to the leaders, judges and kings. They were considered to be wise, and persons whose judgment was valued and whose advise was followed. Wisdom was generally coupled with age, with accumulated experience and particularly sensitive discrimination—qualities which were highly desired by the community.

However, we may also note some doubt about the traditional and conventional wisdom that links superior judgment and wisdom with age and the aging process. It is not at all unexpected to find the expression of such skepticism in the pages of the book of Job. In his discussion with his friends, Job states the accepted maxim, in the early part of his argument—"With the ancient is wisdom; and in the length of days understanding" (Job 12.12). However, one of his interlocutors differs, In the heat of the ensuing argument and in his devotion to an all-knowing deity, Elihu, the son of Barachel says to Job: "I said, days should speak and multitude of years should teach wisdom. But, there is spirit in man; and the inspiration of the almighty makes them understand. Great men are not always wise, nor do the old understand judgement" (Job 32.7–9).

Here we discern a crack in the impregnable wall of faith in the wisdom of the old. It is only one instance of the skepticism that characterizes so much of the book of Job. Much of it, of course, brings the indignant and doubting Job to the edge of apostasy. But it is Elihu who attacks the conventional wisdom regarding the superior judgment of the old in an attempt to discredit the claims of his older friend. Moreover, there is a stress on the "spirit of man," apparently regardless of age, and the "inspiration of the almighty," which is not the exclusive claim of the old.

In modern times, the belief in the "wise old heads," as is noted in the prominence of the elderly in places of authority and influence in our society, has hardly dissipated. Yet it should be observed that the modern science of psychology is bereft of any clear and systematic treatment of the concept of wisdom. Perhaps some other concepts have taken its place in the compendium of human characteristics. Intelligence, knowledge, learning, abstracting ability, and other skills may have replaced it. Perhaps these may be viewed as components of the global term "wisdom," and have been dealt with operationally as separate entities.

A recently published symposium on the subject of wisdom (Sternberg, 1990) attempts to clarify the meaning of the term and relate it to the corpus of present-day theoretical and empirical psychology. In their review of the volume, and in the final chapter of the book, Birren and Fisher (1990) point out that there are as many definitions of wisdom as these are authors of chapters in the edited anthology. Their own summary definition, at which they arrived after a thorough analysis of the twelve preceding chapters, is worth quoting, for it clearly reflects the multi-dimensionality of the concept of wisdom: "Wisdom is the integration of the *affective, conative,* and *cognitive* aspects of human abilities in response to life's tasks and problems. Wisdom is a balance between the opposing valences of intense emotion and detachment, action and inaction and knowledge and doubt. It tends to increase with experiences and therefore age, but not exclusively found in old age" (p. 326). This brief definitional summary clearly indicates that the concept of wisdom is rather complex and multidimensional. Scientific psychology, with its penchant for the analytic and systematic *modus operandi,* has dealt, in considerable detail, with the several component concepts listed in the definition of wisdom. It has studied affects and emotions, cognition and intelligence, and motivation as well as human volition in great and often meticulous particularity, but it has not dealt with the more global notion of wisdom as such. As the conclusion of the symposium from which I quoted indicates—it remains a task for the future.

What is of special interest in the present context is the relationship between wisdom and aging. The quoted summary definition is in accord with some of the observations that wisdom is indeed a function of experience, and therefore of age. To be sure, it is not exclusively the property of the aged, and may be found in many younger individuals. It is consistent with the comments made by Job's younger interlocutor, Elihu, who questions the ever-present wisdom and good judgement in the aged. In modern times we have implicated the processes of memory and learning, and several others, garnered over years and decades from the subjects of gerontological investigation (Eisdorfer & Lawton, 1973).

At any rate, although wisdom as the earmark of the aged does not remain unassailed or unassailable, it maintains its position to a considerable extent in modern popular thinking and behavior. It may well be that this notion underlies the more positive view of the aging process espoused in some of the systematic research with the aged. One longitudinal study, for example, questions "The popular belief that aging ushers in a massive decline in psychological functioning or a narrowing down of ways of living; (this view) finds no support in our evidence. On the contrary, most of the parents (aged) we studied are psychologically well functioning and healthy persons" (Maas & Kuypers, 1974, p. 201). This finding may be related to the description of Moses, of whom it was said at the time of his death, "his eye was not dim and his vigor had not failed" (Deut. 34.7). Recent gerontological research (Poon, 1980; Storandt & Vandenbos, 1989) generally discourages a monolithic view of aging; instead, there is an emphasis upon great individual differences in the degree of onslaught upon the physical and psychological functioning of the aged. One caveat must be mentioned, however; it is that diversity itself may be a function of age. A good deal depends, for example, whether the person under consideration is "old," "young old" or "old old." The terms "old" or "aged" are rather imprecise and may cover a wide range of years. In part, this imprecision leaves the issue of change and impairment of functioning to further investigation and exact definition.

FACING THE END

Erikson's (1950/1963) conceptualization of the last stage of life—ego integrity vs, despair—is the stage least well-defined. It involves a review of one's life, an acceptance of it, and a readiness to face the inevitable; a readiness to accept one's own death. The "life review" concept, introduced by Butler (1963, 1975) which reflects the attempt to make sense of one's life, is the precursor of the achievement of integrity. This pattern of reflection is not particularly noted in biblical figures. What is notable is the connectedness and continuity, the assignment of tasks for the future generations. Thus, Jacob dwells in considerable detail upon the characteristics of his sons, their future and the future of the generations to come (Gen. 49). Similarly, the blessings given by Isaac (Gen. 27) and the instructions of David (1 Kings 1–2) present a picture of continuous involvement and integration of the future with the present. Death was considered as a sort of transitional state, governed by YHWH, and mitigated by the faith in him.

Aging in biblical times was accepted as the inevitable process that it is. It's the fate of human beings, the "Lord's will" and nature's way, or the deity's way, of passing the staff of life from generation to generation. Modern society and modern psychology do not accept aging fatalistically. Prolongation of life, as a result of modern, medical interventions, has produced increasingly sizable numbers of the "old old" (octogenarians and above) and has stimulated greater concern with their lifestyle. A 1993 conference on *Vitality for Life*" has evolved "Research Initiatives Concerning Behavioral Solutions for the Maintenance of Health and Vitality in Late Adulthood" (American Psychological Association, 1993).

AGING WOMEN

Aging women are rarely referred to in the Bible, and the reference to their aging process is rather circumscribed, for it deals with one central issue. This issue, of course, involves woman's major function—that of having children. Sarah, who had been childless and reached a ripe old age, was suddenly surprised by messengers of YHWH predicting that the following year she would have a son. One of the messengers said to Abraham: "I shall visit you again next year and your wife Sarah will have a son. Sarah was listening at the entrance of the tent ... now Abraham and Sarah were old ... and it ceased to be with Sarah after the manner of women, so Sarah laughed to herself saying 'after I have withered can I have pleasure, and my sire is old'." (Gen. 18.10–12). Sarah could not believe that after reaching the menopause she would be able to give birth to a child. This condition, the menopause, was the defining feature of aging in a woman.

Another episode is taken from the book of Ruth. Naomi, the mother of two sons who were married to Moabite women, was about to return to the land of Judah, after her husband and sons had died. The two daughters-in-law wanted to accompany her, but she tried to dissuade them from accompanying her to her native land of Judah. Naomi said, "Why will you go with me? Are there any more sons in my womb that they may be your husbands? ... even if I should say I have hope and have a husband tonight, would you wait for them until they are grown?" (Ruth 1.11–13).

Here, Naomi advises her daughters-in-law to return to their parental homes in Moab, for there is little hope for them in joining her on her return journey. She too stresses the fact that her childbearing days are over, saying, in effect, "I am too old to have a husband ... and I am unable to supply you with new husbands."

In the description of aging in these instances, we note that sensory or psychological factors do not enter into the picture. The sole issue is that of the onset of the menopause and the infertility of the woman as a result of the determining physical fact.

Modern science is cognizant of the fact that the onset of the "change of life" takes place comparatively early during the modern lifespan, and the issue of the menopause is hardly, if ever, mentioned as a special characteristic of old age. No reference to the symptoms of aging listed for men is made in the case of biblical women. The "dimming" eyesight, and loss of function and of capacity to enjoy life, are not part of the description of aging women. This, of course, is consonant with the more limited treatment of females in biblical narratives generally.

In sum, there are several aspects of the old and aging that emerge from the biblical narratives. These appear to be quite consistent with the conclusions and generalizations based on empirical studies of modern gerontology.

First is the general observation regarding the loss, or reduction in acuity, of sensory and cognitive functions as a result of the aging process, mitigated by the facts of individual differences in the effects and the appearance of these deficits. Maintenance of sensory and cognitive acuity, and physical vigor, in some instances, mitigate the alleged doom of deterioration, based on conventional wisdom.

Second, the positive aspects of reaching old age are seen in the institutionalization of the position of the "elders" in the Bible. They are considered to be the source of good judgement and, therefore, the consultants in the formation of social and governmental policy. Wisdom is attributed to them and to the aged generally. It consists of good judgement, intelligence, and affective control, presumably due to, or based upon, long experience in life.

Third, the attribution of wisdom to the aged is occasionally challenged in the Bible. This challenge is a contribution to the notion of the diversity and individual differences in the predicament of the aged.

DEATH: THE END OF THE LIFE COURSE

"Death is a fact of life"—so the saying goes. We are dying our lives and living our death. In a sense, this elliptical statement is biopsychological in nature, for the first part ("we are dying our lives") refers to the biological process of aging that starts at birth, to entropy. The second part of the maxim ("we are living our death") stresses the existential and psychological issues, the constant awareness of the final event—death. Throughout life, we often imagine its arrival, "we live it," and we contemplate it. It is an aspect of what Korzybsky had in mind by referring to the human being as a "time-binding animal," capable of living in the past as well as in the future, and capable of imagining the termination of that future (Korzybsky, 1926/1949). Erich Fromm (1947) also stresses this as a unique characteristic of human beings, unequaled in the rest of the animal kingdom.

Erich Fromm (1947) comments at length on the unique capacity of humans to contemplate their own death. Such contemplation is not rare nor infrequent in the life of the individual. Albeit we do everything to postpone the inevitable event on the time scale, we "live" it nevertheless. Throughout our lives we are aware of the sword of Damocles dangling over our heads. Generally, thoughts of death vary normatively along the age scale. We are aware of the inevitable throughout the lifespan, but aside from special conditions, such as depression or life-threatening illness, contemplation of death is age-related. Young people, albeit unconsciously, think they will live forever, so the saying goes; there is little reflection upon their own demise. However, as a person moves along on life's journey and is increasingly aware of the statistical probability and the normative reality regarding the relationship between age and the incidence of death, the frequency of thoughts and contemplation of the subject soars markedly.

There are numerous references to death in the Hebrew Bible. The death of patriarchs is described in a matter-of-fact manner, for they died at a ripe old age. We are told, for example, that "Abraham passed away and died in a good old age, an old man and full of years, and he was gathered unto his people" (Gen. 25.8). An almost identical report is given about the death of the patriarch Isaac—"and the days of Isaac were one hundred and eighty years. And Isaac passed away and died, and was gathered to his people, old and full of years, and his sons Esau and Jacob buried him" (Gen. 35.28–29). Finally, the third patriarch and grandson of Abraham, Jacob (Israel), after he finished giving his blessings and predictions to his sons and two of his grandsons who were to form the twelve tribes of Israel, made some arrangements about his own burial. Thus, "When Jacob finished with his instructions to his sons, he gathered up his feet into his bed, and passed away, and was gathered unto his people" (Gen. 49.33). In the case of Jacob, however, the text described Joseph, the favorite son, kissing his father, and weeping upon his death. A mourning period was also declared.

In all these instances, there is preparation for death which includes blessings of the sons (daughters are not mentioned); a description of their individual characteristics, and, to some extent, the prediction of the future course of their life and the life of their offspring. Thus, we know that Abraham gave everything he had to Isaac, his only legitimate son, but that he also gave presents to the sons of his concubines. We may recall that Isaac gave his best blessing to the younger son Jacob, who had earlier posed as the older son Esau, who was entitled to the birthright. The blessing could not be withdrawn once it was given, although Jacob's deception was discovered. Isaac was pressed by his son Esau, who finally also received a blessing, but the prediction for the future clearly leaves him in second place, albeit temporarily. "And you shall live by your sword and you shall serve your brother, but it shall come to pass when you will dominate and break the yoke off your neck" (Gen. 27.40).

We also learn that when the time comes, the dying person also leaves last instructions regarding his place of burial. Israel's (that is, Jacob's) instructions are recorded as follows: "And the time of Israel's death came near, and he called his son Joseph and said ... do not bury me in the land of Egypt. I will die with my father, you shall carry me out of Egypt and bury me in their burial place" (Gen. 47.29–30). Similar instructions were given by son Joseph to his brothers some years later (Gen. 50).

All three patriarchs died at a ripe old age. Death was expected and was prepared for through leaving their affairs in order. This order also included specific instructions for the disposition of the body and the place of the burial. Death was clearly a part of life. Death in old age was readily accepted and anticipated. There is a clear sense of the establishment of continuity between the past and the new generations (grandchildren). The past and continuity are especially clear from the expression which is repeated over and over again "and he was gathered unto his people" (that is, his ancestors). Death was a preparation for the future of the community and a return to the past involving an enhancement of the previous generations. Death was viewed as a bridge between the past and the future—the process of joining the ancestors and instructing the younger generation. In a sense, the older persons portrayed in the Bible are examples of what Erikson (1950/1963) characterized as the last two stages of ego development. We definitely see the *generativity* in the establishment and guidance of the new generations. Also reflected is Erikson's notion of *integrity* at the end of life. The special ingredients of integrity such as practical wisdom, acceptance of the self, and belief and trust in the meaning and order of life as buttressed by the faith in YHWH, are often demonstrated in the biblical accounts of the patriarchs, as well as some of the heroes of later generations.

Death in the Old Testament (OT), as described above, does not imply that the issue was resolved theologically. Bultmann (1965) points out that "YHWH is the god of life in a quite exclusive sense. Death and its realm stand outside the stream of power which has subdued all areas of life, and the absence of a theological point of orientation for the concepts of the state of death resulted in the fact that within the Yahwistic faith these have been preserved in an undecided state ... in the OT" (pp. 10–11).

In modern times, descriptions and theoretical formulations of the dying process based on clinical observations of the dying are available in the gerontological and thanatological literature. A rather popular stage theory concerning the final period of life was offered by Kubler-Ross (1969) who based her conceptualization on observation and clinical experience with a large number of terminally ill individuals. The author posits five stages, consisting of *denial* as a first reaction to the prospect of death; *anger,* based on the "why-me feeling"; an attempt at *bargaining* for the extension of life, followed by the onset of *depression;* and a final *acceptance* of the inevitable. Although widely accepted by laypersons and professionals alike, this schema has not remained unchallenged from a scientific perspective (Kastenbaum, 1975). Discussion of such stages is made possible by the advances made by modern science and medicine which allows fairly approximate prediction of the time of death. Such a prognostic luxury was not available to the ancient Israelites.

Death was an act of God, although as we have noted, premonitions in the sense of structural and functional changes and symptoms abounded and permitted a sense of the impending end. The more optimistic theological views about an hereafter were the creations of Christianity and rabbinical Judaism in the post-biblical era.

ON MOURNING

All societies have customs, rituals, and procedures—many rather formalized and traditionally practiced—for marking the death of a member of the community. Following the death of a close relative or other beloved person, in biblical times, involved the wearing of sackcloth and ashes upon the head, like the wearing of black or white in some present-day societies. But our concern is not so much with the externalities and the institutionalized symbolic behavior following a death as with the psychological aspects of the departure of a significant person from the family and community.

In the post-biblical period, Judaism, as well as Christianity, developed elaborate theologies concerning the hereafter of life after death—in heaven, hell, or in some other way-stations in between. However, during the times covered by the Hebrew Bible, only a mythical residence in "Sheol" after death is mentioned. Very little detail is given regarding this place. Death was clearly viewed negatively, as an undesirable event, and often as a punishment, for committed sins, exercised by YHWH or his emissaries. Hence, the loss of a beloved person was mourned for varying periods of time, without emphasis on denial as a defensive operation. Nor was it assisted by the kind of theology that was developed by later generations which were comforted by the belief in a rewarding hereafter. Furthermore, in modern times, we are told that in many instances the defense of denial is frequently part of the work of mourning, involved in the process of separation. The denial and suppression, if not repression, of the awareness, admission, and acceptance of an important loss are often exercised at the expense of the mourner's well-being and psychological integrity. These are instances in which full separation from the beloved object has not taken place, for the work of mourning had not been accomplished.

In most societies, institutionalized periods of mourning facilitate various behaviors, rituals, and expressions of sorrow that constitute the work of separation from the departed object. As we note in the case of the patriarchs—"Abraham came to mourn Sarah and weep for her" (Gen. 23.2). When Jacob died, his son, "Joseph, fell upon his father's face and wept, and he kissed him ... and the Egyptians mourned him for seventy days" (Gen. 50.1–3). During the post-patriarchal period, similar patterns are observed. For example: "The children of Israel wept for Moses thirty days; so the days of weeping and mourning for Moses were ended" (Deut. 34.8). Similarly, when the prophet Samuel died, "all of Israel lamented him" (1 Sam. 28.3). In the first two instances, we see both the personal act of mourning for the departed wife (Sarah) and the departed father (Jacob), while in the others we note the more formal institutionalization of the mourning period for Moses when the entire community is involved in departing from its beloved charismatic leader. The individual mourning is expressed more directly; the affect, the weeping—in the case of Abraham and Joseph. Communal expression seems to involve mourning and lamentation, although in the case of Moses weeping is also mentioned, but the number of days (30) seemed to be stipulated by custom.

Reaction to death and subsequent mourning may be found in some episodes drawn from the long saga of the life of King David. Even before he ascended the throne, the loss of his true and trusted friend Jonathan, the son of King Saul who fell in the battle with the Philistines, is recorded in the most beautiful and poignant verses of the Hebrew Bible. Upon learning of the fallen Jonathan, David lamented: "How the mighty have fallen in the midst of battle. Oh Jonathan, you were slain in the high places. I am distressed for you my brother; you were very pleasant to me; your love for me was more wonderful than the love of women" (2 Sam. 1.25–26). The agony and distress of his true and trusted friend, who saved his life on a number of occasions, is clearly expressed in this affectively loaded eulogy delivered at the beginning of the realization of the loss, and separation, from the object.

And again, when David's rebellious and traitorous yet beloved son, Absalom, was cut down and slain on the field of battle, we hear the father's lamentations when he learns of his son's death: "And the king was disturbed, and went up to the chamber over the gate saying as he went—'Absalom, my son, my son, my son Absalom, I wish I would have died in your stead, Absalom, my son, my son'." (2 Sam. 19.1).

A father's pain and agony are genuinely expressed in these words. The shock and trauma of the sudden death of what the psychoanalyst would call "highly cathected objects" brings about the outpouring of emotion expressing the torment of loss and bereavement. In both instances, in the case of the death of Jonathan and Absalom, we witness the immediate reaction as the first phase of the mourning process and the commencement of what Freud, in his work on *Mourning and Melancholia* (Vol. XIV), called the "work which mourning performs" (p. 243). He writes of the difficulty experienced in relinquishing the beloved object and in accepting the bitter reality of its nonexistence. It is a gradual process, before the object is given up and no longer has a hold on the living-loving person, "and when the work of mourning is completed the ego becomes free and uninhibited again" (p. 245).

As mentioned earlier, there are more formalized, ritualistic kinds of behavior which are part of most cultures, in which the parting from the deceased is much more formalized and normative. The wearing of sackcloth and ashes, the observance of varying periods of abstinence, as well as formal group lamentation were aspects of the death process then, as they are in many modern cultures. The Bible, however, is not clear about the mourning process and the particular "work" involved, such as denial, the temporary loss of the sense of reality, the final acceptance of the loss, and the recovery of full reality awareness. We note the reactions of raw affect and genuine response to personal loss, and the possible catharsis implied in the expression of grief and dysphoric affect, which are the beginnings of the work of mourning. Implied are the affective and cognitive processes defining final separation.

SUMMARY

In ancient Israel, the life course was divisible into three major period—childhood, adulthood, and senescence. Dependency and impulsivity characterize the earliest periods; activity and achievement, the second one; and the third period is mainly described in terms of wisdom, failing health, and withdrawal and disengagement. The final subdivisions, such as Erikson's "ages of men," based on psychological factors characteristics of modern developments, was not discernible in biblical texts. An outstanding example is the transitional period of adolescence, which is primarily a late 19th and early 20th century conceptualization.

Complete and absolute parental authority over offspring, often regardless of age, is the rule in the biblical era. The desirability and effectiveness of corporal punishment as a tool of discipline is generally shared.

Despite the determinism of behaviors in the theological tradition, adults' responsibility in performing the sundry tasks imposed upon them by the social system is paramount. Fairly clear age boundaries are specified to various tasks involving public service, in war and peace. The emphasis on experience is the source of attribution of wisdom to the elderly.

Although death was viewed negatively and often seen as a punishment by the deity, it was accepted fatalistically and with equanimity by the aged; a "hereafter" was not clearly conceptualized, and death was seen as a return to "lie with the ancestors." Existence after death is not specified. Death was often prepared for and advice to the younger generation was a part of the separation process. Mourning for the old was ritualized and formalized, and the expression of strong affect was present, especially in the case of premature demise.

CHAPTER 3

Sexuality

HETEROSEXUALITY

Early in the book of Genesis, the inevitability and predestination of the mutual attraction between men and women is clearly stressed. It is the fate of man and woman to join together. One of the creation stories refers to man being the origin of woman; God created woman out of the man's rib (Gen. 2.23), and the Bible tells us, "Therefore, a man leaves his father and mother and cleaves unto his wife and they become one flesh" (Gen. 2.24). It seems that the destiny of the sexes is to cling to each other, and to reunite; by being with each other they become one whole again. Sex and marriage are viewed as people's nature and fate.

Generally, marriages were arranged in ancient times of tribal existence; often, the parents of the couple knew each other and planned the union—a situation that persisted until recently in the modern world, and is still characteristic in many of the world's societies. Marriages were often arranged for economic reasons or reasons of kinship and family connections. Notions of love, and especially of romantic love so prevalent in modern Western society, are relatively rare in the biblical narratives of ancient Israel.

However, quite a number of examples of love, or romantic love, both in and out of the marital state, may be found in the biblical texts. After Abraham's emissary found Rebecca as a

45

suitable bride for his son Isaac, the two are brought together and we are told that Isaac took Rebecca to his mother's tent, "and she became his wife and he loved her" (Gen. 24.63). It may be readily noted that he loved her, after she became his wife. The text makes the distinction between becoming a wife and cohabitation and love, which, apparently, goes beyond the mere marital state. Moreover, the part-sentence just quoted is completed by the following phrase: "and he was consoled for the death of his mother." Isaac's mother Sarah had died some time before, and as her only, long-awaited son, upon whom she must have showered a great deal of affection, he missed her very much. Thus some of the love he felt for his late mother, true to the Oedipal formula, was transferred or sublimated into the love for his new bride. The symbolism of taking her to his mother's tent cannot be ignored.

Moving on to the next generation, the marital struggles of Jacob, Isaac's son, draw our attention. After he was tricked into marrying his uncle Laban's older daughter, Leah, Jacob consented, nay, was eager, to work an extra 7–year stint for his father-in-law in order to marry Rachel, whom he really loved, and make her his wife. The Bible comments that although Jacob worked for 7 full years for Rachel, "they seemed but a few days, because he loved her so" (Gen. 29.20). The intensity of his love for Rachel seemed to make 7 years of labor pass quickly, while he remained in Laban's household and may have been continuously in contact with his heart's ideal.

The book of Judges tells us the story of Samson, who loved a Philistine woman of Timonah. Now, the Philistines had been the enemies of the Israelites for many years, and Samson's parents protested against his involvement with this woman. But Samson married her nevertheless, for he loved her.

Although the purpose of marriage was generally conceived as a means for the perpetuation of the species—to be fruitful and multiply—there are some occasions when the relationship between two partners is not exclusively defined by this dictum. The ingredient of love and affection in the marital union not infrequently transcended the obligation of procreation. Marriages persisted successfully, despite childlessness. Abraham and Sarah were married for a long time prior to the birth of their son Isaac. Rachel remained as Jacob's beloved and preferred wife despite her period of barrenness.

At the very beginning of the book 1 Samuel, we are told of a relevant episode about Elkanah, the son of Jeroham, who had

> two wives; the name of the one was Hannah, and the name of the other Peninah; and Peninah had children, but Hannah had none. And this man went up out of his city every year to worship in Shilo ... and when Elkanah made his offering he gave to Peninah and all her sons and daughters, portions. And to Hannah he gave a double portion, for he loved Hannah. And the Lord closed Hannah's womb. And her adversary provoked her and made her fret, because the Lord closed her womb. Year after year, when she went up to the house of the Lord she angered her so, that she wept and did not eat. And Elkanah, her husband, said to her, Hannah why are you crying? Why aren't you eating? Why are you so upset? Am I not better to you than ten sons?" (1 Samuel 1.1–8).

This narrative represents an interesting deviation from the notion that a marriage had to produce children, especially male children. Elkanah's profession of love and the actual behavior that is consistent with it, ignores the infertility of his wife. Essentially, he is telling Hannah that his love for her does not depend upon her capacity to bear his offspring. Moreover, he favors her by giving her a double portion, and professes his devotion to her and her great value to him. The Hannah-Elkanah episode is remarkable for the flexibility that is revealed in the Bible with regard to the fertility injunction. Again, consistent with many other instances detailed in the scriptures, there is often a discrepancy between the moral law and religious obligation enunciated in the Torah (in the books of Leviticus, Numbers, and Deuteronomy) and the actual behavior of real persons described in the stories of the other books in the Tanakh. Moreover, most of these stories demonstrate that these discrepancies between law and behavior are related in a matter-of-fact manner, without accompanying denunciation or censure. Perhaps, in this particular instance, Elkanah's disappointment at Hannah's infertility was mitigated by the fact that his other wife produced the heirs in the family. Thus, he showed his obedience (by having children with Peninah) and was magnanimous with Hannah who, after all, was barren because "the Lord closed her womb." Rehoboam, the son of king Solomon, and his heir to the throne "loved Maaca, the daughter of Absalom, more than all his wives and concubines" (2 Chron. 11.22).

Finally, in this connection, it would be appropriate to quote from what may probably be the most secular book of the Bible, *"The Song of Songs."* The poet expressed himself as follows: "For love is strong as death, jealousy is cruel as the grave; the flashes thereof are flashes of fire, a very flame of the Lord. Many waters cannot quench love, no rivers can sweep it away" (8.6–7). The entire book of Song of Songs (or the "Song of Solomon") is an exquisite love poem that stands out in world literature. Thus, we have noted in numerous examples, the power of love, heterosexual love, as it was demonstrated in actual life. The literary expression further validates this point and adds to it poetry, beauty, and inspiration.

In modern times, we do not only recognize the power and expression of love, but are also concerned with a more detailed analysis of this complex state in human relationships. Modern definitions of love, such as those offered by Fromm (1947) and Sullivan (1953), stress the unselfish and altruistic nature of love. Fromm (1947) offers the following definition: "Love is the productive form of relatedness to others and to oneself. It implies responsibility, care, respect, and knowledge, and the wish for the other person to grow and develop" (p. 110). H. S. Sullivan notes that a state of love exists "when the satisfaction or the security of another person becomes as significant as one's own satisfaction and security" (p. 20). Tillich, the theologian, sees love as a combination of two major elements, those of "attachment" and "caring." Another component is also suggested—that of confidential communication.

Studies of the phenomenon of love reported by modern social psychologists direct our attention to the cognitive aspects that underlie the state of love. Aside from the physical components in the mutual attraction of couples, numerous other factors are involved. Similarity in sociocultural and socioeconomic background, religious background, and the perception of similarity of attitudes and values related to these factors, are a few of the many ingredients of love and mutual attraction. All of these are at the basis of the so-called "personality profiles," whose matching is aided by computer technology and are a part of the burgeoning industry developed in recent decades in the United States.

ADULTERY

Rather early in the history of the Hebrew nation, the commission of adultery was strongly condemned. The seventh commandment, "you shall not commit adultery," clearly spells out the prohibition of sexual behavior which is potentially so destructive to the social fabric of the nation. In the book of Leviticus, following the listing of the ten commandments, there is a further admonition—"Don't defile the wife of your neighbor with your semen" (Lev. 18.20). Finally, the corresponding punishment is spelled out a couple of chapters later, as follows: "A man who commits adultery with another man's wife ... with the wife of his neighbor (friend) shall be put to death—the adulterer and the adulteress" (Lev. 20.10).

From the Draconian measures recommended or prescribed, it would not be too far-fetched to hypothesize that adultery was a very strong drive against which a strong defense had to be erected. Yet the only blatant example of this type of behavior recorded by the Bible is not so drastically punished, and involves a relatively high degree of tolerance, almost approaching the level reached in present-day Western society.

DAVID'S SIN

The quotation from the Bible that illustrates this point involves the popular king David, who: "One evening ... walked upon the roof of the king's house, and from the roof, he saw a woman washing herself, and the woman was very beautiful. And David inquired and sent after the woman, and took her; and she came unto him and he lay with her ... and she returned to her home. And the woman conceived and told David—'I am with child'." (2 Sam. 11.2–5).

To make matters worse, the king sent the woman's husband, Uriah the Hittite, into the frontline of the ongoing war, whereupon Uriah got killed and king David married his widow, who was already pregnant with his child. To be sure, the king was severely castigated by Nathan the prophet, but he continued his successful reign for many years afterwards. Moreover, the royal privilege not only extended to condoning the behavior without the severe punishment prescribed by Mosaic law, but the son of this union, Solomon, was selected to continue the Davidic dynasty. Furthermore, what is important to note, is that the prophet lashed out against David for taking away the only woman that Uriah had, while David himself already had a number of them.

Other examples of unfaithfulness and adultery, and the punishment of such behavior, are hard to find in the scriptures. This is another instance of tolerance of a serious infraction, albeit an infraction committed by royalty. But, again, the biblical narratives involved few applications of the laws, for there is no evidence of a rigid or well-developed judicial system of the kind developed in later centuries. The case was in the hands of the monarchs, priests, and, as in the case of avengers, in the hands of the people themselves. Some such instances may be found in the next section concerned with rape.

Since modern psychology presumably is a "value-free" science it is not much concerned with adultery, only insofar as it is symptomatic of the dissatisfaction of the participants in their marriages. It remains a violation of the legal code (without the Draconian punishment of the Bible), but it involves concern with the welfare of the families, implicated in such temporary affairs, and the consequences for the children who may be members of the respective families.

CONCERNING RAPE

Forced sex, or rape, is viewed negatively and regarded as a serious offense in most societies—ancient and modern. In the Israelite code that evolved, the attitude toward the act is mitigated by the circumstances and the status of the victim. As we noted before, if an adulterous relationship is involved, the punishment according to the Mosaic code is clear and extremely severe. If a man comes across a "betrothed" young woman and forces her into a sexual relationship, then the Draconian measure is applied; his punishment is death.

In the case of the engaged (or betrothed) woman, there are circumstances that absolve her from guilt. The punishment is meted out to the man only if the sexual attack takes place "in the field," outside an inhabited area where the cries and protestations of the woman may be heard. Presumably, in such a case the woman did not consent, and, therefore, only the man is guilty. However, the punishment is visited upon by both participants if the sexual act took place in the city or urban area, where the vocal protests of the woman involved may be heard. If they were not heard, her consent is assumed, rape is ruled out, and the situation is defined as consensual and adulterous and punishable by the death of *both* participants. It is an instance of cohabitation, but not rape.

Rape of an unmarried (not betrothed) woman is not judged as harshly. The rule laid down in the book of Deuteronomy reads as follows: "If a man finds a girl who is a virgin, who is not engaged, and he seizes her, and lies with her, and they are found, then the man who lays with her shall give the girl's father fifty shekels of silver and she shall be his wife" (Deut. 22.28).

The man is obliged to marry her and, in modern parlance, "make an honest woman of her." However, should the woman's father refuse the man, and not give his daughter into marriage, the dowry money is to be paid to the father anyway. It may be noted that the act of rape *per se* is not punished severely.

Although the official legal code did not specify severe punishment of rape of an unmarried woman, apparently custom and tradition regarded such an event as an extreme insult to the family. In such instances, the honor of the family was surely avenged by its male members.

SCHECHEM AND DINAH

Schechem, the prince of the Hivite tribe that was a neighbor of the Israelite clan of Jacob and his extended family, came across Dinah, the young daughter of the patriarch. He caught her and raped her. Although he fell in love with her and offered to marry her, Jacob's sons did not take kindly to him and to the ultimate insult to the clan. Because of the violation of their sister, brothers Simon and Levi conspired and slew all the Hivite males of Schechem's clan. In response to the father's criticism of their drastic action and his more conciliatory attitude, they posed the rhetorical question, "Is our sister to be treated like a whore?"

(Gen. 34.31). The rape of a family member was the ultimate insult to the entire clan of Jacob and motivated the cruel revenge. Most likely, in this pre-Mosaic period, the more tolerant reaction, involving payment and marriage, was inoperative. Moreover, according to the Bible, ethnic differences were an additional factor.

AMNON AND TAMAR

In introducing the episode that follows, it is worth calling attention to the nature of the family structure of ancient Israelite society some three to four millennia ago. It was a polygamous, and more specifically, a polygynous society. Rather complex relationships are created as a result of the structure of such families—consisting of a single father (master) and several (if not numerous) mother/ wives, and many children; brothers, sisters, half-brothers and half-sisters. Such was the structure of the royal family of King David, which was similar to, and characteristic of, most of the families in the upper strata of the ancient society.

One of King David's sons, Amnon, became enamored of his half-sister Tamar, whose full brother was Absalom. The lovesick Amnon feigned illness, upon the advice of one of the palace entourage, and requested that Tamar bring him some food to eat. "Tamar took the cakes and brought them to her brother Amnon, inside his house. But when she served them to him, he caught hold of her and said to her: 'Come lie with me, sister.' But she said to him: 'Don't brother, don't force me! Such things are not done in Israel. Don't do such a vile thing. Where will I carry my shame? And you, you will be like any scoundrel in Israel. Please speak to the King; he will not refuse me to you'." (2 Sam. 13.10–13).

When Tamar was in this predicament, she pleaded with Amnon to do the honorable thing and obtain their father's blessing for the union. She wanted a proper marriage: "But he would not listen to her; he overpowered her and lay with her by force" (2 Sam. 13–14). Tamar left the house, rent her clothes and put dust upon her head (a sign of mourning), and screamed as she walked. Her brother Absalom knew what happened to his sister and who the culprit was. He told Tamar to be quiet and not brood over it.

For a long while, we are told, Absalom did nothing to Amnon, nor did he say anything, but he hated him very much, because Amnon had violated his beloved sister. He bided his time. Some 2 years later, at a gala gathering of the royal princes, Absalom gave his servants the order to assassinate Amnon, "when he is merry with wine." The servants carried out their master's instructions and thus, the shame of Tamar was avenged.

The episodes related above refer to different periods of history; the Schechem story belongs to prehistory, while the Amnon-Tamar story took place during the historical monarchical period of the Israeli state. However, the resolution of the rape issue is identical in each case; the brothers avenged the sexual attacks on their sister. Implications of the commission of a great affront and insult to the clan are clear. It seems that the violence against the individual, the woman involved, was secondary to the besmirching of the honor of the collective—the family and the clan.

It may also be noted that formal Mosaic rules provide for monetary compensation to the father of the aggrieved party and a chance of marriage, but there was no other punishment of the violation of the person and the physical and psychological aggression involved. Concern with the issue of violation of a woman's rights in sexuality was to await cultural development many centuries later.

The concern of modern society with this issue is definitely more psychological; it is a concern with the feelings and self of the victim, not only with the violation of sex, but with the degradation of the person. Some sense of this concern is indirectly communicated by the description of the raped Tamar reacting to her traumatic experience.

Homosexual rape is not at all unknown in the scriptures. Specific instances of actual individual rape are not to be found. Yet reference to the threat of rape by groups of men would indicate that it was not such an uncommon event. The men of Sodom and Gommorah tried to force Lot to send out his house guests to them so that they might "know" them (Gen. 19.4–8). Similarly, the men of Gibeah (Judg. 19.21–24) demanded that the male visitor at the home of one of the town's residents be handed to them so that they would "know" him. Thus, the threat of homosexual rape, apparently "gang" rape, was not an extraordinary phenomenon of the darkest side of the Israelite society during the early biblical patriarchal and tribal period. It is interesting to note, although difficult to explain, that homosexual rape is omitted from the Mosaic code of sexual behavior in the books of Exodus and Deuteronomy.

The Gibeah episode had rather dire consequences. Instead of the man coming out to meet the rabble that demanded to have intercourse with him, his concubine was dispatched in his place, "so the Levite took hold of his concubine and thrust her outside for them. They assaulted and abused her all night till the morning. . . ." (Judg. 29.25). This episode precipitated a bloody war between the tribes of Israel. The gang rape was instead displaced unto the woman who died that morning.

ON PROSTITUTION

Sexuality, as a commodity for sale, outside the bonds of marriage, was not unknown by any means in the Israelite ancient past. It is quite obvious that "the world's oldest profession" was alive and well, and flourished, in the old biblical days. As a matter of fact, the Hebrew word *zona* (meaning "prostitute" or "harlot"), and the various forms of the verb from which the word originated, appear quite often in the biblical texts, in a number of different contexts and connections.

In the book of Leviticus, the Israelites (men, fathers) are admonished as follows: "Do not prostitute your daughter so as to make her a whore and the land will not become prostituted and full of lewdness" (19.29). Several points of significance are involved in this dictum. First, the parent, the father, most likely, was the one in whose power lay the fate of the daughter. The use of young girls to boost the family economy was not altogether unknown. It is not clear, in this context, *how* the prostituting process occurred or was undertaken, but parental direction and or consent was implied.

Second, the reason for this prohibition concerns the effect of prostitution upon public behavior and sexual morality. The spread of prostitution is viewed as an act of lowering the moral level of the society.

Third, it is of interest to observe that a daughter's entry, and initiation, into the "oldest profession" was not looked at from the personal viewpoint of the daughter herself, the young woman involved, but from the broader concern for the society at large. The father owned the child and could do anything he wanted with his chattel.

Although the Israelites were cautioned against prostitution, there is considerable evidence of the practice of this profession. Of special interest was the institutionalized form of prostitution, connected with religious rites and perpetuated by the Hebrews under the influence of Canaanite and other religious influences. Male (*kadesh*) and female (*kedesha*) prostitutes were part of the religious services of the Amorites and other Canaanite tribes, and were maintained as part of the syncretism in the religion of the ancient Hebrews. The well-known anthropologist and Hebrew scholar, Rafael Patai, comments that "In the early days of the Hebrew tribes, after they had conquered Canaan, and undoubtedly under the influence of the indigenous Canaanite practices, prostitutes were attached to local sanctuaries serving the visitors and pilgrims. Both men and women served in this capacity as adjuncts of the shrines" (1960, p. 134). These practices, apparently, persisted in Jerusalem and in other communities until the Babylonian exile at the end of the sixth century B.C.E.

Female sexual activity prior to marriage was apparently quite widespread as a part of religious observance throughout the ancient middle East. In *The Golden Bough,* the classic work of J. G. Frazer (1922/1960), we are informed that in such diverse places as Cyprus, Phoenicia, Babylon, and Greece, the custom of women to prostitute themselves to strangers, often for a fee that was turned in to the sanctuary, was prevalent in the service of Astarte, Baalath, and other fertility gods and goddesses. Furthermore, Frazer states that "there was a law of the Amorites, that she who was about to marry should sit in fornication seven days by the gate" (Frazer, 1960, p. 384). This, apparently, was a standard prenuptial procedure.

A number of references to harlots and prostitutes, holy or otherwise, appear in the Biblical literature. An interesting episode of this kind tells of Tamar, the daughter-in-law of Judah, who disguised herself as a Kedesha or ritual prostitute, caught the attention of her father-in-law, and was impregnated by him in order to regain her family rights and status (Gen. 38).

Tamar was married to Judah's son who died and left no progeny. She was promised a younger son as a husband, according to the Levirate law. This law would have provided that the male offspring would carry on the first husband's legacy. However, a younger son did not become available, and a new heir was not produced, so Tamar took matters in her own hands, and followed a different path to security by concerning a son with her father-in-law.

The two women who lived together and gave birth to sons at the same time and who resorted to the wise judgment of King Solomon were described as "harlots" (1 Kings 3.16). In these and other instances, the use of the term prostitute is nonpejorative; it is employed matter-of-factly and as a description of the occupation or the occupational status of the individuals involved.

Despite the prevalence of the practice of prostitution, which was either a private enterprise or institutional function connected with religious rites, the verb "to prostitute" or "whoring" is pejorative throughout the Bible. The term "whoring" connotes untrustworthiness and promiscuous behavior. The term is frequently employed in the context of the Israelite unfaithfulness to YHWH, and the concept of promiscuity in the worship of the extant host of different deities of the neighboring tribes and nations. "Whoring after other gods" was ubiquitous and subject to frequent preaching and admonition on the part of the priests and prophets throughout the pre-monarchic period, during the monarchic period, and after the Babylonian Exile as well.

Thus, when Moses was about to die, "The Lord said to Moses: 'Behold, you shall sleep with your fathers, and this people will rise up and go *whoring* after the gods of the strangers of the land" (Deut. 30.16). In another passage from the book of Judges, we see a similar comment that the Israelites "would not listen to their judges, but they went on whoring after other gods" (2.17).

Later, the prophets employed the figurative expression quite extensively in their orations. The furious chastisement of the Israelite people by the prophet Ezekiel is a rather extreme example of this genre: "You have built your high places ... and you have opened up your legs to every passerby and multiplied your whoredoms'." (Ezek. 6.25).

A rather unusual message from YHWH was reported by the prophet Hosea: "The Lord said to Hosea: 'Go get yourself a wife of whoredom and children of whoredom, for the land will whore away from YHWH'" (Hosea 1.2). Scholars have been puzzled by these strange instructions allegedly received by the prophet. It appears to be another device for demonstrating the symbolic relationship between YHWH, the husband, and his wife, the people of Israel. The wife, the nation of Israel, is seen as unfaithful to the deity, as whoring and promiscuous in her pursuit of other "lovers" (i.e., gods). Patai concludes that the sin of idolatry was almost indistinguishable, in Biblical mentality and phraseology, from the sin of adultery (1960, p. 77).

As we have seen in an earlier section of this chapter, infidelity and adultery were prohibited and severely punished by the code of conduct of the Israelites. However, prostitution, as we noted above, was part of the social reality and structure of ancient Israel. It was apparently a social institution, and in the early existence of the nation, a religious institution as well. When we consider the attitudes expressed toward whoring together with the actual tolerance and implicit acceptance of prostitution as a profession, there appears to have been a certain ambivalence in the ancient era—an attitude that may, viewed realistically, persist in present-day modern society.

The persistence of prostitution in the societies of the Western world and elsewhere is an indication of the half-hearted rejection of this institution in those societies. It is similar to the apparent ambivalence, and even hypocrisy, that continues to reign in modern and postmodern society with respect to sexuality in general. With few exceptions, the codes of most societies condemn the practice of prostitution; yet it is widespread and the laws against it are often not enforced. This may support the notion of the power of sexuality, championed by modern psychology and psychoanalysis, as well as the characterization of the human species as fickle and promiscuous in nature. Widespread infidelity, adultery, and the frequency of divorce provide additional support for this notion.

INCEST AND THE INCEST TABOOS

Prohibition against the mating and marrying of close relatives is almost a universal rule in human societies. The society and culture of ancient Israel is no exception. A series of laws and principles of sexual behavior relevant to incest is spelled out in some detail in the third book of the Pentateuch-Leviticus. Along with many warnings that Moses pronounced to the people of Israel, as the emissary of YHWH himself—warnings regarding idol worship, child sacrifice, and other abhorrent practices of the surrounding polytheistic peoples—he also stressed the principles of incest prohibitions in some detail: "None of you shall approach any near of kin to uncover their nakedness. . . . The nakedness of your father and the nakedness of your mother you shall not uncover; she is your mother and you shall not uncover her nakedness. The nakedness of your father's wife you shall not uncover. . . . The nakedness of your sister, the daughter of your father, or the daughter of your mother, whether born at home or away from home, you shall not uncover their nakedness. The nakedness of your son's daughter, or the daughter's daughter ... the nakedness of your father's wife's daughter ... she is your sister" (Levit. 18.6–16).

In addition, it is further specified that the "nakedness" of the father's sister, mother's sister, brother's wife, father's brother's wife, daughter-in-law, and sundry other kinsmen should not be uncovered. It is clear from the wording and the context that the "uncovering of nakedness" refers to sexual intercourse. In other parts of the Bible, persons who violate these laws or rules are "cursed" (see Deuteronomy) and elsewhere in the text, transgression is even punishable by death. Actually, there seems to be a discrepancy between the violation of the taboo and the actual punishment that was meted out to the culprits involved. Here are several examples which illustrate the violation of the incest taboo and the resulting treatment that implicitly ignores the severity of punishment originally enunciated by the nation's leader and intermediary between YHWH and his people—Moses.

Lot and His Daughters

One of the clearest and most blatant episodes involving incest is narrated in the book of Genesis. Following the devastation and destruction of Sodom and Gomorrah, because of the sinfulness of their people, Lot, the nephew of the patriarch Abraham, escaped into the desert with his two daughters. His wife was not with them for she had turned into "a pillar of salt." The biblical story proceeds as follows:

> And Lot went up out of Zoar and dwelled in the mountain, and his two daughters with him ... and he dwelled in a cave, he and his two daughters. And the older said to the younger—our father is old and there is no man to come to us as is the custom. Come, let us make our father drink wine, and we will lie with him and we will preserve seed from our father. And they made their father drink wine that night and the older daughter came in and lay with her father and he did not know when she lay down, nor when she got up. Then, the following morning, the older said to the younger—I lay last night with my father, let us make him drink wine tonight also and you go and lay with him and preserve our father's seed. And they made their father drink wine that night and the younger daughter arose and lay with him and he was not aware when she lay down nor when she got up and both daughters were with child by their father (Gen. 10.30–38).

As a result of the conspiracy of the daughters and the participation of their "anaesthetized" father, the two nights were quite productive for the daughters bore sons which, in fact, did preserve the seed of their father. Two sons were born and their descendants, according to the Bible, formed the tribes of the Moabites and the Ammonites.

What is of interest is that despite the disapprobation of incest specified in the Mosaic rules quoted above, the Bible's editors report the adventures of Lot's daughters in a rather matter-of-fact manner. There is no reiteration of the incest taboo in that context nor any reference to the impropriety and sinfulness of the behavior. There is even a hint of acquiescence with, and approval of, the behavior of the daughters, for a great goal was served. Of course, historically, the episode of Lot and his daughters allegedly takes place long before the appearance of Moses on the scene. But, it is somewhat surprising that the editors or redactors of the Bible left this blatantly deviant folk-tale in the text of the "Holy writ." Yet, this tolerant attitude persists, as may be illustrated in the episodes that follow.

REUBEN'S FOLLY

Generations later, something happened for which disapproval is indicated, but again, no serious punishment follows. Israel (Jacob) was away on a long trip, during which his younger and favorite wife Rachel died. After she died he returned to the family enclave "And Israel journeyed and pitched his tent beyond the tower of Edar. And it happened when Israel dwelled in that land, Reuben went and lay with Bilhah, Israel's concubine. And Israel heard about it" (Gen. 36.21–22). Although there is no evidence of reprisals on the part of father Israel against his oldest son for what we may call his "Oedipal acting-out, it was quite clear that his father bore him a grudge. It became abundantly clear when he spoke to his sons on his deathbed, commented on their character, and predicted their future. On that occasion he said: "Reuben, you are my first-born ... unstable as water, you shall not excel because you went up on your father's bed and defiled his couch" (Gen. 49.3–4). Obviously, Reuben's father commented on his impulsivity and weakness of character, but not his violation of the incest taboo. There is the reference to personal pique or resentment, but no concern with cultural-religious prohibitions. Again, in this case the period is still pre-Mosaic, and, therefore, the injunctions against incest were not codified and were not yet part of the religious law. It is interesting that in this instance, as in the case of Lot, the biblical editors included the story as part of the compendium. In a sense, it is still prehistory, and located prior to the full institutionalization of Hebrew monotheism.

TAMAR'S DECEPTION OF JUDAH

Jacob's fourth son, Judah, had three sons. The oldest, Er, was married to a woman by the name of Tamar. By law, or custom, upon Er's death, his brother Onan was supposed to take his place, especially since Er did not have any children, but Onan did not wish to supply the household of his brother with an heir. Then Onan died and the youngest of the brothers, Shelah, was too young to marry the widow of his oldest brother. So, Judah sent her to the house of her father to wait until his youngest son becomes of age.

Over the years Judah did not fulfill his promise to give his last son to Tamar as a husband. So Tamar disguised herself as a prostitute and lured the unaware Judah, who slept with her and impregnated her. Thus, Judah, albeit unknowingly, violated the prohibition against sexual involvement with one's daughter-in-law (Gen. 38; see the discussion of prostitution, above).

Judah's was not a conscious violation of the incest prohibition, but it occurred nevertheless. We are not told what Judah's and Tamar's subsequent relationship was upon his discovery of her true identity. She produced twin sons following this temporary union. But Tamar certainly knew what she was doing, and knew that she violated the incest taboo by enticing her father-in-law into this illicit affair. No punishment is mentioned on this occasion.

Of interest is another biblical fact that may be mentioned parenthetically. One of the twins born to Judah and Tamar was Peretz, whose descendant, Boaz, married Ruth the Moabite. She gave birth to Obed, who was the grandfather of David—the famous warrior and king of Israel, circa 1000 B.C.E. (Ruth 4.21–23).

AMNON AND TAMAR—BROTHER AND SISTER

The incest tales related so far belong to what may be called the "prehistory" of Israel; the time before the formation and birth of a full-fledged national entity. The present story, however, dates from a much later period, after the kingdom had been established, and during the reign of King David, which may be viewed as a more "historical" era.

In the section above discussing rape, the episode of Amnon and Tamar was discussed in some detail. It was a description of an instance of rape within the extended royal family of King David. In the present context, rape is not the issue, but incest is. The fact was that Tamar was a "daughter of the father's wife"; in other words, she was a half-sister.

I quoted earlier from the book of Leviticus. Part of the quote reads: "The nakedness of your sister, the daughter of your father, or the daughter of your mother ... you shall not uncover." From this we learn that the incest taboo extended to the half-sister, the daughter of the father, as well. Hence, Amnon was not only guilty of rape, but of the violation of a taboo as well. Incidentally, the taboo is reiterated in the book of Deuteronomy as follows: "Cursed be he who lies with his sister, whether daughter of his father or his mother" (Deut. 27.22).

It is clear from the text that the violation of the taboo was not the sole cause, but it was surely the rape of his sister, that motivated Absalom's assassination of Amnon. King David and others knew about the taboo violation, but nothing was done about it. The behavior was disapproved, but it was not punished, as specified in the code of Moses. This laxness was apparently part of the ancient tradition. For example: Leah and Rachel, who were sisters, married the same man—Jacob. Sarah herself was actually a half sister of her husband Abraham. It would appear that the apparent tolerance of incest behavior in the Bible may represent a transitional period in the life of ancient Israel. It was not until later centuries that the incest taboo was strengthened and the prohibition more strictly enforced. Western culture is heir to the incest taboo tradition.

Further Comments

Regarding the series of prohibitions involving incestuous sexual behavior, two additional observations may be made.

First, all the admonitions against the violation of the incest taboo, are directed at the male of the species. The nature of the violation was apparently viewed as a one-way street; that is, all sexual behavior originates with the male, involving the tabooed object, the female. It demonstrates the traditional patriarchal view of the man as the "wooer," aggressor, and initiator of the contact, with the woman as a passive object, the recipient of masculine attention.

Second, the listing of women who are forbidden as sex objects and with whom sexual intercourse is prohibited is somewhat incomplete. Let's review a more literal translation with a different version of the relevant passage in the book of Leviticus: "Any man, any man—to any kin of one's [own] flesh you are not to come near, exposing their nakedness. The nakedness of your father and the nakedness of your mother, you are not to expose. She is your mother, you are not to expose her nakedness. I am YHWH. The nakedness of your father's wife, you are not to expose ... the nakedness of your sister.... The nakedness of your son's daughter or of your daughter's daughter." (Levi. 18.6–10). This quotation from Fox's (1995) translation of the Pentateuch goes on to extend the list of those whose "exposure of nakedness" is forbidden to include aunts, stepsisters, daughters-in-law, and sisters-in-law, as well as some other, more remote relatives. This is the most literal rendition of the Hebrew text. We note that the reference is to uncovering nakedness, but the meaning of this expression is not readily obvious. The *New English Bible* (Oxford Edition) translates the uncovering of nakedness simply as *"intercourse,"* whereas most other translations stick to the literal "nakedness." However, the interpretation of this passage quite generally refers to sexual intercourse, for the expression is relatively meaningless and would not be accompanied by the strict injunctions, had it been anything else but intercourse. It was a somewhat indirect, "nice" way to refer to the sexual act.

One conspicuous omission from the lists of forbidden sexual objects is rather puzzling; I refer here to the absence of *daughters* from the rather lengthy roster presented in the book of Leviticus.

It may be argued that the preliminary sentence which introduces the entire collection of rules—"any man—to any kin of one's own flesh, you are not to come near exposing their nakedness"—clearly includes one's daughter, for she certainly qualifies as "kin of one's [own] flesh." If that is so, then the question arises—why list all the women relatives that are "kin," for they may be subsumed under the general term used in the introductory statement? It seems that the specification was needed in the case of persons who are not members of the immediate family. Yet, "mother" and "sister" are mentioned. It is a puzzle that is not easily resolved.

A question arises—is this taboo maintained in Western society, and to what extent is it maintained? To answer this question we must turn to some more recent sources concerning this issue.

THE INCEST TABOO IN WESTERN SOCIETY

Although it has been often stated that the incest taboo is universal and has existed from time immemorial, the instances presented from the biblical literature indicated that such a view is not entirely unchallenged. Despite legal and forensic condemnation of the incest behavior, there is, implicitly a certain degree of tolerance of such deviance. And, despite the statements that incest violation was to be punished by death, we have not found any reports in the biblical texts of such an occurrence. Yet, over the centuries, the *laws* and *rules* regarding the behavior have been adopted by the world's religions and legal systems.

In modern psychology, especially psychoanalysis, there is a full recognition of the powerful drive of the incestuous wishes. It is at the basis of the Freudian fundamental concept of the Oedipus complex. Here is an emphasis of the inevitability of the child of one sex having incestual fantasies regarding the parent of the opposite sex. It seems that incest is a very basic urge, or else why should there be such universal condemnation of the act?

In a 1932 letter (Jones, 1957), the father of psychoanalysis writes to one of his followers, Marie Bonoparte, as follows: "It is curious but perhaps easily understood—that just the most powerful prohibitions of mankind are those that are hardest to justify. That is because the justifications are prehistoric, taking their root in man's past. The situation with incest is just the same as with cannibalism. There are, of course, real grounds in modern life against slaying a man in order to devour him, but no ground whatsoever against eating human flesh instead of animal flesh. Still, most of us would find it impossible" (p. 454).

"Incest is not so remote and indeed happens often enough. We can readily see that if generally practiced, it would be just as harmful socially today as in ancient times. This social harm is the kernel which has undergone an apotheosis after being adorned with a taboo. In individual exceptional cases, incest would even today be harmless although it is true it would still be unsocial as abrogating one of those social restrictions necessary to the maintenance of civilization" (Jones, 1957, p. 454). In psychoanalysis, what is most important is not so much the actual violation of the incest taboo. Instead, the focus is on the effect of the indecisive repression of incestuous wishes, as a function of the taboo, upon the personality of the individual.

In present-day American society, important changes have apparently taken place with respect to the incidence of the violation of the taboo. Some 30 years ago we were told: "Although sanctioned in a few privileged classes and in some sectarian groups, incest behavior is uniformly condemned in virtually all societies, from illiterate to modern. The few cases that do arise and are detected in Western societies are less than one offender per million persons in English speaking countries" (Weinberg, 1963, p. 349). A more recent summary of the incidence of incest behavior concludes that "the traditional estimate of one in a million is no more than a wish." The authors (Forward & Buck, 1978) report that: "Various studies estimate that up to one in every four women in the United States is a victim of sexual molestation, by the time she reaches eighteen years of age ... 38 percent are incestuous ... one out of every ten women" (p. 3).

The changes in incidence reported are due to a number of factors.

First, the question arises whether "sexual molestation" is truly part of the definition of "incest," which implies intercourse. The more recent figures may be inflated by a more liberal definition of the incest taboo.

Second, the earlier definitions of incest referred to the prohibition of consanguinous behavior—that is, sex with the immediate members of the nuclear family. The later definitions of incest are much broader, and include half-brothers and sisters-in-law, step-siblings, and even "live-in lovers."

Third, there is no doubt that modern society is more open, and with the development of psychologically minded cultural attitudes, there is greater self-examination and confession of behaviors that have previously been held strictly private and concealed from the outside world. This is not to say that all incest behavior always comes to light, and that there is no sizable number of violations that do not come to the attention of the courts or of the psychotherapists.

Considering all that, one might conclude that we do not have any accurate figures. The numbers are, most likely, greater than "one in a million."

The literature on the topic in contemporary society is rife with examples of the discovery of unpunished incest behavior. Many such revelations appear in retrospect, as a result of therapeutic evocation of repressed memories of parental incestuous behavior during childhood. The "horror" of incest is still very much with us as its destructiveness to individuals and to families of lasting duration.

MASTURBATION

One of the laws laid down by Moses in the extensive code of the book of Deuteronomy concerns the obligations of the younger brother of a man who dies and who leaves his wife childless (that is, without a male heir). In that event, it is the duty of the wife's brother-in-law, the brother of her dead husband, "to come to her and marry her. And the oldest son born shall establish the name of the dead brother whose name will not be erased in Israel" (Deut. 25.6–7). There are also stipulations of certain humiliating punishments for the man who refuses to do his duty. This is known as the law of the *Levirate*.

A rather unique compromise between refusal to obey the law and adherence to it is illustrated in the story of Onan, the younger son of Judah: "And Judah took a wife for his son Er, his firstborn, whose name was Tamar. And Er was wicked and YHWH slew him. And Judah said to Onan: Go to your brother's wife, and marry her, and raise up issue for your brother. And Onan knew that the issue would not be his, so whenever he slept with his brother's wife, he spilled his seed to the ground, so as to not raise up issue for his brother ... what he did was wicked in the eyes of the Lord" (Gen. 38.6–10).

It is not at all clear what the "wickedness" of Onan consisted of—refusal to accept a holy obligation, the means by which the avoidance was accomplished, or both. It seems, however, that subsequent generations continued to react most to the *means* by which Onan avoided his duty—the wasting of valuable sperm—or masturbation, rather than providing issue and inheritance rights to the family of his dead brother.

Over the centuries, "spilling the seed to the ground" has been condemned by the major religions of the world. Yet, as far as the Bible is concerned, the Onan episode (from which the term Onanism was culled and used for centuries as synonymous to masturbation), is the only one which directly concerns the act of masturbation. Moreover, Onan's behavior consisted, apparently, of the act of withdrawal during intercourse ("coitus interruptus"), and not of masturbation as it is generally understood (as self-stimulation). It would appear that the *sin* committed was that of wasting the seed. It is the latter concept that led to the eventual generalization about all acts of masturbation by males, where the "waste" of sperm is involved.

It is not surprising that masturbation on the part of *females* is nowhere mentioned. The reasons are readily understood when we consider the biblical context. In the first place, the relative insignificance of women, as illustrated for example, in their remaining anonymous and nameless in most biblical sources, seems to reveal relative inattention to their private behavior. Secondly, the importance of the "seed," the semen, in the perpetuation and expansion of the family, tribe and nation—the adherence to the dictum of "be fruitful and multiply"—is reduced and degraded in the act of masturbation. However, it was *male* masturbation that was viewed as the destruction or depletion of the supply of semen necessary for deposit into potentially childbearing women. No similar waste or destructiveness was perceived in the case of the female of the species.

Even in modern times, male masturbation has received much greater attention than female self-gratification. But there is a recognition of the ubiquity of the behavior, both as part of the developmental phase of life, as well as during the period of adulthood and even later maturity. Until the recent past, masturbation has been considered as a sign of "depravity," if not outright sinfulness. But this attitude finds rather slim support in the Bible; that is, in the Old Testament. It seems that the act of Onan has been overinterpreted, exaggerated, overexpanded, and overgeneralized in its importance by the subsequent generations of wise men, priests and religious aficionados of both Judaism and Christianity.

Since the 17th and 18th centuries, with their greater concern with abnormal behavior and its treatment, and the advent of a more liberal approach on the part of some of the clergy and the medical profession, a number of sins, such as homosexuality, incest, and masturbation, have been interpreted as causes or symptoms of mental illness, or mental disorder, or insanity. Thus, during the early decades of the 19th century, when the state hospital movement flourished in the United States, masturbation was cited along with impiousness and alcoholism as a major cause of insanity.

The following excerpt from an article published in the March 6, 1839 *New Hampshire Sentinel,* concerning the *Sixth Annual Report of the Massachusetts Lunatic Hospital,* is a reasonable statement of the state of psychiatry and psychopathology at that time: "It breathes the spirit of science and philanthropy. It demonstrates that insanity is a disease, or when incurable, yet capable of great amelioration by proper medical and moral treatment. It points to the causes which are productive of insanity, some of which may be avoided by those forewarned of the consequences. The three highest are *Intemperance, Ill Health, and Masturbation*" [italics added] (p. 42).

This is an interesting example of the conversions of a past sin, a prohibition attributed to the Bible, into a more modern version, a major cause of "insanity" or mental disorder.

With the development of psychoanalysis and with greater attention to child behavior, the ubiquity of the masturbation phenomenon became more recognized in contemporary society. It is variously estimated that about 95% of adult males and 50–80% of females have masturbated (McCary, 1967/1973). It is to be remembered that the term has broadened in its meaning over the centuries and that it applies to any form of stimulation of the genitals in an attempt at sexual gratification. This extended definition of masturbation even applies to infants. Orgasm does not even seem to be the necessary ingredient. It would appear that even if the generalization of the biblical activity of Onan is adopted to incorporate all orgastic behavior, much of what is defined under the heading of "masturbation" would not fall into that category.

Masturbation has become a major topic with the development of psychoanalytic theory and practice. It is viewed as a normal feature of early infantile development and, especially, during the person's adolescence. It becomes a serious psychological issue when, for a variety of reasons, in adulthood, the masturbatory activity remains the main source of sexual gratification. This behavior is viewed as abnormal if it persists in adulthood as the exclusive or major mode of sexual gratification. It is a symptom of social isolation and unconnectedness with people in the environment. It often accompanies withdrawal of a schizophrenic nature—the extreme expression of isolation and relinquishment of social interaction.

Paradoxically, while under the influence of psychoanalysis the term "masturbation" has come to designate any kind of self-stimulation occurring as early as infancy; but at the very same time, its pathological significance, especially as a causative factor in the etiology of mental disorder, has disappeared from the pages of modern psychiatry texts. However, the deliberations of Freud's inner circle at the beginning of the century (Freud, Vol. XII, 241–254) have produced little consensus concerning this matter. Fenichel (1945) summarized the matter pithily by concluding that masturbation is to be considered as abnormal only when it is an adult's preferred mode of sexual gratification and concomitant with an inability to gain, or incapacity for interactive sexual satisfaction.

This is a far cry from designation masturbation as one of the major *causes* of mental disorder. Most frequently, the problem of exclusive gratification of sexuality via masturbation is created when "parental or adult attitudes toward the act have instilled in the child anxieties and fears that affect its development adversely" (Kolb & Brodie, 1982, p. 695).

Over the centuries, masturbation got its bad name and evil status not from the original Bible, but from the exegetic literature, from the Talmud, Mishnaic writings and from the New Testament, and from the Christian fathers who established the strong prohibition and the implied sinfulness of masturbatory practices. A great deal of guilt and low self-esteem became associated with the act of masturbation, and hence became a source of great psychological stress and consequently woven into the fabric of the theory and etiology of psychopathology.

CONCERNING DEVIATIONS FROM HETEROSEXUALITY

Aside from the numerous prohibitions of sexual intercourse between adults of the opposite sex who are not married to each other, there are a number of negative pronouncements concerning unconventional or non-normative types of sexual behavior. The injunctions in the book of Leviticus are directed against male homosexuality and against bestiality committed by either sex.

It is of particular interest that female deviation, that is, female homosexuality or lesbianism, is not even mentioned in the Bible. Apparently, this type of behavior was not identified nor recognized by the ancient Hebrews. It was neither observed, reported, nor considered significant enough to comment about it in the appropriate compendia of rules of behavior, nor in the detailed presentation of the forensic and legal codes of the tribes and the nation.

From the viewpoint of the injunction to "be fruitful and multiply," it can be readily understood why homosexuality was totally rejected by ancient Hebrew law. It violates the dictum, for obvious reasons that the homosexual union is nonproductive; it does not bear fruit and does not contribute to the multiplying of the nation. It is clearly against the enunciated goal of nation-building that is frequently mentioned in the scriptures. Hence, the very harsh punishment of men engaged in homosexual behavior; but, the punishment of men only. The phenomenon of female homosexuality was apparently unobserved or not recognized as such. And, if there was an inkling of such possible behavior, it was not viewed as a danger or a threat to the growth and expansion of the nation. All marriageable women apparently had husbands and were engaged in intercourse that resulted in impregnation, regardless of their sexual inclinations. If pregnancy did not occur, it was seen as an act of God and, possibly, as a punishment that the Lord "withheld the child from the womb," or, that the Lord "closed the womb." Possible rejection of heterosexuality on the part of women was inconceivable; after all, it was viewed as women's major function in life to provide their husband with heirs (preferably male), be fruitful and multiply, and replenish the land. In the patriarchal, andro-centric society, the man initiated the conjugal relationship.

This state of affairs continued over the centuries, and has changed to some extent in the 20th century, but in only a limited segment of the world's population. When males do not pursue the heterosexual path, they tend to be viewed with suspicion by their peers. In the 19th century, this suspicion was based in the rejection of homosexuality, which was seen as abnormal and unnatural and in need of correction and treatment. The enlightened humanism dictated a more kind approach to homosexuality than dictated by Mosaic law or by its derivatives in Christianity, medicine, and psychiatry; rather than stoning and execution, a grudging tolerance became the order of the day. After many decades in limbo, homosexuality figured in the list of mental disorders of the psychiatric community's diagnostic manuals. It was not until the early 1970s that this entry, the listing of homosexuality among the psychopathological disorders, was expunged from the rosters of those condemned to the asylums and hospitals, and removed from the catalogs and learned tomes of the psychiatric profession.

In this respect, historically speaking, female homosexuals or lesbians have had a better time of it. Those who were not selected by avid male suitors, or who rejected all comers, may have been pitied, but, by and large, they were left alone. Actually, they were left to associate freely, and with impunity, with the other "unfortunates" of similar ilk. Even in the 19th and 20th centuries, female homosexuality was neither much noticed, nor condemned, nor taken over by the medical-psychiatric establishment. Diagnostic records of the various institutions concerned with this matter will bear me out on this score. At any rate, if we are to follow this line of reasoning, no interference with the process of nation-building of the Israelites was perceived in close friendships among women. Such friendships, if noted, were not suspected to be sexual in nature, and were not censured as instance of an "abomination."

In the book of Leviticus, we find the following injunction: "You shall not be with a man as with a woman; that is an abomination" (18.22). In a later chapter, not only disapproval is the result, but "They shall be put to death; their blood shall be on their own heads" (20.18). It is interesting to note that the prohibition is spelled out and addressed to men only; lesbianism is neither mentioned nor proscribed.

MEN OF SODOM

A couple of outstanding episodes illustrating a rather aggressive sort of homosexuality may deserve mention in this connection. The first episode, first discussed above in the section on "Rape," is a special illustration of the wickedness of the men from Sodom and Gommorah, the doomed cities of old. Two messengers (or angels) were reported to have visited Lot and wished to depart immediately after executing their mission. It was God's warning regarding the impending destruction of the wicked cities. However, Lot was very hospitable, as was appropriate for the host in patriarchal times: "But Lot was so insistent that they came into his house and he made them a feast ... and they ate. Before they had lain down to sleep, the men of Sodom, young and old, surrounded the house, and they called out to Lot and said—'where are the men who came to you tonight? Bring them out, so that we will know them.' Lot went out and closed the door behind him. He said—'please, brothers, do not act wickedly. Here are my two daughters, do with them as you wish, but don't do anything to the men, for they came under the shadow of my roof'." (Gen. 19.4–8).

"To know," in the Biblical sense, means to perform the sexual act; to have intercourse. Not only were the men of Sodom pursuing homosexual gratification, but they wanted to force the issue—essentially, to commit rape on the men who were Lot's guests. Lot does not seem to express horror about the intended homosexual behavior, but instead about the force to be applied, and about the indignity and insult to his guests who were under the shadow of his roof. Lot was even willing to sacrifice his daughters in order to protect his guests. But, the sacrifice apparently was not necessary. The angels worked a miracle that saved the situation, and Sodom and Gommorah were utterly destroyed shortly thereafter.

THE GIBEAH EPISODE

A similar incident took place during the period of the Judges (Judg. 19.21–24) in the town of Gibeah. It is almost an exact parallel of the Lot story, when a wayfarer and his wife were taken in by one of the townsmen as his guests. "They washed their feet and ate and drank. While they were enjoying themselves, some of the worst men of the town surrounded the house … shouting 'bring out the man who came to your house so that we may know him'." The evil men of the town were apparently not interested in the woman who came with the man; they were only interested in the man. The host sent out his own concubine instead, and she was abused all night.

It seems that the crowd in this case was not strictly homosexual, but, as Patai suggests, bisexual. His further comments about the Biblical redactors: "What they condemn and execrate is the intended violation of the Sodomite and Gibehite mobs of the visiting strangers. This would have been rape, and as such, just as sinful as rape of a woman and in fact, worse, it would have been also a violation of the sacred institution of hospitality" (Patai, 1960, p. 153). However, this explanation is not altogether satisfactory in view of the willingness of the host to placate the mobs by offering them women instead of the visiting men.

What is of interest is the fact that despite the formal prohibition against homosexuality, the quest of males for sex with other males was not a rare occurrence at all. The tendency was not very vigorously condemned in actual life and behavior. In a sense, these facts and the apparent discrepancy between frequent behavior and the prohibitions of the Mosaic code is a rather general principle which we have encountered in the incest taboo violation and will note in other contexts as well. Homosexuality disappears from the Biblical scene, and is not mentioned in any of the later books of the canon. The taboo against homosexuality has been strongly reinforced in subsequent centuries, both in Christianity as well as in Judaism.

Although homosexual behavior remains anathema to most

organized religion and was until recently prohibited by the secular codes, the practice has remained widespread and flourished, especially during the last generation. This may only be an apparent increase due to the greater openness and permissiveness of contemporary American society. Conventional wisdom alleges that there has always been a sizable percentage of the population that engaged in homosexual practices (Kinsey, Pomeroy, & Gebhard, 1948). But in the past, the behavior was covert and not open to public knowledge. Only recently, people have "come out of the closet" and the numbers of self-admitted homosexuals has risen markedly.

Modern psychiatry has identified homosexuality as a psychopathological condition. During the first half of the 20th century, it was labeled as "psychopathic personality with pathological sexuality." The second edition of the American Psychiatric Association's *Diagnostic and Statistical Manual of Mental Disorders* (1952) includes homosexuality under the general rubric of "sexual deviations"; the diagnosis will specify the type of pathological behavior such as homosexuality or transvestism." The second edition of the manual (1968) continues the same category of sexual deviations. In it are included "individuals whose sexual interests are directed primarily to objects other than people of the opposite sex." There is a further qualification, that such a diagnosis does not apply to people who engage in such deviant behavior because no normal sexual object is available. The rampant homosexuality among previously heterosexual men who are in prison is an example of this stipulation.

It was not until 1973 that the American Psychiatric Association voted to exclude homosexuality from the realm of the psychopathological. The 1994 APA manual no longer lists homosexuality among the disorders or deviations. It is viewed as a "variant" of sexuality, not a mark of abnormality or pathology.

Over the years, the sciences of psychiatry, neurology, genetics and psychoanalysis have attempted to get at the root and cause of this variant behavior. So far, there is little that can be said in support of any one theory to the exclusion of any other. It may well be that, at present, the formula of genetic predisposition, or *anlage,* combined with favorable environmental circumstances that produce the particular pattern of behavior, is

the most defensible statement concerning the origins of homosexuality.

SUMMING UP

Overall, sexuality is regarded in a positive light in the Hebrew
Bible. Although procreation and perpetuation of the species was
of the utmost value, love and pleasure of an erotic nature, as
described in the Song of Songs in particular, is not neglected
nor certainly proscribed in any way. Asceticism, sexual abstention for its own sake, and self-deprivation in the sexual sphere
did not appear as part of the extant culture until after the Hebrew Bible had been finalized, "sealed and delivered," so to
speak, by the priestly editors.

Adultery is the only major sexual prohibition to appear in
the decalogue, the cardinal statement of ethical behavior of
the Judaic religion; this is more commonly known as the "Ten
Commandments." The sinfulness and prohibition of any kind
of sexual promiscuity is forbidden, and the principle is reiterated in several sections of the book of Genesis. Promiscuity serves as a paradigm and a metaphor for religious
fickleness. The sin of whoring after other gods and turning
away from YHWH was repeatedly preached by the prophets.
Nevertheless, examples of the violation of the commandment
against adultery and promiscuity abound in the Bible and
still remain the bane of modern society on the eve of the 21st
millennium. The violation of the seventh commandment (that
is, adultery) was a threat to the very fabric of ancient society; this violation threatened both the sanctity of marriage
and the safety and stability of the family.

No such prohibitions were invoked by the practice of male or
female prostitution, which was implicated in the premosaic religious rites and practices and persisted in the Israelite culture.
It may be speculated that the practice of the profession served
some function for members of the ancient society, as it does
even now, in modern and postmodern societies.

Recreational sex was certainly not considered in biblical
writings, but sexuality whose function is solely procreation

was regarded very positively, but primarily as an obligation and as a means of family and nation building. It is the absence of such obligations that underlies the draconian punishments for "nonproductive" sexuality such as homosexuality and bestiality. Persons engaged in such practices are "cursed" and are subject to capital punishment. Similar punishment was visited upon Onan (from whom we derive the term "Onanism") who let his "seed drop to the ground" instead of copulating with, and impregnating, his dead brother's wife, and thus providing him with an heir, according to the law of the levirate. Onan's behavior was also, like homosexuality and bestiality, a form of nonproductive sex. However, masturbatory activity as such, outside these special circumstances does not seem to have been considered in the Hebrew Bible.

Perhaps there was a recognition of the ubiquity of this behavior, but also an awareness that its occasional practice is not inimical to nor does it interfere seriously with, ultimate procreation and population growth.

As far as the commission of rape is concerned, it was viewed as an instance in which the loss of self-control results in disrespect—an affront to and an insult of the family of the woman attacked. In a sense, it was considered as an act of aggression combined with heterosexual expression (as in the case of Schechem) or homosexuality (as in the case of Sodom and Gommorah, and Gibeah). With few exceptions (e.g., Saudi Arabia; see Lindsey, 1991), the greater liberalism and permissiveness of the era of enlightenment in recent centuries has eliminated the use of draconian measures in response to the violation of these traditionally proscribed behaviors. Modern society remains, however, cognizant of the need for the perpetuation of some constraints, in the service of a civilized and humanitarian society.

CHAPTER 4

Aspects of the Biblical Family

THE STRUCTURE OF THE BIBLICAL FAMILY

As has been noted elsewhere in this work, the ancient Israelite society was patriarchal and androcentric. It was also polygamous in nature. More specifically, it was polygynous in nature—men being married to more than one wife. Families consisted of a father, the head of the household, more than one wife-mother, and the children of several wives. This was a sort of extended family, consisting of a number of nuclear subfamilies—depending, of course, on the number of wives married to the man of the household. Each nuclear family unit included the children born to that specific union.

There was also a second-order type of family consisting of concubines and maidservants, who bore the master's children and were part of the extended household. The ranking of the wives within the larger unit is not clear, nor institutionalized. However, some of the wives or concubines were more preferred or favored by the master of the family, and were rewarded accordingly. The status of the maidservants and of the concubines was somewhat lower than that of ordinary wives; they were often subservient to the legitimate wives who had greater power and authority in the family hierarchy. Sarah, for example, had the authority to expel Hagar, the Egyptian maidservant and surrogate wife of Abraham, despite her status as a concubine and despite the fact that she was the mother of Ishmael—the son of Abraham (Gen. 21).

This kind of family organization was most likely fertile ground for envy, competition, and strife between wives and between their respective offspring. Wives competed for status in the eyes of the master, the head of the polygynous family. The jealousy of the two wives of Jacob, may be seen as one example. Childless Rachel, early in her marriage, was obviously unhappy about the superior status of her older sister Leah, the first wife of Jacob, who gave him many children (Gen. 30). A similar source of unhappiness and jealousy occurred in the case of Hannah, the wife of Elkana (1 Sam. 1).

Rivalry between siblings involved not only competition within the nuclear unit, but within the extended family as well; rivalry was not only between consanguinous brothers, but also between those brothers who shared the same father but different mothers. An aspect of the jealousy of the older brothers with respect to young Joseph may be an illustrative example of this point (Gen. 37). This state of affairs was especially reflected in the accounts of the struggles for royal succession in the reigning families of the kingdoms of Israel and Judah, detailed in the books of Kings and Chronicles of the Tanakh. Although the principle of primogeniture was the official canon in ancient Israel, accounts of the flouting of this principle may frequently be found in the Bible, and are dealt with later in the present chapter.

It should be noted that the references to sibling rivalry are almost exclusively concerned with the male of the species. Competition among sisters has been of relatively little concern to the biblical chroniclers; partly because they were not counted as heirs, and the principle of primogeniture was hardly relevant in that case. Additionally, as mentioned earlier, feminine salience in the biblical narrative is generally much lower than of the males in the patriarchal society.

In the following pages, the issue of sibling rivalry in the ancient Hebrew family, both nuclear and extended, is pursued, and the consequences and possible developmental trajectories of such struggles are discussed in greater detail. In our comparisons of personality development and adult status, related to birth order, one needs to be fully cognizant of the fundamental differences between the structure of the biblical family and that of the modern family. Much of the psychological literature is based on close observations and clinical analysis of the close relationships within the modern nuclear family. The work of Freud, Adler, and others in the psychoanalytic tradition is most relevant and influential.

RIVALRY BETWEEN SIBLINGS

In many cultures, the status of the oldest child, especially if that child is a son, is most favorable. He has the "birthright," or the favorite status in the patriarchal type of family. In a sense, he is second to the head of the family as far as potential power and economic rights are concerned; he is the chief heir to the family land and to other worldly goods. In royal families, even today, it is the oldest child who inherits the throne. Throughout history, the position of the favorite oldest son has been challenged by younger sons on numerous occasions. This sibling rivalry has carried over into modern times, although neither throne nor inheritance may be at stake. Psychologists have viewed the causes of that rivalry as not connected with royal status or special economic privilege, but with psychological status and affectional advantages. The rivalry has almost been viewed as a universal and as axiomatic.

CAIN AND ABEL

The first description in the Bible of this competitive relationship between two brothers appears in the book of Genesis. The reference, of course, is to the sons of Adam, the first man. Cain, the oldest son, was a farmer, "a tiller of the ground," while Abel, his younger brother, "was a keeper of sheep." Both Cain and Abel brought their offerings to the Lord: "And the Lord had paid heed to Abel and his offering: But unto Cain and his offering he paid no heed" (Gen. 4.4–5). This discrimination in favor of his brother Abel angered Cain very much. "And Cain talked with Abel his brother: And it came to pass, when they were in the field, that Cain rose up against Abel his brother, and slew him" (Gen. 4.8). Thus, the jealous Cain was unable to bear his younger brother's higher status and recognition, and acted out his murderous impulse.

It is interesting to note, parenthetically, that Abel was the most generous in his offering ("he also brought of the firstlings of his flock and of the fat thereof"), while his brother Cain just "brought the fruit of the ground." Biblical commentaries attribute to this act the greater recognition given Abel, which was the cause of his death at the hands of his own brother.

Esau and Jacob

A second episode involving the relationship between two brothers is also described in the book of Genesis. This is not a clear example of sibling rivalry as such, but some of the implications of competition for status are definitely there.

Even before the twins, Esau and Jacob, were born to their parents, Isaac and Rebekkah, "the children struggled together within her" (Gen. 25.22). Esau was designated as the older of the two: "And the first came out ... and they called his name Esau" (Gen. 25.25). His status as the oldest son had been clearly established. It is in the following paragraph that follows that we see how different the two sons were, and how the older Esau relinquished his birthright to the younger brother Jacob.

"And the boys grew: and Esau was a cunning hunter, a man of the field; and Jacob was a plain man dwelling in tents. And Isaac loved Esau, because he did eat his venison: But Rebekkah loved Jacob. And Jacob prepared a pottage: and Esau came from the field, and he was exhausted. And Esau said to Jacob, 'Feed me, with this red pottage for I am exhausted' ... and Jacob said, 'Sell me this day your birthright.' And Esau said; 'Now I am at the point to die: and what is this birthright to me?' ... and he sold his birthright to Jacob" (Gen. 25.27–33). Thus, Esau sold his birthright for a "mess of pottage." Apparently, the birthright was an important source of envy on the part of the younger brother, Jacob, who exploited a weak moment and made a profitable transaction.

However, Isaac, the father of Esau and Jacob, was apparently unaware of the fact that Esau relinquished his birthright. So, when the aged and blind Isaac was about to die, he summoned his older son Esau to give him the blessing, as befit the first-born. But, at the instigation of Rebekkah, her favorite son, Jacob, disguised himself as Esau and received the blessing instead. "Therefore God give you of the dew of heaven, and the fatness of the earth, and plenty of corn and wine. Let people serve you, and nations bow down to you; be lord over your brethren, and let your mother's sons bow down to you ..." (Gen. 27.28–29). Hence, the privileges of the oldest son were twice wrested by Jacob, from his older brother, Esau.

Upon finding that he was again outmaneuvered by his younger brother, "Esau hated Jacob because of the blessing wherewith his father blessed him; and Esau said in his heart, 'The days of mourning for my father are at hand then I will slay my brother Jacob' " (Gen. 27.41). Were it not for Rebekkah, who packed Jacob off to her brother's house in Haran, the Cain-Abel tragedy would have been reenacted. The only revenge left to Esau was in the path of matrimony. He took himself a Canaanite wife, which he knew would displease his parents who disapproved of the intermarriage.

JACOB'S SONS

The saga of Jacob's own family and offspring is not devoid of brotherly struggle. Joseph, the eleventh son of Jacob, was his father's favorite. He remained the favorite, although one more son (Benjamin) was born 6 years later, the second son of Rachel, who died at birth. The other sons, all ten of them, were not at all happy about the special status accorded by Father Jacob to Joseph. Their dislike was enhanced by Joseph's inordinate pride and belief that he was better than the others (see the section below on "dreams"), and that his brothers should show their respect for him.

When the opportunity presented itself, when Joseph was with them in the fields, his brothers sold him into slavery and reported to their father that he has been killed by a wild animal. The role of the oldest son on this occasion is described by pointing out his greater responsibility. At first, Reuben, the oldest son, stopped his brothers from murdering Joseph. It was only during his absence that the other brothers sold their father's favorite son to a passing caravan on the way to Egypt.

Even on his deathbed, when his sons gathered around him, Jacob reserved his greatest blessings for his favorite Joseph. In this last speech, the patriarch characterized his sons and foretold their future. His remarks about most of the brothers, with the exception of Judah, who was likened to a lion and who was predicted to gain the praise of his brethren and the better of his enemies, were not at all complimentary. Reuben is considered as "unstable as water," (Gen. 49.4) Simon and Levi, "cursed by their anger, for it was fierce" (Gen. 49.7). The others were not so sharply condemned, but were predicted to have modest achievement and success.

But "Joseph is a fruitful bough, even a fruitful bough by a well, whose branches run over the wall ... The blessings of your father have prevailed ... they shall be on the head of Joseph ..." (Gen. 49.22–26). For him, the most generous blessings were reserved and the brightest future was predicted.

DIVERSITY: THE DIFFERENCES BETWEEN SIBLINGS

A feature related to the phenomenon of sibling rivalry is the overwhelming trend of marked differences in appearance and character between siblings. Of course, the expectation of similarities between siblings of the polygynous family, characteristic of ancient societies (and a few modern ones as well), is considerably reduced, due to the fact that although the children share the genes of the father, they differ markedly on the mother's side. This difference depends, of course, upon the particular wife among the two or more wives of the biblical family who brought children into the world.

Throughout the Bible, the description of siblings highlights the substantial physical and psychological contrasts between siblings, even those born of the same mother. The sons of Eve had markedly different interests and careers. One was a farmer, closely tied to the soil (Cain), whereas his younger brother (Abel) was engaged in animal husbandry, a herder, and probably less territorial and more nomadic than his brother (Gen. 4). Esau and Jacob, fraternal twins, were genetically similar, as ordinary siblings are expected to be. Yet the Bible's description of them features and accentuates their personalty and physical differences. Esau, the first to be born, and this the "older" sibling (twin) at birth, "came out red all over, like a hairy garment" (Gen. 25.25), a characteristic which apparently, clearly distinguished him physically from his younger brother, Jacob, who was described as holding on to his brother's heel at birth. It is tempting to conjecture that these contrasting physical positions symbolized, nay, even predicted, Esau's and Jacob's future relationship to each other, as well as their behavioral characteristics—such as their leadership vs. followership, or activity vs. passivity. And as the two brothers grew up, they seem to have followed different paths. Esau was an "expert hunter, a man of the field; and Jacob was a plain man, dwelling in tents" (Gen. 25.27). We are also informed that Esau was his father's favorite, while the younger, Jacob, was preferred by the mother, Rebekkah. Clearly, the experience of the two sons was quite different from the very beginning, in the relationship with their parents. They were different in appearance, and different in their ordinal position. And there must have been an interaction between Jacob's lifestyle of Jacob—staying home—"being a dweller of the tents," and the fact that he was his mother's favorite. Esau, on the other hand, was rarely home, but was favored by the father for the tidbits that he brought him from the hunt. Here we see clearly the interaction between genetically similar and similarly endowed brothers who had the same father and mother, but differential life experiences and interaction within the family system. Here is an example of siblings who pursue different life paths, "separate lives," consistent with a modern analysis of what makes children of the same family so different. It is apparently not only the different gene combination of the two parents, but the differences in the non-shared experiences of their lives that directs them from the very beginning.

Undoubtedly, in the case of the biblical example, the pair experienced different relationships with their parents, and subsequently were exposed to, and interacted in, additional "nonshared" (Dunn & Plomin, 1990) events and experiences which fashioned and directed dissimilar developmental life trajectories. Alfred Adler's early work is relevant here and seminal in this connection (1919, 1927).

What is of further interest is the psychological analysis, characterization, and future perspective which Jacob delineated with respect to his twelve sons while on his deathbed. This progeny issued from four different mothers (see Table 4.1).

Leah had six sons, whereas Jacob's remaining three wives,

Table 4.1 Parents and Birth Order of Sons Mentioned in the Text

Parents	Oldest Son	Other Sons
Adam and Eve	Cain	Abel (2)
Abraham and Sarah and (Hagar)	Ishmael	Isaac (2)
Isaac and Rebeccah	Esau	Jacob (2)
Jacob and Leah	Reuben	Simeon (2), Levi (3) Judah (4), Issachar (9), and Zebulun (10)
(Zilpah)		Gad (7) and Asher (8)
and Rachel		Joseph (11) and Benjamin (12)
(Bilhah)		Dan (5) and Naftali (6)
Joseph and Osnath	Mannasseh	Ephraim (2)
Joash*	Gideon (?)	
Amram and Yocheved	Aaron	Moses (2)
Jessie*	Eliav	David (7)

Notes: Bracketed names are those of maidservants or substitute wives. Numbers in parentheses indicate birth order. The order of the families follows the temporal sequence as it appears in the Bible.
*No names of wives given in the biblical text.

Zilpah, Bilhah, and Rachel, had two sons each. We shall note some of the words spoken by Jacob about Leah's six sons and not compare them with the others of different mothers.

The patriarch, Jacob, for reasons noted elsewhere in this chapter, was very critical of his and Leah's eldest son, Reuben, who under ordinary circumstances would have been his father's favorite. Reuben was described by Jacob as "unstable as water, and will not excel." His two younger brothers, Simon and Levi, were characterized as instruments of "cruelty," because of the act of uncompromising revenge that they visited upon their neighbors following the rape of their sister Dinah. Judah, the fourth brother was seen as the one with leadership potential: "your father's children shall bow down before you" (Gen. 49.9) and one from whose descendants "the scepter shall not depart." Even in this partial listing of Jacob's sons by the same wife, Leah, the Bible demonstrates the great differences and diversity of traits of character and potential for future direction and development in offspring of the same parents. The old patriarch, Jacob was fully cognizant of the individual differences among his sons.

Being the oldest was traditionally and historically a favorite position in the ancient Hebrew family and society. Being the oldest is, of course, an experience not shared by any of the siblings who subsequently appear on the scene. Each had a different "order of birth," or a different ordinal position in the sibship which, to a considerable extent, created their different and nonshared experiences, both inside and outside the family milieu. It is not surprising, therefore, that there is considerable dissimilarity between siblings who grow up in the same family, which presumably presents the "same" environment for its members.

We are now ready to move beyond the issue of individual differences and diversity within the family system. At this point, we shall consider in greater detail the personality characteristics that tend to develop in siblings as a result of their ordinal position as well as the trajectories of their careers in life. Examples of biblical figures will be cited and discussed in the light of some recent psychological findings.

THE SIBLING RELATIONSHIPS

Modern times have spawned many theories regarding the psychology of child development as a result of closer observation of families and children. Whereas the examples of biblical sibling rivalry center upon periods of later development, upon adolescence and early adulthood, in modern times our focus is upon the earlier periods of infancy and childhood, on the detailed intrafamilial processes involving children and their parents. Psychoanalysis is one of the pioneering fields which placed great emphasis on the notion of sibling rivalry and its effects upon later personality development. In his well-known classic, the *General Introduction to Psychoanalysis* (1924/1972), Freud makes some observations which have, by now, become so commonplace that they may be viewed as axiomatic. He describes "The little child [who] does not necessarily love his brothers and sisters, and often is quite frank about it. It is unquestionable that in them he sees and hates his rivals, and it is well known how commonly this attitude persists without interruption for many years, till the child reaches maturity, and even later ... every opportunity is seized to disparage the newcomer; attempts are even made to injure it, and actual attacks upon it are by no means unheard of" (pp. 214–215). Alfred Adler, one of the early disciples of Freud and also one of the early dissidents who left the fold, writes about the older child's feeling of being "dethroned" when the second one appears. He comments about the "sense of tragedy" resulting from the loss of power experienced by the older child. Both Freud and Adler stress the persistence of these rivalrous sentiments well into later life. Unquestionably, this is an important ingredient of the "non-shared experiences" that make genetically similar siblings so varied and different in character (Dunn & Plomin, 1990).

On the other hand, in an early review of various studies on family structure and socialization (Clausen, 1966), the author agrees with the general idea of rivalry, but seems to question the ubiquity and the exclusiveness of the hard feelings on the part of the "dethroned" sibling: "The older may (and perhaps most inevitably, does) regard the younger as a rival and may initially express jealousy and hostility, but he may also be extremely proud and protective of his younger sibling" (p. 19). Undoubtedly, accommodation takes place; Esau and Jacob ultimately settled their differences, as did Joseph and his brothers. The Cain and Abel solution is not inevitable.

We may conclude that the rivalry of siblings is a long-standing feature of intrafamilial relations and sibling interaction. The rivalry appears to be keenest when the stakes are high, when the possession and attention of the parents is most crucial, when the dependency of the young and the need for affection and protection are at the peak. But, as the years go by, when the horizons broaden and the individuals have more opportunities for gratification of needs and have gained a great measure of autonomy, independence, and self-esteem, the feelings of competition and the accompanying hostility toward the rival sibling diminish markedly. However, the early experiences involved do not become eradicated completely, but remain at some level of awareness, and persist as a part of the psychodynamics of the adult person. Some of these issues will be considered and discussed in the next section concerned with the relationships between birth order and personality.

Sibling rivalry seems to be a persisting psychological issue as long as there are families of two or more children. It seems to be almost inevitable that, when the children are close in age, they compete for the same supplies—whether that be parental affection, status, objects that money can buy, or any other items that are marked by scarcity and desirability. According to some recent reports (Viehe, 1991) the struggle may even turn out to be "perilous," when siblings abuse each other and are in some limited ways reenacting the Cain and Abel drama. The results may not be as lethal, but they are hurtful and harmful nevertheless. According to a recent study, about half of the sample 100 children "abuse a brother or a sister every year."

BIRTH ORDER, PERSONALITY, AND DESTINY

Modern dynamic psychology has shown an interest in the effects of the child's ordinal position in the family upon his or her development and status in adulthood. More than a hundred years ago, Sir Francis Galton observed that a disproportionately large number of British scientists happened to be first-born children. Various studies have subsequently stressed the first-born's more *reflective* nature when compared with their younger siblings. Greater popularity and success in *interpersonal relations* has been attributed to the youngest or later-born children in the family. Overall, the results of literally hundreds of studies of birth order have not arrived at solid and consistent conclusions regarding its influence upon personality development.

The clinical observations of Alfred Adler, one of the pioneers in the field of dynamic psychology, have been influential in stimulating much of the research on the effects of birth order upon personality development. Adler points out that the oldest child, the first-born, is "in an excellent position" for he has the undivided attention of his parents and is the center of attention. However, he eventually is "dethroned" when the second child is born, and he does not like the new situation. Adler and others have also noted that the first-born in later life is anxious to preserve the *status quo* and, therefore, tends to be more conservative and even power-oriented (Adler, 152–153).

Adler further elaborates the advantages of the eldest child by pointing out that "among many peoples, in many classes, this advantageous status has become traditional (p. 153)." This data is quite consonant with the anthropological studies of *primogeniture* summarized by Frazer (1975). The preference for the oldest son and his special inheritance rights are well-known in the traditions of modern societies and is consistent with Adler's observations. Evidence of this tradition abounds in the Bible, biblical law, and the legal codes of the modern world. Hence, the oldest son does not only enjoy a favorable position as he grows up, but is especially blessed with a position of power, family leadership, and economic control of family resources upon reaching adulthood.

Despite this tradition, there is ample evidence in the Bible of another pattern: that of *ultimogeniture,* the preference for the younger or youngest son. There are a number of interesting instances in which the younger son is the preferred one, possesses more desirable qualities, and is ultimately the most successful. There seems to be a fairly consistent trend of showing the ascendance of the "underdog" and his rise to power and distinction (Niditch, 1987).

A number of examples that illustrate the points made above will indicate quite consistently the tradition of ultimogeniture as it is demonstrated in the Bible and in biblical times. The first instance, discussed in the context of sibling rivalry, appears in the book of Genesis where the fratricidal tragedy is described. "The Lord received Abel and his gift, but Cain and his gift he did not receive ..." (Gen. 4.4–5). Thus we note that the younger brother, Abel, was viewed more favorably, although the tragic event of his being murdered by his brother, Cain, cuts his life short.

The case of Ishmael and Isaac is another example of the favoritism shown the younger son. At his barren wife's suggestion, Abraham slept with her Egyptian maidservant Hagar so that a family will be established (Gen. 14). Thus, Ishmael, the son born to Hagar, was the first son born to Abraham. However, some time later, Abraham's wife Sarah bore him a son—Isaac. Then Sarah became concerned about the inheritance rights of her son. She prevailed upon Abraham to drive out Ishmael and his mother from their household (Gen. 20). Here, again, ultimogeniture asserts itself; the younger son inherits, and the older one is exiled. The matter is, of course, complicated by the fact that the sons were of different mothers who had different status—wife vs. servant—to begin with. Nevertheless, the point regarding the favoritism enjoyed by the younger child is clearly demonstrated.

ESAU AND JACOB

Two aspects of the story of Esau and Jacob should be stressed. First, that the right of the first born—primogeniture—was a well-established tradition among the early Jews. Second, that Jacob, the younger brother, by exploiting the special circumstances of his brother's hunger and exhaustion, as well as through his impulsivity (inability to postpone gratification), arrogates the special privilege to himself; he buys the birthright. Thus, again, ultimogeniture triumphs over primogeniture.

This state of affairs is further exacerbated when Jacob, at the urging of his mother Rebecca, by means of cunning and deception, also obtains his dying father's blessings, by pretending to be the older brother Esau. We need not dwell, at this point, upon the animosity that this deception caused in Esau—who was tricked twice—but we note again that the younger son obtained the favored blessing and, consequently, the favorite position as the senior heir in the family. It seems that history repeats itself, a similar pattern is passed on to the next generation in the story of Isaac and Ishmael. Ishmael was born to Hagar, the servant of Sarah, the wife of Abraham, at Sarah's own request, for she herself was barren. However, some years later, Sarah gave birth to her son Isaac. then, she banished Hagar from the household, along with Ishmael. She was upset because Ishmael was laughing at her son Isaac. So, "Abraham rose early in the morning, took some food and a waterskin full of water and gave it to Hagar, he set the child on her shoulder and he sent her away, and she went and wandered in the wilderness of Beersheba" (Gen. 21.14).

Hagar and her oldest son of Abraham survived the ordeal, but Isaac's position as the favorite was established. Again, we may quite readily note that the oldest has fallen from grace and the youngest turns out to be a "prince among his brothers"

(Gen. 49.26). Moreover, there is some consistency in the characterization of the oldest as impulsive and lacking in self-control; Cain, Esau, and Reuben all seem to share this major trait.

JACOB AND HIS GRANDCHILDREN

The same trend tends to carry over unto the next generation; Israel (Jacob) perpetuates it, as we see in the blessings he bestowed upon his own grandchildren, Menashe and Ephraim, Joseph's sons born in Egypt.

When these grandchildren were presented to Israel for their blessing by the aging patriarch, he placed his right hand, ordinarily reserved for the oldest son, on the head of Ephraim, the youngest son, and his left hand on the head of Menashe. This occurred despite the fact that Joseph presented the older Menashe on his right and the younger Ephraim on his left.

When Joseph noticed the reversal of the direction of the patriarch's hands, "he was displeased and removed the hand from the head of Ephraim unto the head of Menashe;" his father refused and said "I know my son, I know he too will become a people and prosper, but his younger brother will be greater than he and his seed will become a full nation" (Gen. 48.17–19). One can hardly avoid perceiving the parallel between that scene and the one that Israel (Jacob) had originally acted out in relation to his older brother Esau. It seems as if the old patriarch was compelled to reestablish and perpetuate a pattern which he himself had initiated many years earlier; the dethronement of the older in favor of the younger, and the ultimogeniture as a replacement of the traditional primogeniture.

MOSES

Moses was perhaps the most important leader, religious guide, and lawmaker of ancient Israel. According to the Bible, he was brought up in the Egyptian Pharaoh's court, and was 3 years younger than his brother Aaron. The long struggle of the Israelites to escape the yoke of oppression of Pharaonic tyranny is described in detail in several chapters in the book of Exodus. It was Moses who led the Israelites out of the land of Egypt, shaped them into a national entity, and brought them the Law which is embodied in the Ten Commandments, and numerous other regulations detailed in Deuteronomy, Exodus, and Leviticus. To quote: "And the Lord said to Moses, I make you like a god to Pharaoh, and Aaron will be your spokesman (prophet). You will say what I shall command and Aaron your brother will talk to Pharaoh, and he will send the children of Israel from his land" (Exodus 7.1–2).

It is interesting to observe that the Bible tells us that Moses was the one selected to receive the direct message from God and pass it on to the people, this, despite the fact that he had a speech impediment. He was favored by being selected as a sort of extension of the deity itself, and Aaron was the translator, interpreter and messenger-the mouthpiece, via which the messages of God were transmitted to the people of Israel.

It is of further interest that Aaron, the older brother and the priest in charge of ritual, was readily persuaded by the populace to return to the very threatening idol worship by making the golden calf—a clear offence against the uncompromising monotheism pursued by brother Moses. Again, the older brother Aaron shows weakness of character and lack of resolve by submitting to group pressure as compared with Moses, the younger, steadfast leader and direct emissary of YHWH himself. In some respects, Aaron's behavior is similar to the disrespectful behavior of the oldest son, Reuben, toward his father Jacob, and to the impulsive fratricidal behavior of Cain. Moses, the younger brother emerges as the principled and undisputed leader of his people who receives his messages directly from the deity. He was the stronger and the more effective leader of the two brothers.

GIDEON

The period of the "Judges," prior to the establishment of the kingdom of Israel, was one of constant struggle and warfare with the tribes in and surrounding the land of Canaan. One of the frequent adversaries who invaded the countryside and destroyed the crops of the Israelites was the tribe of the Midianites. According to the book of Judges, the Israelites were destitute and cried out to YHWH for help. Of course, the Bible tells us that the children of Israel had sinned by being unfaithful to their God and, as a consequence, their troubles with their neighbors the Midianites mounted. The need for defense against the marauders was imperative: "Now an angel of YHWH came and sat under a terebinth ... which belonged to Joash the Abiezerite. The Midianites were marauding and pillaging the countryside, and therefore Joash's son Gideon was threshing the wheat in the winepress in order to keep it from the Midianites. The angel ... showed himself to Gideon and said: you are a brave man and Yahweh is with you ... go and use this strength of yours and free Israel from the hand of Midian; I send you. Gideon responded: How can I save Israel? Behold my clan is the weakest in Manassah and I am the youngest at my father's house" (Jud. 6.11–15). In the end, Gideon, the youngest in his father's household, became a leader of his people and a successful military commander who subdued the Midianites, the land was at peace for 40 years—"all the lifetime of Gideon."

Again, ultimogeniture prevails and triumphs. Gideon's first reaction, arising from the traditional preference for the oldest son, was that he was not the one destined for the exalted position of the leader of his people. But, with the direction of the Deity, he rose to the occasion with phenomenal success.

DAVID

After King Saul fell in disfavor with the Lord and with Samuel the prophet, it was time to select a replacement to be anointed as the new king. Samuel made Jesse the Bethlehemite parade his seven sons before him, but none was deemed appropriate for the throne: "and Samuel said to Jesse: 'Are these all the lads?' And Jesse replied: 'There is still the youngest one who is tending the sheep.' Then Samuel said to Jesse: "Send for him and bring him over, for we will not sit down until he comes ... And the Spirit of the Lord came upon David" (1 Samuel 16.11–13). And David was anointed as the second king of Israel.

Clearly, in this instance, the youngest was favored over all the older brothers in the family. Moreover, he turned out to be the most successful king in the history of Israel. He was a musician, poet, warrior and leader who united the people and established the dynasty—the House of David.

MODERN DATA

In their 1970 review of the scientific literature on siblings and birth order, Sutton-Smith and Rosenberg concluded that "in general, the firstborn are more achieving, affiliative and conforming" (p. 107). Their conclusions are largely based on test data and observations of young subjects, but are not necessarily related to adult status, personality development, and later career direction and success. The biblical anecdotes related in the previous pages do not deal with the early life of the great achievers, for as we noted previously, concern with childhood and early development even in modern society is, historically speaking, relatively recent.

A comprehensive review of the issue of birth order by Ernst and Angst (1983) is extremely critical of the bulk of studies concerned with the relationship between birth order and personality. Their criticism rests on methodological grounds, such as failure to use adequate controls and background factors (e.g., size of family, age interval, and socioeconomic status). Ernst and Angst nearly demolish the conclusions of the vast array of studies and observations published over the last few decades. However, so many studies *did* report positive results that the question raised by the authors themselves—whether a meticulous meta-analytic approach would not be productive and yield different conclusions—should be definitely entertained. In the meantime, little or no support is offered by the authors to the characteristics of the alleged "first-born personality." Due to the faulty methodology, they in fact reject the notion of a "firstborn personality." They do see no support for the greater anxiety, conformity, affiliation, need for achievement, creativity, empathy, and a number of other traits which supposedly characterize the firstborn. One positive finding is granted: "A firstborn personality ... usually appears when self-selected parents compare the characteristics of their children. Firstborns are described as more sensitive, serious, and responsible, and as less impulsive, happy, socially active and outgoing" (p. 186).

In summary, the first-born of the Bible seem to have been quite different from those described in modern psychological literature, although those descriptions are not unanimous, and the universality of those characterizations is very much questionable. The biblical first-borns were, particularly in the book of Genesis, rather impulsive and generally less successful in their careers than the late-born. Cain explodes in his anger against Abel; Esau cannot postpone gratification and makes a catastrophic decision in order to satisfy his hunger; and Reuben violates the taboo and sleeps with his father's concubine. On the other hand, their counterparts are actually more favored; Abel is favored by God; Jacob receives the prime blessing; and Joseph is his father's favorite from the start). The later-borns are socially and materially more successful, and outdistance their older siblings by far. From the traditional point of view they were the "underdogs" (Niditch, 1987) whose cunning, social sense, and skills at manipulation catapulted them to great heights. Generalizations regarding manipulation on the part of the later-born may be questioned; their consistent success in the Bible is undeniable.

Much of the theorizing regarding birth order, and especially the personality of the first-born, is based on the Adlerian notion of the "dethronement" of the older child due to the competition of the latecomer for parental care and affection. This state of affairs may exist when the age difference between the older and the younger child is such that a certain "kingdom" had been established by the older before the younger sibling appeared on the scene. According to various authorities, such a situation is most plausible when there is a 3– to 4–year age difference. When the age difference is much smaller, for example, a year, a year and a half, or two, the "royal" status of the older is not so clearly established, and the jealousy and feelings of dethronement are much less likely to occur. A much larger age difference would also mitigate against the rivalry and competition; the older, more independent and mature child is no longer concerned with the time and affection of parents expended on the new arrival.

It is reasonable to speculate that children in the families of ancient Israel, following the dictum of be "fruitful and multiply," did not space their children very far apart. Most likely, children were born almost annually during the woman's fertile years. Consequently, the likelihood of jealousy among siblings in the earlier ages was less, as was the sense of dethronement. Hence, the development of such characteristics as anxiety about possible loss of status, and the need for achievement to satisfy parental expectancies, were less likely to be reflected in the later personality development of the firstborn.

Effects of birth order or ordinal position in the family upon the personality and life trajectory of the offspring is undoubtedly more credible in our present society than was the case in ancient times. Birth order in those times was especially complicated by the practice of polygamy. For example, the oldest child of a later wife might be the youngest in the multi-wife polygamous family; this was the case of Joseph, who was Rachel's first-born, but was the youngest in the large family of Jacob the patriarch who already had children by Leah and two additional "maidservants." Thus, it is doubtful that the reported results, albeit inconsistent, regarding the impact of birth order on personality and life success are strictly comparable to those described in the Bible. We can, however, attempt to understand the reasons for the consistent success of the later-born as compared with the first-born siblings.

It is quite possible that there was such resentment of the traditional privilege of the first-born, that is, primogeniture, on the part of a broad sector of the population who did not belong to that exclusive category—including the scribes and redactors of the manuscripts—that out of that resentment emerged selective reporting of the unusual capacities and achievements of the later-born. Another possible explanation is traceable to the speculations offered by Frazer (1975), who postulated the notion that ultimogeniture historically preceded primogeniture, and that the biblical period represents a period of transition from one system of inheritance to the other.

Although there is some evidence for the last-mentioned hypothesis, the universality of primogeniture is overwhelming. Because of this privileged position the egocentricity of the first-born gets in the way of his achievement, as compared with the competitiveness and increased social skills of his younger counterpart. We note this trend in the instances detailed in this section, but not in the characteristics of older children described in modern psychological literature.

SUMMARY

The universal familial interaction noted in the modern Western nuclear family (Freud 1924/1972) and expressed in the rivalry between children is definitely present and observed in the ancient family constellations of the bible. Personality and career trajectories as a function of position in the family, or birth-order positions, seen in the modern family are unlike those reported in the biblical literature of that ancient era. Contrary to the special privileges assigned to the first-born son by law and tradition in the Israelite family, the more favorable status in adulthood, according to the biblical narratives, is achieved by the younger or youngest son. It may well be that the motive of overcompensation for the feelings of inferiority on the part of the younger child propels him to greater effort, achievement, and success (Adler, 1927). Here we note another example of the discrepancy between the normative rule and the account of actual events and life as it was lived in ancient Israel. Perhaps it is another instance of the success of the underdog—the eternal optimism of the downtrodden.

A recent comprehensive contribution to the issue of primogeniture vs. ultimogeniture was made by F. J. Sulloway in his 1996 work *Born to Rebel: Birth Order, Family Dynamics and Creative Lives.* This work may be described as a systematic sociohistorical and biopsychological approach to the problem. According to the author, "Most innovations in science, especially radical ones have been initiated and championed by lateborn. Firstborn tends to reject new ideas, especially when the innovation appears to upset long accepted principles" (p. 53). Sulloway stresses the sociobiological aspects involved in the intrafamilial relationships. In this connection he quotes a 1864 remark by Charles Darwin: "But, oh what a scheme is primogeniture for destroying natural selection (p. 54)." It seems, however, that the biblical rules of primogeniture did not thwart many of the developments of the laterborn who were not squelched by the rules of primogeniture. Certainly, the success of such laterborns as Moses, Joseph, David, and others seems to have stimulated subsequent generations to pay attention to this phenomenon. Their creativity and innovativeness is quite consonant with the sociohistorical and psychobiological explorations of recent vintage.

CHAPTER 5

Building the Family

WHY CHILDREN?

MOTIVATION FOR PARENTHOOD

From the very beginning of the patriarchal era, the value of children was stressed in the Bible. Not only was it a religious command of YHWH—"Be dutiful and multiply and replenish the land"—but it was also seen as an act of nation-building and self-preservation. Repeatedly, the Deity invokes the sense of history and the future. The patriarchs, and some of the leaders who followed them, were promised by YHWH that their "seed" would persist and grow into a mighty nation. This altruistic concern for strengthening the nation and assuring its future was probably an important motivation for procreating children, the more the better. Considering the little resistance to disease and other acts of nature that might threaten the very young, the survival rate of infants was relatively low; having many children assured the retention of a larger number of children in the family and their availability to contribute to the family and tribal economy in the future. The greatest blessing that YHWH bestowed upon the early patriarchs was that of fertility, of a multiplicity of children— "As many as the stars in the sky and as numerous as the sand by the sea" (Gen. 22.17). The greatest tragedy to be visited on a woman was to be "barren" or childless; a curse from the Lord, "who closed her womb." We find a number of instances, especially in the book of Genesis, where the childless woman prays to God to alter her miserable state.

This state was unhappy for a number of reasons. First, it was counter to the old biblical religion's command to be fruitful and multiply. Second, it was necessary to produce a male heir for the perpetuation of the family's social and economic status. Third, especially in families with more than one wife, having children assured the wife's status vis-a-vis her competitors in the multigynous family. Four or more children strengthened and assured the family's economic standing by enabling more hands to participate in the family enterprise. Finally, the contribution to the strength of the tribe and nation was, of course, not to be overlooked. More recruits for the tribal and national armies assured independence and prosperity.

BARREN WOMEN

Several interesting instances may be cited of the value of the birth of a child, and its effect on the status of the ancient Hebrew woman. After Sarai (later known as Sarah) proposed to Abraham, her husband that he take Hagar the Egyptian maidservant as a substitute wife to be her proxy as the bearer of his son, we are told: "and he came to Hagar and she conceived; and when she saw that she had conceived, her mistress was despised in her eyes" (Gen. 16.4). A couple of generations later— "And when Rachel saw that she bore no children, she envied her sister; she said to Jacob, her husband: 'Give me children or else I die' (Gen. 30.1). We now go one of the later books of the Bible, the book of Samuel. We are told about a man by the name of Elkanah who had two wives, Hannah and Peninah: "Peninah had children and Hannah had none ... the Lord had shut her womb ... and her rival provoked and angered her, because the Lord had shut her womb" (1 Sam. 1.3–6).

What we readily note is the miserable state of the childless woman; she is exposed to contempt and derision on the part of her competitors, and she herself experiences envy and low self-esteem. Thus, in a negative sense, the motivation of biblical women to have children was also that of avoidance of ridicule and demeaning attitudes on the part of their more fertile sisters. Having children was axiomatic and automatic; that was the unquestionable fate and the universal expectation of women. Motherhood was perceived as a woman's main function in life; deviation from that preordained path was undesirable and un-acceptable by the society at large. Hence, having children was perceived as the aim and obligation of the woman and a surren-der to the will of God, for only he controlled fertility. A depar-ture from that pattern represented both a denial of one's destiny and an indication of punishment by the deity ("the Lord closed her womb").

As far as the motivation of the male parent is concerned, the emphasis seems to have been somewhat different. Here, the birth of an heir (masculine) who will take over the land and *perpetuate the name* of the family was paramount. Moreover, the desire for many children to provide a work force for the master's enterprises, such as farming and raising sheep illus-trates the importance of the economic factor. Finally, the avail-ability of the younger generation to care for, and protect, their elders was a consideration and a definite anticipation in the fulfillment of the Torah's Fifth Commandment ("Honor your fa-ther and mother").

In Modern Times

It is amazing how many of these ancient motives for having children persist in modern societies as well. A sizable number of studies concerning the motivation for parenthood, or the value of children for their parents, have been reported in the psychological literature during the past few decades. Modern Western society has introduced various means of controlling pregnancy and, hence, of controlling the attainment of parent-hood. The introduction of various contraceptive and prophylac-tic substances and devices has removed the inevitability and fatalism inherent in the parent status which was true of the life of men, and especially women, of biblical times. Modern West-ern society makes it possible to prevent pregnancies as well as to allow their following the natural course. Pregnancies and parenthood can be made to follow a timetable preferred by the individuals involved, within certain age limits. Hence, the deci-sion to have or not to have children is not a matter of destiny or fate, in the vast majority of people, but a course of action subject to the motivations and expectations of the couples involved.

As a result of advances in science, medicine and technology, and as a result of the greater complexity of society, the motivation for parenthood has become more complex and multidimensional in nature. Religious fundamentalists in secular societies, and many people in Third World societies, often reflect some of the underlying motives characteristic of the biblical patriarchs and their descendants of ancient times.

As a result of serious attempts to study the causes of world overpopulation, a number of investigators have concerned themselves with such topics as *Family Design: Marital Sexuality, Family Size, and Contraception* (Rainwater, 1965), *The Psychology of Birth Planning* (Pohlman, 1969), and *The Childbearing Decision* (Fox, 1982). These researchers report that becoming pregnant, and making the decision to become a parent, has entered an era of personal planning and control. The ancient attitude that having children is "in the hands of the Lord," i.e., the attitude of fatalism, has by and large given way to self conscious thought and motivation. This is not to deny, that for reasons of religion or limited contact with modern thought, the fatalistic attitude still persists in sizeable sectors of the world's population.

On the other hand, Alva Myrdal, more than 50 years ago (1968/ 1941) was concerned with the issue of *underpopulation* that was plaguing her native Sweden. In her survey, the issue of motivation *for parenthood* is dismissed rather cavalierly by stating: that "it is tacitly taken for granted that some desire to have children exists in mankind and that this desire has remained fairly constant. It can hardly be analyzed, but has to be cloaked in some sweeping terms such as a desire to marry, inclination to found a family, love of children, and desire to have some of one's own" (p. 53). In her fatalistic attitude Myrdal concentrates her efforts in the study of the "motives against childbearing," which were more directly linked with Sweden's national problem at that time.

RECENT CONCEPTUALIZATIONS

Based on preliminary interviewing and other empirically obtained information, several studies have identified four main motivational and attitudinal factors for having children. These also resulted from a survey of the extant literature in the 1960s. The four attitudes identified were as follows (Rabin, 1965):

1. *Altruistic motivation.* Refers to affection for children, concern for them, and the need to express nurturance in relation to them.

2. *Fatalism.* Refers to a notion of predestination (predeterminism); a feeling that this is "the order of things" and that the reason one was brought into the world is to procreate and perpetuate the species.

3. *Narcissistic motivation.* Involves the hope or expectation that the offspring will reflect glory upon the parent, and prove his or her virility and fertility, as well as their biological and psychological adequacy. Perpetuation of the name and stock are paramount.

4. *Instrumental motivation.* Refers to the expectation that the child to be born will be a vehicle in the achievement of parental goals, be they economic, psychological, or social.

These categories are broad and abstract. However, their validity has been supported in a number of empirical studies and by a factor analysis (Counte, Garron, & Branda, 1979; Rabin, 1965; Rabin & Greene, 1968).

A much more extensive system of value categories was introduced by Hoffman and Hoffman in 1973, and later reviewed by Michaels (1988). The nine categories of values involve needs that children are expected to satisfy for their parents. A brief statement of these categories follows.

1. *Adult status and identity.* Fulfillment of the need to be accepted as a mature and responsible adult of the community.

2. *Expansion of the self.* A need of transcendence of one's life, the expansion of one's horizons, and the need for someone to perpetuate and carry on the self after one's death; a sort of need for "immortality."

3. *Morality.* Satisfaction of the need for religion, moral improvement and altruism; doing things for the good of society.

4. *Primary group ties; affiliation.* The need for love, intimacy, and affection within the family circle.

5. *Stimulation, novelty, and fun.* Children viewed with pleasure as presenting new experiences and opportunities for pleasurable experiences.

6. *Creativity, accomplishment, and competence.* Here the value is that greater achievement and creativity that can be attained by helping children grow and develop.

7. *Power, influence, and effectance.* Essentially, this value refers to the power gained as a result of having children and exercising control over them.

8. *Social comparison; competition.* Involved herein is the expectation that the child will be a source of prestige for the parents, especially when the child's status and achievement may be compared with those of children in other families in the community.

9. *Economic utility.* This need is clearly one present in many societies, ancient and contemporary. It involved the expectation that the child will be an important economic asset to the family—it may be expressed in the form of assistance with parental occupation or in the form of contribution to the family support from the fruits of one's own labor. The economic utility of adult children to their aging parents is a rather important value in many societies.

This more detailed scheme of values contains and overlaps, to a great extent, the motivations listed earlier in the studies of Rabin (1965), Rabin and Greene (1968), and Counte et al. (1979). For example, the "narcissistic" category, broadly defined, could contain value categories 1, 2, 6, and 8; the "instrumental" motivation is very much related to value categories 5, 7, and 9. What is important in this context is to see the relationship between the "implied" motivations and values in having children, elicited from the biblical stories, and those emanating from analyses of empirical findings in contemporary societies. Needless to say, the term "contemporary societies" does not refer to some kind of monolithic enclave of the world's population. We must be aware of the tremendous differences and great diversity existing, even in this modern day and age, between "postmodern," modern, and developing societies, the latter being much closer to that observed in the ancient biblical documents.

Considerable overlap may be noted with the comprehensive list of values of children for modern and biblical parents. The exact quotation from Genesis is: "Be fruitful and multiply, and replenish the earth, and subdue it" (1.28). Aside from YHWH's command to have children—the religious and moral obligation— there is also an inherent statement of the exercise of power— replenish the earth, subdue it, dominate it. This surely is the equivalent of values 3 (morality, religion ...) and value 7 (power and influence) listed above. Certainly, value 8 (social comparison, competition) was clearly seen in the instances of rivalry and envy felt by the childless women such as Sarai, Rachel, and Hannah. The latter value is closely related to value 1 (adult status and social identity) which was clearly a part of the value of children perceived by adults, both male and female, in biblical times. There are frequent references to men and women who have, are blessed with, many children, clearly viewed in highly positive terms. Finally, value 9 (economic utility) was undoubtedly an important value underlying the motivation for having children, much as it apparently is in present-day societies whose economies are very labor-intensive. Having sons who are potential warriors and protectors of the family, clan, tribe and nation, was also very important. But, generally, the biblical texts do not give us a direct indication of personal motivation for parenthood in males as it does in the case of women.

Several of the nine values listed are not found in the texts of the Bible. The values of "expansion of the self," group ties and affection, stimulation and fun, and achievement and creativity do not appear in the contexts of parental expectations. It seems that these for the most part narcissistic motivations, are a later historical development, and part of the psychological climate of present-day Western societies. The emphasis in these motivations seems to be the satisfaction of the broader needs of the parents' growth and fuller self-realization. These are primarily the ideals of a secular society, in which individualism and the worship of the self reign supreme. To be sure, these tendencies are part of a motivational system which is complex and multidimensional and combines some of the patterns of biblical times with the more recent ideological development and empirical findings of modern psychology.

INFERTILE WOMEN, SURROGATE WIVES, AND THE "CURE" OF ADOPTION

Having children, especially sons, was a very important, if not *the* most important, goal of the woman in biblical times. As we noted before, the motivation for having children was strong, based on religious, social, economic, narcissistic, altruistic, and psychological foundations. The biblical dictum of "be fruitful and multiply" was the overarching principle that powered the aspirations of the ancient family. Having children, especially male children, established the status of the wife in the frequently multigynous families. Childlessness was considered a great tragedy for the biblical woman. In families of several wives, jealousy was rampant; the childless wife saw herself as inferior and inadequate when compared with the others who were blessed with offspring. The woman who remained childless was often mocked and ridiculed by her more fortunate, fertile competitors in the extended household. The unhappy woman would cast about and seek help from the holy men and seers, and pray to the Lord to "open her womb."

Infertility, or barrenness, is mentioned nearly a dozen times in the Hebrew scriptures. Considering the state of knowledge about nature in general in biblical times, and about human biology and reproductive physiology in particular, it is not at all surprising that it was the woman, almost exclusively, who was implicated and blamed for infertility. All of the biblical references that deal with barrenness involve women who are incapable of having children. The possibility that the male of the species might somehow be involved, that he might be infertile and might bear the responsibility for childlessness is apparently not entertained. The only reference that I found in which barrenness is hinted at and indirectly connected with the masculine gender appears in the book of Deuteronomy. It is in the context of a prophetic speech by the leader, Moses, to the people of Israel: "You shall be blessed above all people; there shall be no male or female barren among you or among your cattle" (Gen. 7.14). It is noteworthy that this is not a description of an actual case of barrenness, but an expression of a hypothetical possibility. All the actual cases of infertility cited and described involve women, such as Sarai, the wife of Abraham, Rachel, the wife of Jacob, and Hannah, the wife of Elkanah. Perhaps the main reason that the subject of male infertility received no attention is in part due to the fact of the multigynous family. Generally, as we shall see, the "other" wife or wives in the family did have children—a fact that would exonerate the husband and place the onus on the infertile woman, who is presumably punished by God, who "closed her womb."

SARAH AND RACHEL

Sarai (later known as Sarah), the wife of the first Hebrew, Abram (later known as Abraham), was barren, without child. Since she wanted to have a family, she resorted to a method which was apparently common in those days. She resorted to the surrogate system, by giving her husband her Egyptian slave girl, Hagar, for a wife, with the explicit intention that the son to be born will be hers. Things did not go too well in this instance because Hagar, "when she knew that she was with child, despised her mistress" (Gen. 16.4). Here, the slave girl, the surrogate wife appointed by the mistress herself, by the legitimate wife of the master, was contemptuous of her mistress for her failure to have children of her own.

A similar pattern is repeated two generations later when Rachel, one of the wives of Jacob, Abraham's grandson, was also childless. The desperate Rachel is quoted as saying to her husband: "Give me children, or I'll die"; Jacob became angry and said: "Am I God that I prevented you from having children?" Then she said—"Here is Bilhah my maidservant, go to her, and she will give birth upon my knees" (Gen. 30.1–3). In this case, the request for a surrogate is almost identical to the one made by grandmother Sarah, in giving Hagar to Abraham for a wife. It may be added that Rachel's desperation was further accentuated by the fact that her older, and less loved, sister Leah who was Jacob's first (and other) wife did have children and made Rachel especially jealous. For the most part, the status of a childless wife in a multigynous family was rather tenuous.

ADOPTION AS CURE

In both instances described above, Sarah and Rachel anticipated that the child once born was to be their own. It was a form of adoption of the servant's offspring. In the passages cited, I deliberately omitted a crucial phrase in each quotation. The reason for that omission is the questionable aspects of the standard translations of the phrase.

The standard edition, the King James version, of the Old Testament presents similar translations of the passages quoted. Sarai is quoted as saying: "I pray thee go in unto my maid; it may be that I obtain children by her" (Gen. 16.2). Rachel is similarly quoted as saying: "Behold, my maid Bilhah, go in unto her, and she shall bear upon my knees, that I may also have children by her" (Gen. 30.3). Other, latter-day translations of these passages in the modern Bibles follow the same lead by stating that the barren women expected to make up a family by adopting the children born to the servants as their own. The New English Bible, for example, translates the last quoted passage about Rachel as follows: "Here is my slave girl Bilhah, lie with her so that she may bear sons, to be laid upon my knees, and through her, I too may build up a family." In a similar vein, Sarai said to her husband Abram, "Take my slave girl; perhaps I shall found a family through her." The interesting point is that both of these passages employ the same word in the Hebrew version, which does *not* in fact refer to building up a family. This business of "building up a family" is to some extent a reflection of the liberty taken by the translators in an attempt to make sense of the passage. In both of these instances, the Hebrew Bible uses the word spoken by Sarah and Rachel that has the root of the verb to build (*bano*). The actual Hebrew word that appears in both passages is *ebone*. The literal and most accurate translation of the word *ebone* is the passive tense of the verb "to build;" the most precise meaning is "I shall be built" or "I shall be constructed." Both Sarai and Rachel employed the word *ebone,* meaning "I shall be built up," and not "I shall have a family" or "I shall build a family."

The implication here seems to be that some change is expected to take place in the person of the mother ("built up") as a result of having a child or children by the maidservant. It seems that the intent was more far-reaching and implies a belief that having children by a surrogate—in a sense, adopting a child—will bring about a "building up" of the childless woman so that she too can have her own children and build her own family. And, at this point, the speculation made upon observations and informal accounts in modern society, of infertile women bearing children following an adoption of a child, may be entertained.

This notion that women in biblical times believed that adopting and caring for children might cure their infertility was stimulated by the more precise translation of the passages referred to above. I mulled it over for quite some time and was hesitant to commit myself to this view. To my surprise, I was not the only one who came to this conclusion.

Recently, and unexpectedly, I came across an article, which, to my surprise made the same point. The piece entitled "Adoption as a remedy for infertility in the period of the patriarchs" appeared in 1958 in the *Journal of Semitic Studies,* under the authorship of S. Kardimon. It seems, according to Kardimon, that "the opinion of Talmudic sages is that the phrase, 'it may be that I shall be builded up through her' signifies that Sarah and Rachel gave their handmaids to their husbands for wives as a remedy for their infertility, that *they themselves* should bear children" (p. 123). The author goes on to state that quite a few commentators in the past adopted this interpretation, but that since the 12th century this interpretation was abandoned as contrary to nature and logic. Through the 19th century some scholars still adhered to the theory of adoption as a remedy for infertility. But, the more rational atmosphere of the 20th century caused the scholars to abandon this theory and go along with the notion of building a family by adoption only and not by becoming fertile. Kardimon quotes a number of authors who, on the basis of primarily anecdotal material and psychoanalytic theoretical speculation, give support to the idea of adoption as a remedy for infertility. He concludes his contribution by stating "Thus, there seems to be a valid foundation to the interpretation by the Talmudic sages that the phrase, "I shall be builded up through her," denotes that Sarah and Rachel were using the adoption of children of their handmaids as a remedy for their own infertility" (p. 123). In the light of *modern* medicine and psychology, such an interpretation would seem both natural and plausible.

One further comment concerning the Hebrew word *ebone* employed both by Sarah and Rachel. As I mentioned, the construction is first-person passive ("I shall be built up," or reconstructed). Only recently did I come across a similar use of the verb, but in the second person (*tibone*). This is found in the book of Job (22.23) when the beleaguered and tragic figure is admonished: "If you return to Shaddai (the almighty), you shall be *built up* (*tibone*) and keep away inequity far from your tents." In this context, the reference is to Job's status and fortune. But the expression refers to a radical change, to a renewal, reconstruction, and restoration. Job, according to his interlocutor, Elifaz, had sinned and is to be reconstructed. Barren women thought they had sinned (and, therefore, YHWH "closed their womb"), but they were "built up"—reconstructed to fertility.

CONTEMPORARY VIEWS

The story does not end here. The decades subsequent to the 1930s and 1940s produced a fair number of empirical observations and systematic studies of the claim that adoption is a cure for infertility. In the first place, it is important to consider the question of the psychogenic basis for some cases of infertility. The question as to whether, aside from various organic, physiological and endocrinological causes of infertility, there are some psychological or psychosomatic factors that can be reliably considered as causative of this reproductive disorder. Some investigators have researched the question of the possibility of there being a condition of *functional* infertility, or primarily psychogenic infertility. A series of systematic studies have appeared in the professional literature during the last few decades. They criticized the anecdotal nature of the earlier work and concentrated on the investigation of large samples of infertile mothers, compared them with fertile women on a number of psychological parameters, and attended to a number of control variables of the samples such as age, period of diagnosis, and so on. A closer look at these data is important if one is to examine the original biblical hypothesis that adopting children brings about a "cure" of infertility. For, after all, the notion of introducing a child in the family implies a psychological change in the family dynamics, as well as in the self-perception of the adopting mother.

In their careful review, Edelman and Connolly (1986) have

summarized the findings of studies in which functionally infertile women were compared with organically infertile women on
a series of psychological and psychopathological personality
variables. According to these authors, the findings are rather
equivocal; psychological causation of infertility is questionable
at best. Some of the studies give partial support to the psychogenic hypothesis regarding infertility. However, others simply do not yield any personality differences between the
functionally infertile women and the fertile comparison groups.

One of the studies considered in the aforementioned review
is that by Harvard researchers Seibel and Taymor (1982). Their
study, in particular, concerns the phenomenon of pregnancy
after adoption. They state: "Although statistical evidence is
overwhelmingly against the relationship of adoption and subsequent conception, it does appear that a small percentage of
patients do achieve pregnancy following adoption. This can,
perhaps, be explained by a reduction of stress, and subsequently
in the alteration in the neuroendocrinologic characteristics of
the infertile couple" (p. 144). They further elaborate by pointing out that stress may play a role in infertility since cate-
cholamines, prolactin, adrenal steroids, endorphins, and
serotonin affect ovulation and are affected by stress. Thus,
we may see some cautious and provisional support for a psychogenic, or perhaps more specifically, a psychosomatic hypothesis regarding the causes of infertility in some functionally
infertile women. Later work concerning the psychogenic hypothesis was summarized more recently and critically as follows: "In general, reviews of this literature on psychogenesis
have concluded that the preponderance of studies reveals no
consistent or striking evidence of psychological causes of
infertility ..." However, the authors point out that "Currently,
over 80% of infertility cases are found to have an organic
cause, and it is estimated that infertility may be attributable
to stress and emotional factors to no more than 5% of cases"
(Stanton & Dunkel-Schetter, 1993, p. 7).

Obviously, there is no unequivocal support for a broad generalization that adoption reduces stress and facilitates conception in functionally infertile women. Nevertheless, there
is sufficient positive support for such a notion that may bring
current science in harmony with the ancient observations

and experiences related in the Bible. Perhaps Sarai and Rachel were in fact "reconstructed" following the adoption of the Servant's children. Both gave birth to children subsequent to adoption to sons who were pivotal in the history and development of the ancient nation of Israel in Palestine.

The notion of surrogacy in bearing children has, of course, become of considerable interest in the United States in recent years. When a woman is paid for bearing the child of another woman's husband, it raises many legal and ethical issues. But, in a sense, it is a revival of an old biblical custom, except for the fact that the maidservant was not hired for this specific purpose, and actually cohabitated with the father, rather than just being inseminated with his sperm.

It may be concluded that although motivation for pregnancy and parenthood has become more complex and multidimensional, it has not subsided over the millennia. Similarly, ingenious methods to gratify the need for parenthood have been developing in modern times, employing contemporary technology; and some may have their roots in the experiences of ancient biblical times.

SUMMARY AND DISCUSSION

In this chapter I have addressed issues that have not received much attention in modern scientific psychology. Yet these are significant human concerns that underlie the very fabric of society, and are fundamental to the replenishment of the passing generations. Having children was a very positive value in biblical times, but in the present era has become fraught with ambivalence. Evidence for that is the fact that in Western society a certain percentage of women do not want nor expect to have children. So much for the "instinct" for motherhood or parenthood. Modern parents, or rather modern men and women, have a choice that was not available in ancient societies.

It should be recognized that wanting children, the desire for pregnancy, and motivation for parenthood are not identical terms. It should also be recognized that then, as now motivation for parenthood may be different for mothers than for fathers. In biblical times, children enhanced the status of the woman in the multigynous family, while males were concerned with the economic value of children and status enhancement in the larger society. But fatalism, the will of God, was predominant, for humans did not consider themselves to be in control of the process. The only possible biblical exception is the case of Onan (see chapter 3) who prevented impregnation by an action which in fact was a form of birth control.

The high level of motivation for having children brought about much desperation and jealousy in the multigynous family. Woman's passive submission to the will of YHWH was not always satisfactory as far as fertility was concerned. Most likely, the deviant behavior of the women who worshipped Astarte, the goddess of fertility, was an expression of some women's frustration with the monotheistic God of Israel (c.f. Jud. 2.13; 1 Kings, 11.5–33; 2 Kings, 23.13).

The attempt to deal with infertility, especially via adoption of a slave's son fathered by one's husband is rather intriguing. The notion of the infertile woman becoming "reconstructed" as a result of the parenting experience must have obtained some validity in ancient times. It is too soon to tell whether rigorous statistical tests of this trend accompanied by psychophysiological changes in adopting infertile mothers in our society is unequivocally supported by research.

CHAPTER 6

Male and Female

I t is the purpose of the present chapter to review the psychological differences between the sexes as gleaned from the biblical narratives. From the descriptions of males and females, their behavior, activities, traits, and characteristics, we should be able to construct a fairly comprehensive picture of the ancients' views of the differences between the sexes. We use the narrative material, relating various episodes and accounts, of anecdotes in the more historical books of the Bible: the first "five books of Moses" and the books of Joshua, Judges, Kings, and Chronicles. From these we shall attempt to form certain generalizations regarding views of gender psychology. We cull from this narrative a pattern that reflects the lifestyle of the ancient Israelites and Judeans, which in turn points to implied differences in gender personalities. The comparison of the similarities and differences between the genders with the present-day postmodern views, based on some recent psychological research and opinion, will round out the present chapter's discussion.

IT'S A MAN'S WORLD

There is little doubt that in the Hebrew Bible the male of the species is the dominant sex. It is not unlike the vast majority of the sagas of the ancient world. Men, for the most part, were the collectors, authors, and redactors of the collection of myths, fables, tales and stories, and the historical accounts that constitute the books of the old scriptures. Men wrote the history of their brethren, they were viewed as the story-makers and as the protagonists and heroes of those tales.

Clear support for this view is to be derived from the use of gendered language in the contexts which might easily have been neutral in nature. The Hebrew language itself clearly denotes gender in every use of verbs and adjectives as modifiers of nouns. In other words, not only are the nouns gender-bound, but the rest of the language refers quite clearly to one sex or the other. Nouns are either feminine or masculine. YHWH and Elohim, the ancient deities, are masculine and address themselves, in the main, to the male of the species. When the plural form is used, females are included by implication. Thus, when the Lord addresses himself to humans, the words *you* or *thou* are being employed. In the Hebrew, as in the Ten Commandments, for example, the "you" or "thou" that is repeated a number of times is strictly masculine. When God addresses himself to human beings, it is the male who is being admonished—strictly speaking, linguistically. Actually, the general usage indicates that when no specific person is being addressed, the male form is employed; there is no "it" word, or a clumsier form such as "he/she." Perhaps the major point to be made is that male predominance is readily observed in the nature and mode of Hebrew language use and linguistic expression.

With few rare exceptions, males are the warriors, the heads, and protectors of the families and tribes; they are the leaders, judges, prophets and kings, as well as priests and property owners. Most notable is the characteristic of male physical strength and combativeness that is emphasized in the descriptions of the ancients. The story of Samson, the aggression of Cain, Esau, and numerous others are illustrative of the great emphasis placed upon the aspects of physical strength, that involve success in war and in the protection of the family or tribal unit, and of the nation.

Dreamers and seers were chiefly males, as the biblical record unfolds their stories. The chief dreamers such as Jacob, Joseph, and Daniel, whose experiences are reported in considerable detail, and the major prophets, are all males. I found it difficult, if not impossible, to locate a single instance of women reporting detailed dreams that are interpreted, and whose interpretation is of some consequence. In general, what we would call now "beyond reality" experience, visions of God and interaction with the Deity, the dialogue with "him" (the male God) is entirely within the domain of the male. The same is true of prophets who communicated with God and spoke in his name, who experienced the visions and heard the voices of the Deity.

We do have a few isolated examples of deviation from this rule. Deborah was known as a "prophetess" and a judge in the early stages of the nation's formation, as was Hulda in the later years.

> And the children of Israel again did evil in the sight of YHWH. So he sold them to Jabin the king of Canaan ... and the children of Israel cried unto the Lord ... for Jabin had 900 iron chariots and oppressed them for 20 years.
>
> And Deborah the prophetess, the wife of Lapidoth, she judged Israel at that time. she sent and called Barak ... and said to him, "did not YHWH tell you, 'Go and draw to mount Tabor, and take with you ten thousand men, and I will draw to you Sisera, the captain of Jabin's army ... and I will deliver him into your hand.' "
>
> And Barak said to her, "If you will go with me I will go, but if you will not go with me I will not." She said to him, "I surely will go with you, but this journey will bring you no glory, for YHWH will let Sisera fall in the hands of a woman." ... Barak went up with ten thousand men and Deborah went with him (Judg. 4.1–10).

The Israelites were victorious in this battle and Deborah composed a beautiful poem, celebrating the victory (ch. Judges); this poem is considered one of the great gems of biblical literature.

This episode dictates some additional observations. First, the fact that a woman occupied the important position of judge in ancient Israel. Second, she was obviously a charismatic leader and military strategist. Third, she was also the wife of Lapidoth. However, there is no clear indication that these women actually "prophesied," that they were inspired by direct visions and communication with the Deity. There is no legacy of prophesies

by the female prophets, and no detailed record of their pronouncements, as is the case with the voluminous records of the
major male prophets Isaiah, Jeremiah, and Ezekiel and of the
numerous minor prophets that constitute a large part of the
Hebrew Bible.

An interesting and influential institution in the ancient society of Israel was that of the "elders." The elders were the wise
men who were called upon for advice and judgment in legal,
social, military, and even theological matters. At no point do we
read of female elders; apparently they were all males. These
were the wise and experienced men who gave advice and support to the ruling leaders—the judges, generals, and kings. At
times, one group of elders was contradicted by another group
with different political alliances; but elders they were, and ultimately one group of wise men or another was dominant and
their direction was followed by the leadership and the people.

Associated with the position of the "elders" is clearly the
concept of "wisdom," which is often used in the description of
men and only rarely in the characterization of women. Wisdom,
the capacity to make reasoned judgements based on past experience, was highly valued in the ancient writings. That capacity
was viewed as resulting from a seasoning and aging ("elder")
process and was almost exclusively within the purview of the
male gender. Age was not the exclusive requirement for the
elders' position. Rehoboam, for example, consulted his father
Solomon's elders, but finally took the advice of a younger group
who were his own agemates (with disastrous results, one might
add) (1 Kings 12). The elders were not necessarily "old," but
mature and functioned with a combination of intelligence and
good judgement.

In addition to strength, other physical traits appear in the
description of some of the males in the biblical texts. Saul, the
first king of Israel, was apparently a rather imposing figure; he
was tall, and readily seen above the multitude. The description
in the book of Samuel (1 Sam. 9.2) states that Saul was "a good
man and none of the young Israelites was better than he, from
his shoulder upward he was taller than all the people."

Remember that when the prophet Samuel began to look for
King Saul's successor, he went to look over the sons of Jesse
the Bethlehemite. The Lord said to kingmaker Samuel, "Don't

look at his appearance or stature for not as man sees (does the Lord), for man looks only at what is visible to his eyes, but the Lord looks into the heart" (1 Sam. 16.7). Nevertheless, Samuel chose the youngest of Jesse's sons, David, who was "ruddy cheeked, bright-eyed and handsome." David's handsomeness must have been a factor in his great popularity with the people, in addition to his bravery and prowess as a dueler with Goliath and as a successful warrior against the Philistines. There is also a hint that his attractiveness may have been a factor in his close friendship with Saul's son Jonathan.

Joseph, who was "handsome and good looking" (Gen. 39.6), was in the service of Potifar the Egyptian, whose wife was very attracted to him. This aggressive and frustrated lady propositioned him on several occasions. Joseph, exhibiting good moral and political sense, spurned these advances. The factor of good looks in the successful male is to be noted, for Joseph proceeded with his phenomenal rise in the Egyptian royal hierarchy to become the most powerful man, second only to Pharaoh himself.

WOMEN AND MEN

As noted in the previous section, women and men are viewed and treated quite differently in the Bible. Ancient Israelite society was clearly male-oriented ("androcentric"), and most of the writings of the scriptures concern the males of the species. It was a patriarchal and patrilineal society in structure, as were the vast majority of ancient societies and cultures. Overwhelmingly, the description of actions and events center around the males of the society.

A survey of the names mentioned in the Hebrew Bible yields some markedly contrasting figures (Meyers, 1992). Of the 1,426 biblical names, 1,315 are those of males, and only 111 of females. Women's names constitute a paltry 8% of the total. Whether this is a reflection of the relative unimportance attributed to women in the society at that time, or whether it is due to the simple fact that practically all the writers and redactors of biblical texts were probably men, is hard to determine with any degree of finality. Certainly, the two aspects are not mutually exclusive. The truth is that a combination of the two elements may have entered in this picture to produce this lopsided proportion of attention to the two genders.

Despite the obvious disproportionately low representation of women *named* in the biblical narratives, there are a good many accounts of behavior, traits and characteristics of women that cover a wide range. The range of these attributes is actually quite comparable to those of men. While the number and frequency of episodes of specific so-called "masculine-gender" behavior, characteristics, or status may be smaller for women, but the diversity of these behaviors may not differ very markedly.

First, let us consider some instances of specific roles of both men and women. Miriam, the sister of Moses; Deborah; and Hulda were identified as prophetesses; the first two in the book of Genesis, and Hulda in the book of Kings. Compare this with the male prophets: in addition to Moses himself who is identified as a prophet, there were Nathan, Elijah and Elisha, plus the numerous others whose names appear as the authors of a number of the biblical texts. With the exception of Deborah, we are told very little about the functions and missions of these women members of the prophetic profession. By contrast, the words and deeds of quite a few male prophets are given in great detail, as will be seen in chapter 7 ("Special States of Consciousness"). The main point, however, is the fact that female prophets did exist. Feminists raise the issue that male editors and scribes, as the recorders of events and personalities in the Bible, may have been biased. Possibly the small number reflects the reluctance and possible narrow-mindedness of male redactors to acknowledge and record a more extensive, if not equal, participation of women and their response to the prophetic calling. None of the women spoke in the name of YHWH, nor were they considered his direct messengers to the people of Israel—a major function of the vast majority of the male prophets.

A more extreme disproportion of female representation is evident in the positions of royalty. Only two women are mentioned as autonomous and independent queens. The first, the Queen of Sheba, was described as visiting royalty to the palace of Solomon; but she was not a member of the Israelite dynasty, she was a foreigner (1 Kings 10). Among the dozens and dozens of kings in the northern (Israel) and southern (Judah) kingdom of the Jewish people, only one name of an autonomous female (not the wife of a) monarch appears. There is a somewhat cryptic passage about this queen. We are told relatively little about the brief reign of Athalia which lasted about 6 years before she was overthrown by another pretender to the crown (2 Kings 11). Nevertheless, the fact that there were any independent queens is an interesting exception to the all-male succession of royalty in the land. To be sure, many women were "the power behind the throne" in Israel, such as Bathsheba, the wife of David, or Jezebel, the wife of king Ahab; but Athalia was the only female ruler in her own right. Greater detail about these queens is presented in the vignettes that follow.

THE EXCEPTIONAL QUEEN OF SHEBA

Considering the historical period—the reign of King Solomon—the report of a rather extraordinary woman, the Queen of Sheba, is quite unique. Not until this period of the biblical era, nor thereafter, was there mention or description of a similar personage. Here is a woman, a queen in her own right (for there is no mention of a king or a husband), obviously independent and traveling at the head of an entourage of slaves, servants, and advisors from her own land on a sort of state visit to the Hebrew kingdom. We are told that she was curious about the wisdom of King Solomon, whose fame had spread beyond the confines of his own kingdom. She was in search of wisdom and knowledge, and wanted to satisfy her curiosity about the phenomenal royal sage of Israel. In chapter Ten of the Book of Kings (repeated almost verbatim in the book of 2 Chronicles 9) we are told of this fascinating visit to the court of Solomon in Jerusalem. . . .

And the Queen of Sheba heard of the fame of Solomon ... she came to test him with riddles. She came to Jerusalem with a very great train of camels carrying spice and very much gold, and precious stones. She came to Solomon and talked with him all that was on her mind, and Solomon spoke to her of all her words; there was nothing hid from the king that he did not tell her. And the Queen of Sheba saw So-

lomon's wisdom, and the house that he had built, and the
food ... his servants ... there was not more spirit in her and
she said to the king—"it is true what I heard in my country
of your words and wisdom. I didn't believe the words until
I came and saw with my own eyes, and behold I was told
only half of it; your wisdom and prosperity exceed the fame
of which I heard; happy are your men and servants" (1 Kings
10.1–8).

After the Queen of Sheba satisfied her curiosity, she bestowed
many valuable gifts upon the king, and returned to her country
duly impressed and gratified.

From the little we know, the Queen of Sheba was apparently
wealthy and powerful in her own right. There is no hint or
evidence that her affluence and command of the expedition to
the land of Israel in any way derived from any other power in
her realm. Her independence in mounting the voyage to the
distant land to visit the King of Israel is matched by that of only
one woman described earlier in the biblical texts. This was the
charismatic Deborah, who was a judge, a prophetess, and a
leader of her people in war in order to rescue and maintain the
national integrity of the nascent people of Israel. The Queen of
Sheba and Athalia are the only two examples in the Bible of
women who occupied the throne as independent monarchs, and
not as the wives of monarchs.

The Queen of Shebah's reasons for making her pilgrimage to
Israel are interesting. First, she was curious about King Solomon's
great success in governing his people, and implicitly, the great
economic and political achievements that characterized his regime. Second, and not unrelated to the first, was to test Solomon's wisdom and learn from it. She presented him with
"riddles," we are told. Although the nature of these riddles is
not specified, it may be speculated that some dealt with semire-
ligious folk puzzles of a metaphoric nature, while others concerned governmental and personal problems—"She talked with
him all that was on her heart." At any rate, there was a good
deal of communication and exchange of ideas, for "he spoke to
her of all her words." Perhaps it was because she was a queen
that this woman was able to act with such a degree of independence and exchange ideas on an equal basis with the male

monarch of another country. The queen was impressed with her host's wisdom and prosperity and rewarded him handsomely for his willingness to share ideas with her. Nevertheless, although officially of equal status as a royal personage in this story the Queen of Sheba, the female, is in a pupil-teacher relationship with Solomon, the male. The woman asks the questions and the man supplies the answers, being in a position of higher authority, supported by greater wisdom and experience.

ATHALIA'S BRIEF REIGN

Since the prophet Samuel's reluctant anointment of Saul as the first king of the Hebrew nation, dozens of monarchs followed during the more than four succeeding centuries. Their reigns, trials, and tribulations are chronicled, in varying degrees of detail, in the books of Samuel, Kings, and in the books of Chronicles of the Hebrew Bible. Indirectly, the royal houses were also involved with the prophecies and books of the major prophets, Isaiah, Jeremiah, and Ezekiel, as well as in the writings of many of the minor prophets. The monarchs who ruled over the several centuries were nearly exclusively males. But only *nearly*. One notable exception was a woman named Athalia.

Queen Athalia ruled for a relatively brief period of 6 years and is the only female monarch in recorded Hebrew history. She was the single exception in a continuous line of male kings and dynasties. It is actually quite a puzzle as to why and how this exception occurred, and how she managed such a feat in a highly controlled and male-oriented society.

Athalia was the mother of King Ahaziah who died after the reign of just 1 year (843–842 B.C.E). "And when the mother of Ahaziah saw that her son was dead, she arose and destroyed all the royal seed ... and Athalia did reign over the land" (2 Kings 11.1–3). But, one of the women of the court hid Ahaziah's infant son and saved him from destruction. As the only survivor of the dynasty, he was anointed king and with the aid of priestly counsel and intrigue, acceded to the throne. Ruthless Athalia was removed form the throne and killed. "She reigned six years over Judah;" no further comment or detail is offered by the biblical authors.

It is rather surprising that this brief episode of female ascension to the throne of the House of David, in the land of Judah is mentioned at all, albeit cryptically, by the scribes of the Bible. Throughout the Bible, we learn of the influence of women upon their husbands in all manner of things, including acts of governance. They were often the "power behind the throne," for good or for evil. We need only mention the influence of Bathsheba on her husband, King David, in naming her son Solomon as heir of the throne.

When King David became old (they covered him with clothes and he could not keep warm), Adonijah, the son of Haggit, one of his wives, proclaimed himself heir apparent and was drumming up support among the gentry as well as the people. Upon the advice of the prophet Nathan, Bathsheba, another of David's wives, the mother of Solomon, another of david's sons and also a contender for the throne. "So Bathsheba went to the king in his private chamber ... bowed before the king and prostrated herself. 'What do you want?' asked the king. She answered, 'My lord you swore to me your servant ... that my son Solomon should succeed you as king ... but here is Adonijah claims to be king' " (1 Kings 1.15–18). Afterwards the prophet Nathan came in and supported Bathsheba's position.

"Then King David said 'call Bathsheba,' and she came and stood before him. The king swore an oath to her: 'As the Lord lives, who delivered me from all trouble, I swore to YHWH the God of Israel thus—that Solomon your son shall succeed me and sit on my throne' " (1 Kings 1.28–30).

Queen Bathsheba certainly exerted her influence, and assured her own safety in the volatile palace atmosphere by having her son Solomon (the youngest) ascend the throne of David in Israel.

Another example is the pervasive evil influence of the Queen Jezebel upon her husband Ahab in the "legal" appropriation of the land of Naboth upon trumped-up charges of treachery and godlessness. Naboth the Jezreelite had a vineyard near the palace of King Ahab of Samaria.

> Ahab said to Naboth thus: "Give me your vineyard and I'll have it for a garden because it is close to my house and I will give you a better vineyard or give its value in silver." Naboth said to Ahab, "Lord forbid that I give you my ancestral land." Ahab went home sullen and angry ... he lay down on his bed, turned his face, and refused to eat. His wife

Jezebel came in and said, "Why are you upset and do not eat?" And Ahab told her. Jezebel said, "Now you must show that you are King of Israel; arise, eat, and take heart; I will give you the vineyard of Naboth the Jezreelite." ... She wrote a letter in Ahab's name ... to the elders of Naboth's town ... she wrote: "Proclaim a fast and give Naboth the seat of honor ... And see that two scoundrels ... charge him with cursing God and king, then take him and stone him to death" (1 Kings 21.1–10).

Jezebel's instructions were carried out to the letter and Ahab took over Naboth's vineyard. Subsequently, in a very memorable encounter, the prophet Elijah, chastised Ahab severely when he came to take possession of the vineyard: "Have you killed and now you take possession as well?"

Jezebel certainly took charge. But, as an actual sovereign in her own right, Athalia stands alone; she stands out. She must have been a ruthless antagonist and clever operator to destroy all the male heirs who were relatives, including possibly her own grandchildren, and to survive, albeit only for a period of 6 years. This event did take place, and a woman competed with men on their turf, against all odds. Athalia was successful—for a short time. It is not known, however, how many instances of women upstarts were squelched, and the events remained unrecorded.

It is interesting to note, parenthetically, that Athalia was the daughter of the infamous Jezebel who led her husband, King Ahab, astray. Athalia's mother was a strong woman; she may have served as a model for her daughter.

CHARACTERISTIC TRENDS

From the plethora of narratives which are detailed in the Bible, we can construct a picture of the typical behavior and characteristics attributed to the male and female personality. In addition, by looking at the relative frequencies of the different personality patterns that emerge, ancient conceptions of sex or gender differences may be inferred. How did men and women differ from each other, and how does it compare with our present-day conceptions following the postmodern advent of feminism? The sections that follow provide more specific narrative and descriptive information concerning actors of both genders on the biblical stage. Moving from issues of status and position to traits and characteristics, there are great differences in biblical descriptions of males and females.

Although the characteristic of physical beauty is not mentioned very frequently in the Bible, there is a clear trend toward greater emphasis of this quality in the case of women. Beginning with the description of the patriarchal wives (Sarah, Gen. 12; Rachel, Gen. 29) to the comments on the appearance of Tamar (2 Sam. 13), Abigail (1 Sam. 15), and others; beauty and good looks are definitely stressed. When it comes to the description of men, the mention of beauty is proportionately less frequent. Yet, even young Joseph (Gen. 39), young David (Is. 17), and Absalom (2 S.14) are also described as "beautiful" or handsome. The Hebrew language does not have differential adjectives for male beauty ("handsome") and female pulchritude.

In the erotic poetry of the Song of Songs, there is only one reference to the beauty of the male lover, but there are numerous references to the attractiveness and charm of his female beloved. Incidentally, the woman in this context is not a mere passive recipient of male love and admiration, but an active lover in pursuit of her beloved. It is even speculated that, of all the books in the Bible, this may possibly be the only one authored by a woman. Be that as it may, one might conclude that beauty as an attribute is applied to both sexes in biblical literature; but the stress on feminine comeliness is generally greater, using relative frequency of appearance in the text as a criterion.

GENDER-FEMALE-NEGATIVE

Among the several different roles in which women were cast and which reflect the redactor's perception of femininity or femaleness are those of temptress and deceiver. The first instance illustration of this point appears early in the book of Genesis (Ch. 3). Here, there is a description of the well-known unsalutary influence of the first woman, Eve, upon the first man, Adam. After tasting the forbidden fruit of the Garden of Eden that "opened her eyes to good and evil," (Gen. 3.5) she ensnared her husband into committing the infraction of the rule imposed by YHWH, the creator of the universe. As a result, they were both severely punished by an irate God.

There is a blatant example of connivance by a woman in initiating a serious deception. This is found in the story of Jacob who obtained his father's final blessing before his death, the blessing that rightfully and traditionally belonged to his older brother Esau. The jacob-Esau story was discussed in greater detail in chapter 4. When the aging, blind patriarch, Isaac, sent out his older, favorite son Esau to hunt for the meat he liked before giving him his final blessing, his wife Rebekah prepared an entirely different scenario. She wanted *her* favorite son, Jacob, to be the recipient of the coveted blessing instead. So she acted craftily and deceitfully by substituting Jacob for his brother, Esau. She instructed Jacob to bring her a pair of kid goats from the flock and prepared the meat for Isaac, her aged and blind husband. Then Jacob, who is also referred to as "*Israel*," put the goat skins on his hands and neck, so that he would resemble his hairy brother Esau. When Jacob (Israel) brought the repast his mother prepared, he pretended to be Esau bringing food readied from the hunt. Father Isaac was surprised that his son came back so quickly from his hunting and had the meal ready. He checked the authenticity of "Esau" by feeling the hair on his hands, but still wondered saying, "The voice is the voice of Jacob, but the hands are the hands of Esau" (Gen. 27.22). Yet despite this discrepancy and his doubts, Isaac considered the son before him to be his first-born, and gave him the blessing that was rightfully Esau's. Rebekah's conspiracy succeeded, but brought about the subsequent resentment and animosity of Esau for his deceiving brother, Jacob.

Rebekah's conspiracy, which involves and is acted out by Jacob—a conspiracy initiated out of consideration for their future welfare—establishes a pattern which will be repeated many years later by Jacob himself. When the aging grandfather Jacob was about to die, he bestowed his major blessing upon the younger of Joseph's sons, Ephraim, instead of the older one Menashe, whose right it was according to the tradition of primogeniture. This episode is described in greater detail in chapter 4.

Rebekah is portrayed in this story as a manipulator and as a conniving woman. She uses her son as the instrument of her deception, and initiates him in this pattern of behavior. It may be argued that her motives were altruistic, she wanted the best for her favorite son. Whether the means justified the end, however, is another question.

The story of Yael provides another illustration. When Sisera, the commander of the Canaanite forces of King Jabin, was defeated by the Israelis, he escaped into the countryside. "Sisera fled on foot to the tent of Yael, the wife of Heber the Kenite ... Yael came out to meet Sisera and said to him, 'Come in here, my lord, come in and do not be afraid.' So he went into the tent and she covered him with a rug. He said to her: "Give me some water, for I'm thirsty." She opened the pitcher of milk, gave him to drink, and covered him up. He said to her: "Stand by the opening of the tent, and if anybody comes and asks you 'is there anybody here?', say no." But Yael took a tent peg, picked up a hammer in her hand, came up quietly to him and drove the peg into his temple, as he was asleep and tired; and he died" (Judges 4.17–21).

In the tale of Yael, we see the female insinuating herself into the confidence of the fugitive general. She invites the weary soldier to rest in her tent, is solicitous of his welfare and covers him up, and gives him milk to make him sleepy, rather than water to quench his thirst. But, when she has him where she wants him, she strikes at the enemy general with a ferocious finality. She prepares the proper conditions, and acts treacherously toward the man, albeit out of patriotic motives. She eliminates a military threat to the safety and integrity of her people. In this, as well as in other episodes, the theme of the strong woman's exploitation of the weak or weakened man's condition is repeated again and again.

The story of Joseph has also been related in chapter 4. The reader will recall that after young Joseph was sold into slavery by his jealous and scheming brothers, he arrived in the household of Potifar, one of the officers of the Pharaoh, the King of Egypt. Joseph found favor in the eyes of Potifar, who entrusted him with the running of his household: " He left everything in

Joseph's hands and he knew nothing except the food he ate. And Joseph was of fine appearance and good looking. After all this his master's wife raised her eyes at Joseph and said: 'Lie with me.' He refused and said to his master's wife: 'My master gave me charge of the house, no one is above me and he denied me nothing, except yourself, for you are his wife; how could I do this wicked thing and sin before God?' And she spoke to Joseph day after day and he did not yield to her request to lie with her and be with her" (Gen. 39.4–8). Thus, we have a portrayal of a proper and righteous man who is loyal to his employer and to his God.

But Potifar's wife was persistent. One day Joseph came to the house to do his work when none of the household was home. She grabbed his garment and said "Lie with me;" he left the garment in her hand and escaped outside. When she saw that he escaped and left the garment in her hand, she called the people of the household and said to them: " 'See, he brought us a Hebrew to mock us; he came to lie with me and I screamed. And when he heard me raising my voice, he left his garment with me and ran away outside.' She put away the garment by her until the master came home. And she told him as follows" (Gen. 39.11–16).

The woman is seen not only as a temptress, disloyal to her husband, and attempting to be unfaithful to him. She is also portrayed as revengeful and deceitful in projecting her own frustrated sexual advances onto the man who spurned her. Unlike Rebekah and Yael, Potifar's wife committed her treachery for largely personal and egoistic reasons. In the other instances mentioned, the deceit was motivated by altruistic concerns; Rebekah's love for her son Jacob, and Yael's concern for the continuing safety and integrity of her people. In the case of Potifar's wife, her motives were pure hatred and revenge of a frustrated and spurned lover and Delilah's treachery was for personal gain.

A more serious treachery is described elsewhere in the book of Judges. We are told of a powerful giant named Samson, who successfully assaults the enemies of Israel—the Philistines. After several attempts to capture Samson failed, the enemy devised a tricky scheme which involved a woman named Delilah with whom Samson had fallen in love. The Philistines came to

Delilah and appealed to her to find out the secret of Samson's phenomenal strength so that they could capture him. Delilah, in compliance with the request of her countrymen, attempted several times to find out Samson's secret, but to no avail; she questioned him constantly, but he always put her off. She persisted with her whining "How can you say you love me when you do not confide in me?" (Judges 16–15). She so pestered him with these words, day after day, pressing him and wearying him so hard that he finally told her his secret: "If my head were shaved, then my strength would leave me and I will sicken and become like an ordinary man" (Judges 16.17). Then Delilah finally realized that Samson told her the truth and passed the word to the Philistines. "She lulled him to sleep on her lap and had a man cut the "seven braids of his hair and his strength left him" (Judges 16–19). In his weakened condition, he was seized by the Philistines who gouged out his eyes and took him to their headquarters in Gaza for display and torture.

Here, again, the woman who gained the love and trust of the hero betrays him to his enemies with the most dire and cruel consequences. Delilah, like Yael, gains the confidence of the man who subsequently becomes her helpless victim.

A prime example of the negative presentation of women is that of the archetypal evil woman, Jezebel, the wife of King Ahab, portrayed in the first book of Kings. Perhaps the redactors of the Bible were particularly hard on Jezebel, in part, because she was a foreigner—a Phoenician in origin—and also because of her strong incitement to idol worship. We are told that the King (Ahab) was very dispirited and depressed because he was unable to effect a deal with his neighbor, the landowner, Naboth. This man owned a piece of property that was adjacent to that of Ahab's. The king wished to acquire this piece of land and wanted to buy it from Naboth. When he offered Naboth the deal, the latter turned him down, for he did not wish to relinquish his family's heritage. Following the refusal of the transaction, Ahab stayed at home and sulked, Ahab "lay down on his bed, covered his face and would not eat" (1 Kings 21.4). When Jezebel discovered the cause of her husband's withdrawal and depression, she said to him: "Come eat, and take heart, for I'll make you a gift of Naboth's vineyard" (1 Kings 21.7).

Jezebel's method of acquiring the property which her husband was unable to obtain by legitimate means was harsh and high-handed. She arranged for witnesses to testify falsely against Naboth that he "cursed God and king" (1 Kings 21.10). Following this trial on the trumped-up charges she presented to the elders Naboth was taken outside the city and stoned to death.

This wanton execution did not pass unnoticed by the conscience of the people—the prophet Elijah, who confronted king Ahab when he arrived to take possession of Naboth's vineyard. In one of the most poignant passages of the Bible, we see Elijah, upon the instructions of God, confronting Naboth thus: "You have murdered and now you also take possession? Where the dogs licked the blood of Naboth, there they will lick your blood" (1 Kings 21.19–20). Thus ended the grisly episode that was initiated by the evil Jezebel; she implicated her husband in the eyes of the Lord, a man who was to benefit from her crime but was too weak to prevent it, disown it, or condemn it.

Notable here is the dominance of the woman, who is considerate of her husband, but cruel and conniving when it comes to others who stand in her way.

It appears that all of the women described in this section acted against men, and not against members of their own sex. Generally, with the exception of Jezebel, these women have no direct confrontation with men. The results these women wished to accomplish were achieved by means of betrayal, deceit, and trickery and not by direct encounter. Rather, a trusting relationship is established with the men involved. Adam was Eve's husband, as was Rebekah the wife of Isaac; Sissera, the fugitive general was destroyed by Yael, a "hospitable" friend of the family; and Samson's secret was betrayed by his lover, the Philistine Delilah. The only one who does not fit this formula precisely is Jezebel. She did not deceive her own husband, who was weak and dependent upon her. Nevertheless, it was a nefarious and underhanded conspiracy in which she deceived the elders to achieve a goal favorable to her husband. Deceit seems to be the common denominator in all of these stories.

Men in this ancient society attempted to achieve their goals on the battlefield or in direct confrontation. In contrast, women developed an indirect pattern of deceit and betrayal as their *modus operandi*. The use of cunning and lies was their way of obtaining desirable results. However, it would be mistaken to draw conclusions and make generalizations on the basis of these particular selections from the Bible. As will be seen in the subsequent pages, there is another side of the picture which leads to marked differences from the characterizations hitherto derived.

GENDER-FEMALE-POSITIVE

Many descriptions and characterizations of women in the Bible are very positive in nature, and contribute to the conceptual complexity of the female character that emerges. The picture does not at all portray women as the objects of oppression and exploitation stemming from the monolithic patriarchal attitude of the ancient world. The picture is much more complex.

One of the earliest descriptions of female generosity, for example, appears when the young Isaac, accompanied by his servant, comes to the land of his father Abraham's birth to look for a bride. "He saw Rebekah ... The girl was very beautiful and a virgin ... She went down to the spring, filled her jar and came up again. Abraham's servant hurried to meet her and said to her—give me a sip of water from your jar. "Drink sir," she answered, and at once she lowered the jar to her hand to let him drink. When she had finished giving him a drink, she said—Now I will draw water for your camels until they have had enough" (Gen. 24.15–19). Upon experiencing this generosity, Isaac and his servant became convinced that the Lord had made their journey a success; they had found the appropriate bride. Aside from beauty and virginity, the quality of kindheartedness of the woman, both to man and beast, is clearly emphasized.

During the period between the Hebrews' arrival in the land of Canaan and the establishment of the monarchy, 150–200 years later (around 1150 B.C.E.), there were a series of tribal leaders or "judges" who attempted to keep the tribes at peace with each other, as well as to ward off enemies from outside the country. These were popular leaders, often war chieftains, both commanders and charismatic figures who were able to mobilize and galvanize the religious and patriotic fervor of the masses, to settle tribal disputes, and battle against marauders and invaders from the neighboring regions. Outstanding among these leaders is the towering figure of the judge and prophetess, Deborah.

Jabin, the King of Canaan, had been oppressing the children of Israel for some 20 years. His army commander, Sisera, was ruling the people with an iron hand. The text describes the circumstances as follows. "At that time, Deborah, the wife of Lappidoth, a prophetess, was a judge in Israel. It was her custom to sit under a palm tree, between Ramah and Beth El in the hills of Ephraim, and the Israelites came up to her for justice. She sent for Barak, the son of Abinoam ... and said to him "These are the commands of YHWH the Lord of Israel ... go and draw ten thousand men ... and bring them to Mount Tabor ... and I will draw Sisera, Jabin's commander and his chariots and his crowd to the river Kishon, and there I will deliver them into your hands." And Barak said to her, "If you will go with me, I will go; if not, I shall not." "Certainly I will go with you," replied Deborah, "but this won't bring you any glory, for the Lord will deliver Sisera into the hands of a woman" (Judges 4.4–10). Subsequently, Sisera was informed about the intentions of the Israelites. He called for his "nine hundred iron chariots" and his troops and prepared for the attack. Then Deborah said to Barak, " 'Arise, for today the Lord will give Sisera in your hands' ... so Barak came charging ... The Lord put Sisera to rout ... before Barak's onslaught" (Judges 4.15–16).

Following the great victory, Deborah and Barak "sang a song" in which the glory of the Lord and the bravery of the participants in the battle were praised and extolled. To date, this epic poem, the "song of Deborah," remains one of the greatest achievements in world literature. However, aside form the literary merit, our concern in this context is with the role, personality, and character of this charismatic leader, judge, and prophetess—Deborah.

Deborah was the fourth in a long series of judges who led the Israelites during the century and a half following the exodus from Egypt, prior to the establishment of the kingdom. It was a transitional period bridging the nomadic tribal era and the consolidated epoch of nationhood and national monarchy. Deborah was the only female judge mentioned in the book of Judges. Not only did she mete out justice to the people, but she was a prophetess as well. The implication is that, like many of the other prophets of biblical lore, she was viewed as a mediator between YHWH and his people, Israel. She communicated the will of the Deity and his admonitions to the several tribes and to the entire nascent nation. Deborah must have been a woman of exceptional qualities to reach this status and position of respect. The people trusted her prophetic ability as the transmitter of heavenly decrees as well as her judicial and military expertise; and, she had much charisma in what seemed to be a primarily male world. She is shown in the story above as the mover and energizer of the male general, Barak, for without her encouragement he did not dare to face the enemy. Finally, there is Deborah the poet who composes and sings the song of thanks to YHWH for delivering the enemy into the hands of Israel's valiant warriors.

One more issue is worth mentioning; Deborah was also a *wife*—married to Lapidoth. It is interesting to note that such a combination of marriage and career was possible even in ancient times; perhaps as the exception, and not the rule.

Now, we turn to a much later period, to the times of the beginning of the monarchy, and the times of Saul, the first anointed King of Israel. When young David grew in popularity after emerging victorious from the famous duel with the Philistine giant Goliath, King Saul became very jealous and rather suspicious, if not entirely paranoid. We learn that Saul tried to eliminate this potential rival for the throne on several occasions. David escaped the wrath of the king and lived as an outlaw in the countryside with his small band of devoted followers. They lived "on the land" by foraging and obtaining their provisions from the farmers of the rural communities around them. Sometimes they were the beneficiaries of the generosity of the farmers and herders of the villages. Occasionally, the threat of the use of force supplied the needed motivation for the local people to provide for their sustenance.

David and his men had gone to the wilderness of Paran following the death of the prophet Samuel, who had anointed him as the future King, even when Saul was still alive. The Bible informs us that "There was a man at Maon who was a man of substance; he owned three thousand sheep in Carmel. The man's name was Nabal and his wife's name, Abigail; and the woman was intelligent and beautiful, but the man was mean and evil ..."

(1 Sam. 25.2–3). David sent his men to speak to Nabal; they told him that his shearers were with them and they did not harm them or molest them, and "now," they said, "is a good time to give something to your servants and to your son David."

But Nabal turned them down flat: "Who is David? ... Nowadays there are many slaves who break away from their masters. Should I give my bread, water and meat to men I do not know?" (10–11).

David's men turned around and came back to their leader empty-handed and told him about Nabal's reception. David alerted his men, and told them to arm themselves and get ready to attack Nabal.

In the meantime, Abigail, Nabal's wife, was told by one of the servants how Nabal, her husband, had rebuked the messengers of David. He also told her: "The men were good to have not molested us, and protected us day and night" (1 Sam. 2.5–17). After receiving this information, Abigail, without her husband's knowledge, commandeered quantities of bread and wine, lamb, and raisins, and sent her men and all the produce loaded on donkeys to David's camp. She followed them to the camp, and upon her arrival prostrated herself before David and offered him the desired provisions while apologizing for her husband's churlish behavior. Abigail saved the day by wisely avoiding disaster and by providing for the needs of David and his band.

In this story, detailed in chapter 25 of the First Book of Samuel, we note for the first time direct reference to a woman's *wisdom* and *intelligence*. Abigail's diplomacy forestalled an attack which would have brought about harm and destruction as a result of her husband's ungenerous and provocative behavior.

The next story is that of Solomon's famous judgment in the case of two women who claimed the same infant as their son. This is an illustration of still another positive feminine trait implied in the biblical literature. When two women came to Solomon to settle their dispute, they told the following story. They lived in the same house and gave birth to their sons about the same time. Then, as the story was related by one of the women, the other woman inadvertently killed her child by lying on top of him. She then stole the live child from the other in the middle of the night while the other woman was asleep, and replaced it with the dead child. Now, she claimed that her child was the live one. Thus, both women claimed the living child as their own.

The king then said, "Fetch me a sword." They brought in the sword, and the king gave the order to cut the living child into two and give one half to one mother and the second half to the other woman. Then the true mother was moved by compassion for the child and said, "Give her the child and do not kill him" (1 Kings 3.26–27). Then Solomon realized who the real mother was and passed judgment accordingly.

Compassion of the woman for her offspring—motherly love—guided her decision to relinquish the infant and let another woman be declared as his rightful mother. Here we are aware of the extreme expression of selfless love for one's own flesh and blood, despite the possibility of losing the precious object. Happily, in this episode, the evidence of that altruistic love was rewarded by the monarch's wise and insightful decision to place the child in this woman's custody.

On the other hand, the blatant immorality and unethical behavior demonstrated by the adversary whose deception is uncovered, presents another aspect of feminine psychology. Pure egotism and self-centeredness, similar to the behavior of Potifar's wife described earlier, present the other polarity of the feminine character. The previous section was devoted to the presentation of lies and deceptions as part of the armamentarium employed by women, characteristically coping with everyday life in ancient Israelite society.

Overall, the foregoing pages reflect the multidimensionality in the biblical portrayal of women: both the negative and the positive in roles, characteristics, and behaviors.

WOMEN ASSERT THEMSELVES

Several biblical passages describe the rather complex and ambiguous relationship between Michal, the daughter of King Saul, and David, the popular warrior, nemesis of the Philistines, and the ultimate successor to the king on the throne of Israel. The insecure Saul was threatened by David's successes on the battlefield and consequent popularity and had tried to get rid of his perceived competitor both in direct and indirect ways. Since his daughter, Michal, was in love with the brave and handsome David (1 Sam. 29), Saul gave her to David for a wife in the hope that the bride price he was about to exact from David (one hundred Philistine foreskins) was so perilous to achieve so as to bring about his demise. However, David did meet the challenge, and Michal became his wife. She even saved his life, at least on one occasion when her father's emissaries came around to execute him, and she helped him to escape. The story gets a bit murky when we read that Saul, after David's escape "had given his daughter Michal, David's wife, to Palti the son of Layish" (1 Sam. 24.44). However, it appears that subsequently, Michal was still considered to be David's wife, as will appear from the following account of events after the death of Saul and after David's ascension to the throne.

As a part of consolidating his kingdom, the new King David decided to transfer the Holy Ark to the city of his own residence and to the center of government. So, the Holy Ark, accompanied by the priests and the Levites was moved ceremoniously to the "city of David." The parade celebrating the transfer of YHWH's holiest symbol was described as follows: "And David danced, whirling around with all his might before YHWH girt in a linen ephod ... and David and the entire house of Israel were bringing up the Ark of YHWH with blasts and the sound of horn. As the ark was entering the city of David, Michal, the daughter of Saul was watching form the window and saw David leaping and whirling before the Lord, and she despised him in her heart" (2 Sam. 6.14–16).

Clearly, Michal disapproved of David's rather undignified and common behavior—"dancing, leaping and whirling" and exposing himself to the ordinary people like a commoner. Michal's condemnation is clearly more trenchant in the subsequent encounter with David upon his homecoming: "And David came back to greet his household: Michal the daughter of Saul came out to meet him and said: 'didn't the King of Israel do himself honor today—exposing himself before the slave girls as one of the riffraff.' And David said to Michal, 'Before the YHWH who chose me over your father and his household ... before YHWH I shall dance and dishonor myself even more ... among the slave girls I shall be honored.' To her dying day Michal remained childless" (2 Sam. 6.20–23).

In this conceptually loaded paragraph, several important issues about Michal and David and their relationship come to the fore. In the first place, Michal is referred to as the "daughter of Saul," not as the wife of David or the wife of Palti, the son of Layish. Apparently, when Saul took Michal away from David, their connubial relationship had ceased. We are not told what happened with Michal's other union with Palti. Yet, it is interesting to note that Michal was a member of David's household. That seems to leave her marital status rather ambiguous.

Second, what is particularly noteworthy is her encounter with David and sarcasm about what appeared to her to be unseemly behavior. Her chastising him for improper demeanor and lack of royal dignity is uncommon and unusual behavior on the part of a woman toward a man in Biblical times. The traditional deference shown by woman in relation to man is completely lacking and the derision directed at royalty is truly astounding. There is no comparable instance in the biblical literature where the wife defiantly confronts her husband and criticizes him so severely. Perhaps Michal's own royal origins influenced her snobbish attitude toward the behavior of the folksy, democratic, and unpretentious king.

Third, it was not at all clear whether Michal was still (or again) the wife of David. Saul had given her to Palti when he was still king and alive, but at the time of this episode, after Saul's death, she was a member of David's household. Also, she is constantly referred to as the daughter of Saul, and not as the wife of David. Be that as it may, one may speculate that a rather strained relationship between the two motivated Michal's negative, mean, and stinging assessment of David's deportment. However, it is not altogether unusual to refer to the wife's origin when referring to as the daughter of Saul in the Bible, for that was the way of distinguishing one wife from another; and David did in fact have a number of other wives, acquired during his exile and afterwards.

Finally, it is somewhat puzzling that the chapter from which we quoted (2 Sam. 6) ends with what appears to be a *non sequitur:* "To her dying day Michal had no children." Perhaps the authors intend to inform us, or at least imply, that her barrenness was considered a curse from the Deity, and may have been a factor in the cool relationship between the royal couple. It is difficult to say whether, conversely, the infertility of Michal affected the relationship, or whether the coolness of the relationship underlies the barrenness. Michal's previous involvement with another husband, David's accession to her father's throne, and his popularity with the crowds (especially the "maidservants") may all have been factors in Michal's harsh reaction to him. Whatever the cause this episode is a clear example of a woman shedding the traditional subservient role vis-a-vis her husband, her "master," and assuming a critical, nay superior, attitude toward his undignified plebeian behavior.

An example of blatant feminine rebellion against masculine royal authority comes from one of the chronologically later books of the Bible. It deals with the insubordination of Queen Vashti to the wishes and commands of her husband Ahasuerus, the mighty Persian emperor, the ruler of a "hundred and twenty provinces."

At the end of a long period of celebration when the king and the queen had their separate parties with their cronies from the royal entourage, the conflict between the royal couple flared up.

> On the seventh day when the king's heart was merry with wine, he commanded ... the seven chamberlains to bring Vashti the Queen before him, with the royal crown, to show the people and the princes her beauty, for she was good looking. But, the Queen Vashti refused to come upon the King's request via his chamberlains. The king was furious and his anger burned within him. Then the king said to the wise men ... , "what shall we do to the Queen Vashti according to the law, because she has not done according to the commandment of the king?" ... And Memucan said before the king and the princes "Vashti the queen has done wrong not only to the king but to all the princes and all the people in the provinces of King Ahaseurus, for when this matter becomes known to all the women as to despise their husbands in their eyes. The king ... commanded Vashti the queen to be brought in before him, but she came not. Now, the ladies of Persia and Media who have heard of the queen's behavior, will likewise say to the king's princes which will arise contempt and anger. If it pleases the king there be issued a royal decree ... that Vashti come no longer before the king ... and her royal estate be given to someone better

than she. And the example of the king will be heard throughout his empire, all the wives will give their husbands honor,
from the great to the small." And the saying was good in the
eyes of the princes and he did according to Memucan, and
he sent letters to all the provinces ... that every man should
rule in his own house ... (Est. 1.10–22).

This quotation is, perhaps, the most clear enunciation of
masculine domination in biblical times. The queen's refusal to
be exhibited before the king's male friends was a direct defi-
ance of traditional male authority, especially in royal circles. It
seems that the threat of the possible contagiousness of this
female insubordination was great enough to prompt a special
decree from Ahaseurus to the people in his realm. He did it
upon the advice of his counselor, who was cognizant of the
potential damage Vashti's behavior might wreak upon the traditional differences in the gender status of the society in his realm.
The threat of women's "willfulness" and independence was not
to be tolerated; the decree was intended to forestall any widespread rebellion. The reaction of the male establishment in this
instance is one indication, perhaps, of the uneasy truce that
existed. It reflects a certain awareness of the potential of rebellion on the part of women and, therefore, a readiness and a
vigilance about preserving male authority.

Similarly, the increase in equality between the genders in
Western society followed a rather rocky path over the centuries
and up to the present time. There are still many men who are
puzzled by the question raised by Freud: "what do women want?"
The answer, or, shall we say, many answers to this question
have been given in a vast literature during the recent decades.
A discussion of these issues in the present context will take us
too far afield.

In addition to instances which demonstrate the success, self-
assertion, and initiative on the part of women in the biblical
"man's world," there is the unusual and uncharacteristic event
of women as a group standing up and being counted. This instance appears in the book of Jeremiah, who pours out his
wrath (in the name of YHWH) on the Israelites who moved to
the land of Egypt and, contrary to his demands, abandoned the
city of Jerusalem. In the name of the Lord, the vengeful prophet

warns the worshippers of other gods (Baal, Ashera): "I shall punish those who live in Egypt as I punished those in Jerusalem—by sword, famine and pestilence" (Jer. 44.13). We read further in the book of Jeremiah: "Then, all the men who knew that their wives were burning sacrifices to other gods and the crowds of women standing by answered Jeremiah:

> We will not listen to what you tell us in the name of the Lord. We intend to fulfill all the promises by which we have bound ourselves; we will burn sacrifices to the Queen of Heaven and pour drink offerings to her as we used to do, we and our fathers, our kings and princes in the cities of Judah and the streets of Jerusalem. We then had food aplenty and were content; no calamity touched us. But, from the time we left off burning sacrifices to the Queen of Heaven and pouring drink offering to her, we have been in great want, and in the end we have fallen victim to sword and famine. And the women said "when we burned sacrifices to the Queen of Heaven ... our husbands knew full well that we were making crescent cakes marked with her image" (Jer. 44.13–19).

Several important issues are revealed in the verses just quoted. First it seems that the women were the principal deviants from the strict Yahwistic observance. Throughout the period of the monarchy it seems that the women were much implicated in "turning" the men away from YHWH in the direction of idol worship, the worship of Baal and Astarte (Queen of Heaven). Much of the spread of this trend was blamed upon the custom of royalty marrying foreign women—from the times of Solomon, with his "thousand wives," through Ahab's marriage to Jezebel the Phoenician. These women brought foreign influences to the Israelitic society; at least, they were blamed for them. Secondly, the women are standing up to Jeremiah. They not only admit their deviation, but indicate that the men too are a part of the pattern, for at least they condoned it. Moreover, not only do the women admit the practice of worship of the Asherot, but also defend their obligation to fulfill the promises they made as a part of that worship. In the third place, this is one of the very rare occasions in the Bible where women are addressed as such; and not included, by implication, in an address to the "people" for Jeremiah addresses them specifically, and not as part of the entire populace or congregation. Fourth, the women give Jeremiah a very reasonable argument; a rather practical argument, in fact, pointing to the fact that the "Queen of Heaven" took care of them; they offer the practical information that they had plenty of food, and no calamity came upon them. This is a primitive theological argument that empirically, the goddess was more effective than YHWH, despite the prophet's protestations and wringing of hands.

Jeremiah, the prophet of gloom and doom, was hardly a popular figure in the Hebrew community at that time. He was imprisoned by the authorities and nearly executed at one time, for his dire predictions about the nation's future. Contradicting this controversial prophet was not a very risky proposition. On this occasion, and perhaps on others which were not noted by the scribes, the women rebelled, asserted themselves and stood their ground. To be sure, the men joined them, but the women never appeared to be the instigators and motivators of the confrontation with the zealous prophet of YHWH. They were rebels and deviants, but did not instigate confrontations.

Jewish monotheism was in trouble; the women pointed out that the men were worshipping other gods, and that the elite, the royal family was similarly involved. These women had popular support, but the very independence they demonstrated in presenting their views was remarkable. It raises some doubt about that characteristic usually stressed by critics of the biblical period: the ubiquitous and complete domination by the masculine. We do not overlook the fact, however, that on this occasion the rift was not between men and women, but between the people and YHWH's messenger. In fact, the women used the fact of the men's consent as a further justification of their polytheistic practices.

DISCUSSION AND CONCLUSION

The treatment of individual lives in biographies of the famous seems to be consonant with the patriarchal-androcentric trends that appear reflected in the Bible. In her book *The Mismeasure of Women,* social psychologist Carol Tavris refers to Gergen's observations that metaphors common in men's biographies are rarely found in those of women's:

> The stories of powerful white men typically fit the tradition-al male narrative. These authors became heroes, pursue their quest, overcome crises and ultimately win victory. Women and children may come along for the ride (Tavris, 1992, p. 303).

The characteristics of these biographies are truly "traditional," for they match the similar features that describe the biblical narratives. We may recall the description of Jacob who is about to meet his estranged brother Esau while being uncertain, nay, suspicious of his older brother's intentions. In that instance, he sends the women and children to the rear, while facing the danger ahead both directly and valiantly. In biblical battles and wars, the women and children are not involved; they are pro-tected. The actors, the "agents," are the men who perform the memorable deeds—whether for good or for evil. There is a stress on *masculine* activity and *feminine* passivity. Some exceptions negate the absoluteness of the dichotomy. There is the leader-ship of Deborah, the violence of Yael, Jezebel, and Athalia, and the wisdom of Abigail, for example. The two different trends that characterize human existence are of interest: *agency* and *communion* this useful, and influential dichotomy was first pro-posed by David Bakan in his insightful work *The Duality of Human Existence* (1966). The dichotomy, or "duality" is that of *agency* vs. *communion.* In Bakan's own words: "I have adopted ... *agency* for the existence of an organism as an individual, and *communion* for the participation of the individual in some larger organism of which the individual is a part. Agency manifests itself in self-protection, self-assertion, and self expansion; com-munion manifests itself in the sense of being at one with other organisms" (p. 15). In addition, Bakan points out that agency is further characterized by isolation, alienation, aloneness, the urge to master and toward repression of thought and feelings. Com-munion, on the other hand, is the lack of separation, contact, openness, and union and unconditional, cooperation. Gilligan, in her work *In A Different Voice* (1982), shares this orientation.

When we view the characteristics of the biblical males, we note an emphasis upon agentic behavior: Battles, wars, violence, direct conflict, leadership, domination, and striving for control and mastery. Although much less is written about women, women and children under their care were behind the battle lines, rearing and watching over the younger generation, protecting them, safeguarding the family, and exhibiting communion as their major mode of dealing with the world. They identified themselves frequently with the Canaanite deities of fertility, with communion, rather than with the agentic monotheism of the YHWH.

The impression is often gained that in the relationship between the genders, especially in the area of sexuality, the male is dominant. Yet, this impression is not entirely correct. Females have asserted themselves in the Bible, for example, the female lover in the Song of Songs (3.1–4): 'Night after night on my bed I have sought my true love; I have sought him but have not found him; I have called him but he did not answer. I said I will go the rounds of the city ... The watchmen, going the rounds of the city met me and I asked 'have you seen my true love?' Secretly I left them behind me when I met my true love. I seized him and would not let him go, until I had brought him to my mother's house."

Another kind of courtship is described in the book of Ruth. Upon the advice of her mother-in-law, Naomi, Ruth followed a scheme whereby she ultimately obtained the husband she was looking for. This is an instance of the instrumental employment of sexuality for the purpose of achieving the aim of security via marital stability: "One day Ruth's mother-in-law, Naomi, said to her, 'My daughter I want to see you happily settled. Now there is our kinsman Boaz; you were with his girls. Now tonight he is winnowing the barley at his threshing floor. Come, wash and anoint yourself and dress yourself. Then go down to the threshing floor, but do not make yourself known to him until he has finished eating and drinking. And, when he lies down, note the place where he lies down. You will come and turn back the covering at his feet and lie down. He will tell you what to do' " (Ruth 3.1–14).

However, this kind of behavior is rather atypical and unusual. As Biale (1992) comments: "Ruth is doubly antinormative: A woman who takes the sexual initiative in a patriarchal culture and a Moabite who becomes the ancestor of King David, despite legal bans on intermarriage" (p. 26). Biale calls it a sort of "sexual subversion of the Bible," for otherwise, with the exception of the Song of Songs, the Bible shows little interest in Eros.

In Chapter Three concerning sexuality, the episodes of Tamar's capture of Judah, and the aggressive pursuit of Joseph on the part of Potifar's wife are additional examples of feminine independence and aggressiveness in the area of sexuality.

In her research concerned with the comparison of men and women in modern America, social psychologist Alice Eagly (1992, 1995) concurs with the notion that men are more agentic and women are communal. Her recent review of meta-analytic approaches to the study of sex difference (1995) points out that many studies, because of their methodology, routinely produced rather small sex differences. But "alternative metrics foster more accurate understanding of how these group differences would appear in daily life" (p. 152). In this and in a later article (Eagly, 1996) she concludes that "Surely, differences between the sexes reflect the social position between women and men, with women manifesting social behavior that is less agentic and more communal than those of men ... men can be described not merely as more aggressive than women, but as more violent and destructive" (1996, p. 159). In the Bible, the agentic aspects of males are amply documented, but due to the less dramatic aspect of communion and due to male authorship of the biblical works, the major feminine characteristic of communion is both underplayed and under emphasized.

Psychologists have been interested in the study of sex differences, and in their manifestations in personality, abilities, and other characteristics. But, more recently, considerable stress has been placed on the issue of the origins of such differences, if indeed they actually exist. For the biblical man and woman, causality was strictly in deistic or theological terms. Men and women are made differently from the very beginning, since the time of Adam and Eve. God made them that way, and God is responsible for any variances in character and behavior that may be observed. In our modern era, in addition to the investigation of the reality of sex differences, their etiology and development has been an important focus, especially since the advent of feminism. Contrary to the old Freudian dictum that anatomy is destiny, the influence of culture upon the institutionalization of maleness and femaleness in terms of status and sex differences has been strongly stressed by cultural anthropologists (D'Andrade, 1966).

Sociocultural determinism is also taken up by social psychologist Tavris (1992), who is a minimalists on certain sexual differences: "On matters of intellectual ability, brain functions, competence morality, empathy, hostility, greed, and need for intimacy and attachment, love and grief and the capacity for sexual pleasure—on these I am a minimalist" (p. 288). Tavris does conclude, however, that there are significant differences between the sexes in some areas, such as caretaking, communication styles, and contexts of emotional reaction. Her important point is that masculinity and femininity are not actually polar opposites, and that "the virtues and vices of human character are distributed across the sexes, arrogance and compassion included" (p. 302). This conclusion is quite consonant with the various characteristics expressed by the multitude of biblical actors, male and female, who make their appearance in the scriptural writings.

CHAPTER 7

Special States of Consciousness

I t is my intention to briefly survey what might be called "biblical psychopathology." First, it may be of interest to deal with the terms *meshuga* (crazy) and *shigaon* (craziness) that appear in several contexts in the biblical literature. Second, the description of certain patterns of behavior which are not explicitly labeled in the Bible, but conform to our current notions of deviance and/or abnormality, will be examined. And finally, issues of psychodynamics and possible causality underlying these disturbances and aberrant behaviors will be analyzed.

"There is no dearth of clinical material in the Bible," states Gregory Zilboorg in a discussion of the scriptures in his *History of Medical Psychology* (1941). He proceeds to offer a series of retrospective diagnoses in accordance with the old Kraepelinian nosology, the classification system of mental disorders. For example: "Hannah, the mother of prophet Samuel was apparently afflicted with a severe neurosis. Saul suffered from recurrent depression, both homicidal and suicidal. Ezekiel was coprophagic. The ecstatic states of some of the prophets are very suggestive of pathological mental states" (p. 29). While we need not necessarily agree with Zilboorg's diagnostic formulations, it is true that the biblical descriptions of behavior we nowadays label as psychopathological are fairly numerous, and are worthy of more detailed scrutiny.

The term *meshuga* which is employed in the biblical literature on a number of occasions. According to some scholars, despite the differences in Hebrew spelling, the word originated

144

or is related to the verb *shago* (to err) or the noun *shgia,* which means error. Thus, the reference is to a mistaken perception of reality which is, of course, at the core of severe psychopathology. Generally, the term *meshuga* refers to irrational thought and behavior, much as the words "crazy," "mad" and "psychotic" are employed in the English language today. The last-named term, of course, is more formal, and carries with it certain medical and scientific implications. Psychosis (the state of being psychotic) is generally defined as a state of severe mental disorder marked by impairment of a sense of reality and of thought processes.

Biblical references to *meshuga* involve much the same implications of irrationality and bizarreness of behavior. Let us examine a few examples in the biblical text.

DAVID FEIGNING MADNESS

On one of the occasions when David ran away from the wrath of the jealous King Saul, he landed himself in the principality of Gath, which was enemy territory. To avoid harm at the hands of the people of Gath, who might consider him dangerous, he feigned madness, which by implication made him harmless. The story goes as follows: "And David ran away from Saul and came to Achish the King of Gath. The servants of Achish said to him: 'Surely this is David ... about whom they tell in the dance that Saul smote thousand and David the ten thousand.' David became afraid of Achish (because of his notoriety as a warrior) so he changed his behavior, scrabbling on the doors of the city gate and dribbling his saliva on his beard. And Achish said to his servants, 'Don't you see the man is acting crazy; why do you bring him to me? Do I lack crazies to act crazy before me? Should this one come to my house?' " (1 Sam. 21.11–16).

In this excerpt, we see that Achish, the king of Gath, was impressed by the strange behavior of the refugee David and considered him harmless; not a threat, merely a nuisance. Apparently, David's calculated, deliberate, and deceptive behavior, the senseless graffiti, and dribbling spittle were sufficient symptoms for the diagnosis of madness on the part of Achish. there is an underlying consensus as to what constitutes madness, on the part of the actor as well as on the part of the observer; madness is suggested by purposeless activity and poor control of bodily functions. Finally, madness seemed to imply harmlessness and lack of threat. Thus, David was not viewed as the powerful warrior who might be a threat and mean peril to the ruler of Gath.

MADNESS AS DISEASE

The plagues and illnesses referred to in the Bible were viewed as punishment visited upon the people by YHWH for their iniquities or lack of loyalty to the Deity. Some of the chapters in the book of Deuteronomy present a veritable catalog of curses upon the people who may be disobedient and disloyal to the revengeful God. For example, in Chapter 28 of Deuteronomy the people are told: "And it will happen if you do not listen to the voice of the Lord your God and do not obey my laws and commandments ... the following curses will reach you: YHWH will smite you with *madness,* blindness, and *confusion of the mind*" (Deut. 28.28).

A few verses further in the text, we read:

"You will be driven mad by the sight of your eyes" (Deut 28.34).

We note two sources of madness. One is the madness that is like any other disease that comes directly from YHWH. The other is the implication that horrible experiences bring about the state of madness; a person is *driven* into madness, "by the sight of your eyes." Observable events, with which we may not be able to cope—we may speculate that these are traumatic events—precipitate the state of madness; a formulation of ego break as a result of ego insufficiency to cope, proposed by modern dynamic psychology. To more fully understand what "the sight of the eyes" refers to, we must turn to a few sentences earlier in the text. There, the verses refer to the sons and daughter that will be taken by another nation and the wealth of the land and the fruit of the labors will be enjoyed by others. It is this helpless and hopeless experience, resulting from the curses, that drives into madness.

MADNESS AND THE PROPHETS

On some occasions, the attribution of madness is made when a person's behavior is unusual and is not understood by the normative observer. It is the nonconformity of some public figures, such as prophets, that labels them as mad. The case of the young prophet who was sent by the prophet Elisha illustrates the point.

Elisha sent the young prophet to Yehu, one of the king's officers, with instructions that he should anoint Yehu as king in private, and run away lest the treasonous act be discovered soon and lest the reaction of the king whom he was to replace be violent. Upon the young prophet's arrival, Yehu who was sitting with his fellow officers, was called out and anointed in privacy. When he returned to his comrades in the court, "They said to him: 'Is all well? What did the madman want of you?' 'You know him—the way he talks and thinks,' responded Yehu" (2 Kings 9.11). They did not believe him and, upon pressure, he revealed that the young prophet had anointed him to be king. They immediately began an ultimately successful campaign to unseat the old king and inaugurate the reign of the new one. While Yehu was at first disingenuous in his response to his fellow officers; he gave in to their requests and subsequently ruled the nation.

Further, in the same chapter of the book of Kings, the threatened king of Israel sent messengers to Yehu, who was gathering strength, to find out his intentions. The watchman, seeing the arrival of Yehu's army, reported him driving in the manner of "madness" (*shigaon*). The reference here is to impulsive behavior; he was driving furiously, on his way to attack the monarch whom he was about to replace. This use of the word "*madness*" in this context conveys yet another characteristic in addition to those of unusual speech and peculiar thinking.

What is of interest in the story of Yehu was that he was labeled as a lunatic, whose thoughts and speech were outlandish and did not conform to general public opinion. This tells us something about the nature and status of the prophets and prophecy. They were not ordinary people; they often exhibited strange behavior, and their message was either difficult to comprehend or to accept. The broader issue of prophets and prophecy is treated in greater detail below.

In the book of Jeremiah, we find the following message of YHWH transmitted by him to Shemaya, the false prophet: "You claimed that the Lord has appointed you to be priest in the place of Yehoyada ... and it is your duty as officer in charge of the Lord's house to put every lunatic [madman—*meshuga*] who sets up as a prophet into the stocks and the pillory" (Jer. 29.26). Again, madness and prophecy are associated, for the distinction between genuine prophets and "false" prophets was never clearly delineated. It was as common to associate madness with the unaccepted or unconvincing prophecy as with the unusual symbolic speech, behavior, and action of "true" prophets. Consensual validation was the general acceptance by a broad constituency whom the prophets were able to convince that they were within the bounds of sanity; the failure to achieve this consensual validation was a sign of madness. In many respects, this state of affairs and the criteria of nonconformity as the basis for psychopathology even persists today (Szasz, 1961).

So, madness as a curse, as an undesirable state, is not unfamiliar in the Bible. However, the particulars of this condition are relatively few. David's "scrabbling" and "dribbling," the prophets' unconventional behavior of the prophets in their ecstasies and the unusual ideas, extraordinary visions, and dreams often placed them in the category of the mad or lunatic. As we shall see in the section on the prophets, those few who were sufficiently talented, charismatic, and in command of a broad understanding of religious lore and political realities, survived to become leaders in guiding the conscience of their people and in providing an enduring record for the generations and centuries that followed.

SOME CLINICAL MATERIAL

In the preceding section I concerned myself with the idea of madness; with the term as it appears in the biblical literature. I gave only a few descriptions of genuine disturbed behavior or symptomatology. I shall turn to some of the instances that dem-

onstrate the Bible's sensitivity in reporting personality and behavioral patterns that are relevant to the scientific-clinical observations of the modern era.

SAUL'S EVIL SPIRIT

An oft-quoted early example of a description of a psychopathological state appears in the first book of Samuel.

These episodes concerning King Saul involve several aspects of
psychopathology. First, an explanation is offered of the "cause"
of the altered behavior. Secondly, a detailed description of the
behavior itself is presented as expressed in several specific
events. Finally, the remedies, or "treatment," are cited for the
condition.

"But the spirit of the YHWH departed from Saul, and an evil
spirit from the YHWH troubled him. And Saul's servants said
unto him, 'Behold an evil spirit from God troubles you.' Let our
Lord now command your servants, which are before you, to
seek out a man, who is a cunning player on the harp: and it
shall come to pass when the evil spirit from God is upon you,
that he shall play with his hand, and you shall be well" (Sam. 1,
16.14–16). The advice of the servants was followed, and David
was selected. He was reputed to be "cunning in playing and a
mighty valiant man, and a man of war, and prudent in matters,
and a comely person, and the Lord is with him" (1 Sam. 16–18).
Considering all these virtues, David became an immediate success. King Saul "loved him greatly ... and he (David) became his
armor bearer" (1. Sam.16–21).

However, what is most relevant in the present context is the
following passage: "And it came to pass, when the evil spirit
from God was upon Saul, that David took a harp, and played
with his hand: so Saul was refreshed, and was well, and the evil
spirit departed from him" (Sam. 1.16–23).

We may readily note that the source of both good and evil is
the Lord, YHWH, the Deity. If the spirit of the Lord is upon
someone, then it is good and fine. However, when the spirit
departs and an "evil spirit"—also from the Lord—comes to affect a person, then it is readily recognizable. There are very few
clues as to King's actual behavior and feeling state, but anxiety
and depression seem to be the most ready explanations for the

observation that he was troubled by an evil spirit. The trouble's periodic nature ("When the evil spirit ... was upon Saul") is also consistent with this supposition. However, the symptomatology of the affliction is much more complex, as will be seen below.

David had great prowess as a warrior and as a popular hero who fought successfully many of the battles that Saul made him undertake. He was an important object of envy and jealousy on the part of the King. Saul saw David as a threat to his throne, although the Bible clearly indicates that in no way was David plotting against him. Nevertheless, Saul's insecurity, partly due to the prophet's (Samuel's) earlier rejection of him, was considerable. He developed what might today be considered paranoid ideas regarding David, and attempted to get rid of him. Thus, we have the "musical therapist," the feared rival, and the successful warrior, all wrapped up in the same person—David.

Another "symptom" mentioned in relation to King Saul is that of "prophesying." Apparently the activity so designated involved going through a variety of motions of rapture, great excitement, and inspiration, characteristic of the prophets when they prophesy. The removal of clothes is also mentioned in this context. In the following quotations, some of these themes are quite apparent.

"And it came to pass on the morning [following David's victory—*Ed.*] that the evil spirit from God came upon Saul, and he prophesied in the midst of the house: and David played with his hand as at other times: and there was a javelin in Saul's hand. And Saul cast the javelin; for he said, I will smite David even to the wall with it. And David turned away from him twice. And Saul was afraid of David, because the Lord was with him, and was departed from Saul" (Sam. I, 19.23–24).

To recapitulate, therefore, Saul was periodically disturbed. There is some evidence of a cyclical nature of the disturbance; each episode is related in the Bible to the theological explanation of causality—the spirit of the Lord. Some of Saul's episodes are described as states when the "evil spirit" affected; apparently anxiety and/or depression were experiences which were relieved by the "cunning" harp-playing of David. Other episodes were characterized by excitement; "prophesying," in that cultural setting, is consistent with a manic-like state.

The term "paranoid" was used above. The book of Samuel is replete with descriptions of Saul's pursuit of David and his attempts to do away with him. David's success and popularity were the seeds of Saul's suspicion. Perhaps Saul had an inkling that the prophet and kingmaker Samuel intended David to be his replacement. This may have served as the element of realism which often starts the development of the paranoid thought process. Throughout the relevant parts of the Bible, however, there is no indication of any actions on David's part which would have justified Saul's fear, suspicion, and hostile acts.

After David escaped Saul's plans to assassinate him, he went to Ramah and joined the prophet Samuel and his band of prophets. The messengers that Saul sent to Ramah stayed on and joined the prophets in their rapturous experiences (prophesying). Then, when Saul himself finally arrived, he too succumbed to the ecstatic experience.

Saul's increasing insecurity on the throne, due to the successes of David and the support and devotion that his own children, Jonathan and Michal (David's wife) demonstrated toward David, was the basis of his depression (lowered self-esteem) as well as the paranoia. The latter may well be described as the "delusional disorders" mentioned in the American Psychiatric Association's *Diagnostic and Statistical Manual of Mental Disorders* (A.P.A. 1994, p. 296–301).

Alleviation of symptoms by means of music is an idea that persists even in the 20th century. Musical therapy is one of the regular auxiliary treatments employed in many clinical settings. The *Music Therapy Sourcebook* (Schulberg, 1981) presents a variety of applications of music in modern clinical settings. Research on the effects of music upon mood and as an antidote to negative emotions, such as anxiety and depression, has been widely reported. The biblical texts include many accounts on the use of music in everyday life as well.

David's skillful playing on the harp was apparently soothing to the king, but did not cure his essential anxiety, depression, and jealousy. We are not informed about the nature of the music that calmed Saul. The Bible presents narratives, but is devoid of musical notations.

THE DEATH WISH AND SUICIDE

WISHING TO DIE

Personal pain and despair often reach such intensity that the sufferer may cry out in agony, wishing for death. The immediate causes for such a state of unbearable anxiety and/or depression may be intractable pain, without relief on the horizon; psychological pain, perhaps resulting from shame or guilt; or a general loss of self-esteem, which make future existence seem hopeless and the outlook bleak and unredeemable. There is an overwhelming wish to avoid facing such a future. Studies show that severe depressives' future time perspective, that is, their capacity of projecting their selves into the future, is extremely limited and foreshortened as compared with nondepressives. Many historical figures of the past were subject to bouts of extreme feelings of guilt, inadequacy, and despair. A number of biblical figures show similar patterns of experience and corresponding behavior.

Moses complained to God when he felt the pressure of the dissatisfied and rebellious people in the desert. They did not always share his vision of the promised land, the brilliant vision which was often clouded by complains and dissatisfactions which in turn, arose from the rigors endured by life in the wilderness. The people wanted meat; they got tired of the *ersatz,* the fake, the substitute called "mannah." They clamored to return to the "fleshpots of Egypt." "They complained to Moses and Aaron, all the people and the entire congregation said to them, 'If we only died in the desert. Why does YHWH bring us to this land, to fall by the sword, our woman and children will be plundered; is it not better for us to return to Egypt?' " (Num. 14.2–3). Moses felt inadequate in his attempt to gratify the people, to maintain their cohesion and sense of loyalty to the goal of reaching the promised land and ultimate independence as a nation. He complained to the Lord: "This whole people is a burden to me; I cannot carry it alone. If this is thy purpose for me, then kill me ..." (Num. 11.14–15). Moses seems to prefer death to the agony of dealing with a troublesome people as its only, and possibly an ineffectual and unsuccessful, leader.

Another charismatic figure, the prophet Elijah, makes a similar request of his Lord and master. Following the killing of many false prophets who were under the protection, and in service, of Queen Jezebel, the wife of the monarch Ahab, Elijah had to escape the Queen's possibly lethal revenge. In no uncertain terms, Jezebel broadcast her intentions to do away with the zealous prophet of YHWH. Elijah fled south, to Beersheba and then "He went into the wilderness, a day's journey, sat under a broom bush, and begged to die: 'It's enough, please Lord, take my life' " (1 Kings 19.4). It appears a bit paradoxical that after running away from the queen's henchmen in order to save his life, the prophet prays for the relinquishment of that life. At first we may gain the impression that there was something rhetorical about Elijah's request to die. Most likely, Elijah was a weary, miserable, hunted man who genuinely wished to end it all. However, as an extremely devout servant of God, he wanted death to come from the Lord himself, rather than at the hand of an idol worshipper—the Phoenician-born Queen Jezebel.

It is not at all surprising that Job, the most tragic figure of the Bible, wished that he were dead. The entire third chapter of the Book of Job is replete with misery and the desire to escape the destiny of an unhappy life of wretchedness and tribulation. Rather than making an appeal to God that he kill him, Job expresses the wish that he had never been born at all. He curses the day he was born and calls out in agony: "Why did I not die in the womb; why did I not die when I came out of the belly?" (Job 3.11). Moses wanted to die because of his perceived inability to cope with the stupendous task of guiding a "stiff-necked" and intransigent people. Elijah was weary of constantly running and fighting the battles of the YHWH against the idol-worshipping sinners under the influence of various polytheistic foreigners. But Job's suffering and anxiety were both more personal and more philosophical. On the personal level, Job had lost everything that made for a happy and rewarding life—wealth, children, and health. But, his greatest pain comes from his shaken faith, from the growing doubts about the relationship of the Deity to the human, about he relation between moral behavior and reward and punishment. Job, who had led the exemplary life, who had been handsomely rewarded for his righteousness and faith in God, was suddenly brutally punished, to his dismay and great astonishment. It was at this point that the suffering became so unbearable.

In each of these examples, the hurt, the anxiety, and the bafflement are so great that nonbeing, death, is preferable to the status quo, the hell to which they are so suddenly and cruelly transported.

Undoubtedly, the circumstances in the lives of these ancient Hebrews—Moses, Elijah, and Job—were so intolerable that they led to profound unhappiness and depression. However, in none of these cases is there a hint of the impulse to do away with themselves—of suicide. Both Moses and Elijah want God to bring about their demise, but at no point do they contemplate themselves taking the initiative. Even Job, whose experience was most traumatic, speaks only of his wish not to have survived his birth and, incidentally, not to have experienced the good life and the eventual destruction of the wonderful life he had built for himself. It is quite possible that Job thought of suicide; we may speculate about it; but the biblical text neither reveals such intentions nor suggest such solutions.

In modern times, much talk about not wanting to live quite often precedes the attempt and often the actual act of self-destruction. Various reports of suicidal ideation as a predictor of suicide may be found in the professional medical, psychiatric, and psychological literature (Shneidman, 1985, and others).

Actual suicide was not unknown in ancient Israel, as we shall presently see from the narratives that appear in several books of the Bible. However, the act does not seem to have been heralded through verbal expression such as that voiced by Jonah after his mission to Nineveh: "Please, God take my soul, for death is better than my life" (Jonah, 4.4). Here, again, there may have been contemplation of the act, but life was seen in the hands of God, end not under control of mere humans. Expressions of grief and anxiety are found in abundance in a number of biblical books, especially the Psalms. These and other mood states are to be considered in another context.

SUICIDE

Self-destructive behavior and suicide were part of the panorama of life in ancient civilizations as they are in modern society, and the Bible presents several illustrations. It is interesting to note that no judgment is expressed therein as to the propriety or impropriety of the behavior.

"Thou shalt not kill" is often quoted as one of the Ten Commandments which Moses received on Mount Sinai. Actually, the precise translation of the Hebrew ("*Lo tirzach*") rendering of this commandment would be: "Thou shalt not murder." The difference between the two versions appears somewhat trivial, but it may be significant. Murder refers to the deliberate taking of the life of another person, but not one's own life. Suicide is the act of killing oneself. The commandment forbids murder, but not killing *per se,* as in the case of capital punishment. This is consonant with the fact that killing oneself is not explicitly forbidden in the Bible. The following episodes which describe the protagonists' killing themselves present the events in a matter-of-fact manner, without censure or condemnation.

Of further interest is the fact that the Deity is left out of this process. God is not perceived as instigating nor compelling that particular course of action. It was strictly a human initiative.

Samson's Heroic Death

Samson, the powerful giant of Israel, routed the neighboring enemies of the Philistines with great regularity. Various attempts to eliminate him by force were not successful. Finally, the Philistines appealed to their fellow countrywoman, Samson's lover, Delilah, to ferret out of him the secret of his superhuman strength. After nagging him upon numerous occasions, he finally relented and confided in her that his strength lay in his hair. She conspired with her countrymen and cut Samson's hair while he is asleep. The Philistines then captured the weakened and helpless giant. They then "... put

out his eyes, and brought him down to Gaza in brass fetters."
While in prison his hair began to grow, and some of his powers returned to him. Then the lords of the Philistines gathered together, to offer a great sacrifice to Dagon, their god,
and to rejoice: "The people saw him and praised their god for
delivering their enemy, the destroyer of the country and the
one who multiplied our dead." The text goes on:

> When their heart was full of joy, they said: Call Samson to
> amuse us; and they called Samson from his prison and he
> stood before them, between the pillars. And Samson said
> to the lad who was holding his hand: Let me feel the
> pillars on which the house stands so that I'll lean upon
> them. And the house was full of men and women, and the
> officers of the Philistines on the roof, about three thou-
> sand men and women, to watch Samson amuse them. Then
> Samson called to God and said: "Remember me and
> strengthen me this once, but this time, oh God, I will take
> revenge for once, for my eyes of the Philistines." And he
> grasped the two center pillars on which the building was
> erected ... and Samson said: "Let me die with the Philis-
> tines." And he turned the pillars with force, and the house
> toppled ... and he killed more in his death than he did
> during his lifetime" (Judges, 16.21–30).

Here was an example of what one might call a heroic and
patriotic suicide; it is an escape from an undesirable and humiliating fate but, at the same time, it involves an important national objective: the punishment of the tribe's enemies, as well
as one's own torturers.

Saul's Last Battle

Some time later in the history of Israel, after passing the tribal
era of the "judges" and the beginning of the monarchy, we are
given a description of self-destruction: that of king Saul on the
battlefield.

The setting is one of the battles in the continuous series of
conflicts between the newly united nation of Israel and its traditional formidable foe, the coastal nation of the Philistines. It is
one of the best known and most poignant descriptions of sui-

cide on the battlefield of the tragic figure of Israel's first king, Saul. Elsewhere we have noted Saul's recurring depressive episodes, but nowhere was there an inkling or report of any suicidal ideas. Through consultation of the soothsayer, the witch of Endor, Saul knew beforehand of his defeat in the battle but he nevertheless led his forces against the ancient foe, the Philistines. In this fateful battle, King Saul's sons had fallen and the enemy snipers began aiming their arrows at the monarch himself. He then realized that his situation was completely hopeless: "And Saul said to his armor bearer, draw your sword and pierce me lest the uncircumcised (the Philistines) will come and taunt me; but the armor bearer refused to do it, for he was very afraid; so Saul took the sword and fell on it. When the armor bearer saw that Saul died, he too fell on his sword and died" (1 Sam. 30.4–6).

Saul's suicide on the battlefield was probably doubly motivated: first, by his loss of self-esteem, for he proved himself a failure in the position of leadership. The second reason seems to be a more tangible one: facing the not-too-palatable prospect of falling into the hands of the enemy and possible torture and other indignities before being put to death. It may also be noted that Saul's action was quite consistent with what we have learned about him during the prior years of his life. He was intensely jealous of David, the successful newcomer who was admired by the people. He saw David as a threat to his kingdom; he was rather insecure about himself and his hold on the throne. Additionally, Saul was subject to what may be called depressive episodes, an "evil spirit from the Lord" (1 Sam. 16.15). Thus, Saul's longstanding low self-esteem and insecurity may have contributed to his self-destructive behavior.

To some extent, the episodes just cited demonstrate similar motivations for suicide. Both Saul and Samson wanted to avoid the experience of indignity, an extreme injury to their self-esteem, through submission to taunting and torture at the hands of the hated enemy. Death, therefore, seemed preferable to such an ignoble fate. Even the armor-bearer who, apparently, identified himself very closely with his king and master, Saul, knew that if caught alive he would suffer a similar end; he followed suit and destroyed himself.

Zimri's Unsuccessful Revolt

Well after the monarchy was established in the land of Israel and the division of the kingdom into the states of Judea and Israel took place, it is recorded that many bloody feuds and bloody uprisings took place. This was especially true in the case of the northern kingdom, Israel.

One example is the case of Zimri, an officer of the royal force who rebelled against the king. He eliminated all the possible pretenders to the throne—the entire dynasty. However, his reign was short-lived and lasted only 7 days: "When the people heard of Zimri's rebellion, and that he slew the king, they coronated the military commander, Omri, in the field that day. Omri and all the people went up and laid siege to the city of Tirtza where Zimri was. When Zimri realized that the city was conquered, he went to the royal palace, set it on fire and died in it" (1 Kings, 16.16–18). In this instance, defeat was inevitable and the future rather dim for the rebelling upstart. To avoid the experience of humiliation, ignominious defeat and probable execution, Zimri decided upon self-immolation.

The Shamed Ahitophel

Quite a different situation is presented in Ahitophel's suicide. King David's son, Absalom, had built up his own constituency without his father's knowledge. When Absalom's rebellion against his father broke out, King David fled the capital, Jerusalem, to escape possible assassination. Ahitophel, who was a respected consultant, was asked for advice by Absalom: "In those days, a man would seek the counsel of Ahitophel as of the word of God" (2 Sam. 16.23). Ahitophel advised Absalom to go after David immediately and kill him, without harming the people in his entourage who followed him out of Jerusalem. However, Hushai, another respected adviser was also summoned by the rebelling son, Absalom, who apparently wanted to receive confirmation of Ahitophel's advice. As it happened, Hushai was a true friend of David, and acted as a sort of double agent in this situation. In his instance, he told Absalom that he disagreed with Ahitophel's counsel, and proposed an entirely different course of action intended to buy time for King David to escape the clutches of his would-be pursuers. As a matter of fact, Hushai sent out a warning to David about his son's violent intentions. "When Ahitophel saw that his advice had not been taken, he saddled his donkey, he went to his home in his own city, gave his last instructions to his household and strangled himself. So he died and was buried in his father's grave" (2 Sam. 18.23). It appears that Ahitophel was devastated when his advice was rejected, and the resulting loss of self-esteem was profound and unbearable. In addition, he must have also realized that Absalom's uprising was doomed to failure and David would continue to reign. His own status was therefore, in jeopardy. Suicide seemed a most logical solution in these most unhappy circumstances.

"Reactive depression" was at one time a diagnostic term in the nomenclature of the psychiatric profession. The reference was to a severe depression that is not "intrinsic" but extrinsic; it is a depressive reaction that is caused by a sudden traumatic experience that is humiliating, resulting in a tremendous loss of self-esteem and/or loss of support, or both. Although this term is no longer listed in the official diagnostic manual of the American Psychiatric Association, environmental events of the nature described above are incorporated in the diagnostic descriptions of the several types of depression, as "precipitating causes" of the disorder. As is the case in most severe depressions, suicidal thoughts and rumination and suicidal attempts, as well as actual suicide, are part of the picture.

All three suicides referred to above were the consequences of overwhelming traumatic circumstances, considered both physically and psychologically. As is the case in severe depression, the future looks bleak; future time perspective is foreshortened. Clearly, in two of the cases mentioned, the chances for maintaining life were very much in doubt. Saul would have been killed by the Philistines who had overrun his position, Zimri's life was in jeopardy because of his rival's victory. These two men had nothing to lose; they were doomed, and chose a more honorable death. Ahitophel was the only one who might have survived his dishonor and humiliation, had he viewed the future in more positive terms.

Overall, it would appear that in all of these examples cited, suicide was a reaction to unbearable external conditions, a reactive response to sudden traumatic changes in one's status as a result of unanticipated turns of events. Many modern suicides seem to be motivated by intrinsic factors involving feelings of alienation and depression. To be sure, external motivations are often also operative in many suicides, but not as exclusively as in the biblical instances.

Finally, as mentioned before, it is interesting to note that in none of these descriptions is there an indication of disapproval of the specific self-destructive solution. Suicides were reported, but in a factual manner. No moral judgments of the acts are pronounced by the authors of the Bible. Apparently, the religious objections to suicide were formulated by developments in the Hebrew community during the post-biblical period.

EFFECTS OF WINE

Wine was used in ancient Israel on many occasions of celebration: ritual, nonritual, or secular. Apparently there was a recognition of the positive as well as the negative consequences of imbibing. On the one hand, the relaxing effect and the feelings of well-being are fully recognized while on the other hand, some of the primarily cognitive, as well as the physically incapacitating, effects are also found in biblical descriptions of the consequences of alcohol consumption.

In the book of Psalms we find the ode to the Lord: "You make the grass grow ... and green things ... bringing bread out of the earth and wine to gladden men's hearts" (Psalms 104.15). Wine in moderation seems to be favored by the aphorist: "Happy the land when its king is nobly born and its princes feast the right time of day, with self control, and not as drunkards ... the table has its pleasures and wine makes a cheerful life" (Eccl. 17.19). The happiness and good feeling brought about by the consumption of alcohol should not be out of control; these sensations need to be moderated. Using wine as a metaphor, Zecharia, the prophet, speaks of "... Ephraim shall be like warriors, glad like men cheerful with wine" (Zech. 10.7). Finally, when King Ahasuerus was celebrating: "On the seventh day, when the king was merry with wine, he ordered ... the seven eunuchs ... to bring Queen Vashti before him ..." (Es 1.11–12). There seems to be a general awareness of the mood enhancing qualities of wine experienced as part of the good life.

Wine, however, does not receive uniformly high marks from the biblical writers; it surely is not an unmitigated success. As noted already, the exercise of control in the use of the alcoholic drink is strongly advocated, the dire consequences of not abiding by that rule are clearly, and sometimes dramatically, spelled out in some of the following quotations.

The book of Proverbs is especially generous in the comments concerning the drinking of wine: "Wine is an insolent fellow, and strong drink makes an uproar; no one addicted to their company grows wise" (10.1) or "Do not keep company with drunkards … drink and greed will end in poverty. The drunk goes.in. rags" (23.20–1).

A most telling and dramatic passage about the physical and psychological effects of drinking may be found in chapter 23 of the book of Proverbs. "Whose is the misery? Whose the remorse? … the quarrel and anxiety? Who gets bruised for nothing? Whose eyes are bloodshot? Those who linger over the wine … do not gulp down the strong red wine … at the end it will bite you like a snake and sting like a cobra. Your eyes will see strange sights and your mind and speech will be confused; you become like a man tossed upon the sea … When I wake I shall look for it again" (30–35). Here is an exhortation of the shocking state of the excessive imbiber. The physical effects—bloodshot eyes, loss of balance, feeling of being tossed on the sea—and psychological effects—confusion, visual hallucinations, speech—describe an alcoholic's bout, stressing the pain resulting from that extreme state. Not only are the symptoms of the drunken state described, but so is the antecedent "misery" and "anxiety," as well as a return to the drink so characteristic of the compulsive drinkers and chronic alcoholics. When he wakes from the stupor—"I shall look for it again!."

In the final chapter of the book of Proverbs we find the following: words of Lemuel, King of Mass, quoting the words that "his mother taught him: "It is not for kings to drink wine nor strong drink for princes … if they drink they will forget the law and twist it against the poor and wretched. Give drink to the lost and embittered; they will drink and forget their poverty and trouble" (31.1–7). Additional issues seem to be introduced in this excerpt: Both stress upon the cognitive factors, and effects on the moral judgment of royalty that may be a consequence of wine and strong drink. Yet, there is a recognition of some of the questionably beneficent effects in anesthetizing the masses; the poor may forget their "poverty and trouble." The Marxist orientation regarding religion as the "opiate of the masses" may have had a precursor in this suggestion of "merciful" political use of wine and strong drink.

In one of many chastising sermons to the Israelites, the prophet Isaiah addresses his audience as "the drunkards of Ephraism, overcome with wine." He further speaks to the elite of the society:

"These too are addicted to wine; priest and prophet are addicted ... every table is covered with vomit and filth ..." (28.7–8). What is stressed in this passage as well as the others quoted is the habitual use of wine and strong drink, and the addiction to it, that is definitely criticized and condemned.

One more interesting item concerning wine involves a sort of asceticism, a feature rather uncharacteristic of the YHWHist religion. The Nazirite makes a vow to the service of the Lord and undergoes a period of self-denial. Prominent in this self-denial is the abstention from wine. Hence, wine was considered a source of pleasure to be relinquished like all other worldly pleasures once one made the sacrifice of being a Nazirite, devoted to the service of YHWH. The specifications were enunciated by Moses: "When anyone, man or woman makes a special vow dedicating himself to the Lord as a Nazarite he shall abstain from wine and strong drink ... during the whole term of his vow he shall eat nothing that comes from the vine ... he shall keep himself holy to the Lord" (Nu 6.2–5). Both the prophet Samuel (1 Sam. 1.22–28) and the warrior Samson (Judg. 13.5) were born to once-barren women who made the promise that they will be Nazirites, "consecrated to God."

Pulling together the different strands of data about the attitudes toward the use of wine and the effects of its use, fairly clear trends may be discovered.

1. The relaxing and good feelings created via the consumption of wine are recognized, and generally, not censured.

2. Effects upon the judgment of the excessive imbiber are clearly noted and condemned.

3. Habituation and addiction to the use of wine and hard drink are condemned and censured.

4. Western society's attitudes and observations are consonant with this general orientation.

ANXIETY, DEPRESSION, AND SELF-CONCEPT

Modern psychology and psychopathology has been concerned with the phenomena of fear, anxiety, and depression from the very beginning. Most central is the concept of anxiety in psychological theories of recent vintage, such as learning theory and psychoanalysis. Learning theory has pointed out the curvilinear relationship between anxiety and learning, making the point that a little anxiety is needed to spur or facilitate the learning process, while excessive or massive anxiety may have a crippling effect on that process. A similar relationship between adequate functioning and degree of anxiety has been championed by the psychoanalysts. Signal anxiety brings about alertness and indicates the effectiveness of ego functioning, whereas the experience of "overwhelming" anxiety instigates all kinds of defensive maneuvers and, when these maneuvers are unsuccessful, ultimate breakdown.

Depression may be the result of the incapacity of the person to ward off anxiety due to his cognitive assessment of his chances for success. Here enters the notion of self-concept, referring to the person's estimation of his or her own capacities and abilities to cope with challenging situations. In depression, the experience of pain and agony may often bring about the ultimate solution, that of suicide: the elimination of the unbearable.

We have seen instances of the application of this final solution in some biblical episodes, but the emotional experience, the pain, the insecurity, and the clamoring for help and support is most poignantly expressed in the verses of the book of Psalms.

In his influential *Learning Theory and Personality Dynamics*

(1950), the late Hobart Mowrer wrote that he searched for the term "anxiety" in the Bible, but in vain; he could not find any direct reference to this concept. However, when he looked at the work of the Psalmist, he found ample descriptions of the states we call anxiety and depression. The experiences, the symptoms are related; only the modern terminology is missing. This state of affairs is not unlike the situations we have encountered previously. The Bible *describes* many of the psychological *phenomena,* but rarely deals with what William James called the *conditions,* or the *causes,* of the observed phenomena.

Mowrer (1950) states that "Although I am unable to find the word 'anxiety' anywhere in the King James version of the Old Testament ... it is surely obvious to the modern reader that the anguish of the human soul with which many of the Old Testament writers were concerned was none other than anxiety and its related states of depression and guilt" (p. 533). He adds further that "Christian writers ... handled the problem of anxiety much less well, psychologically speaking, than did those of the Old Testament. In the middle ages, theology almost wholly replaced anything that might be called psychology, and the naturalism which one finds in David and other Hebrew writers was superseded by rampant supernaturalism" (p. 533).

In addition to this quotation from Psalm 34 ("I sought the Lord and He heard me, and delivered me from all my fears," Psa. 34.5), I am presenting a few similar verses from the book of Psalms which broaden our vision of biblical concern with the human condition.

> Have mercy upon me O Lord, for I am miserable, heal me for my bones are stricken and my soul is also in great panic ... Return O Lord, deliver my soul; save me for your mercies' sake ... I am weary with my groaning; all the night I make my bed swim; I water my couch with my tears (Psa. 6.3–6).

> My God, my God, why have you forsaken me ... O, my God, I cry in the daytime and you do not answer, and in the night I am not silent ... I am a worm, not a man, a reproach of men and despised by the people ... all who see me laugh at me ...
>
> You took me out of the womb and made me hope when I was upon my mother's breasts. I was cast upon you from

the womb; you are my God from my mother's belly. Be not far from me, for trouble is near and there is none to help ...
I am poured out like water, and all my bones are out of joint; my heart is like wax, melted in my bowels, my strength is dried up ... (Psa. 22.2–16).

Hear my voice, Lord, and favor me with an answer ... do not hide your face from me ... though my father and mother have abandoned me, the Lord will take me in (Psa. 23.7–10).

O Lord, do not rebuke me in your anger, nor punish me in your wrath. Your anger has left no part of my body un-scarred, there is no health in my body because of my sin ... I am bowed down greatly. I go about mourning all day long. My loins burn with fever and there is no soundness in my flesh ... My heart beats fast and my strength left me, and the light of my eyes is no longer with me (Psa. 38.2–11).

First and foremost is the feeling of abandonment, of being alone and without protection in an unfriendly and dangerous world. The psalmist is abandoned by his father and mother and is forsaken by the YHWH. Moreover, he is rejected by his fellow humans; they despise him. We see here the agony and unhappiness of the lone soul, but also the low self-esteem, wherein people laugh at him and despise him. The resulting or accompanying depression is quite clear. There is a powerlessness ("my strength is dried up") and bodily disintegration, along with tears and groaning. We note the guilt, the low self-esteem, and the severe emotional reactions. Along with the severe depression and melancholia, the helplessness and the cry for help, one is also impressed with the somatic or psychosomatic symptomatology that is involved with the severe anxiety and depression. It is incontestable that the impression is that of genuine anguish and psychological pain and suffering, the description of which goes beyond the mere assumptions of loss of self-esteem and implied severe depression found in the suicides described earlier in this chapter.

The book of Psalms is not the only biblical source for the description of psychological pain, anxiety, and depressive states. Two other books, Job and Koheleth (Ecclesiastes) are also very much expressive of pessimism and negative affects and perceptions by the respective authors and redactors. Whereas, the psalmist (or psalmists) is often very emotional in his reaction to pain, abandonment, anxiety, and guilt, Job and Koheleth are acutely concerned with the broader philosophical issues of the "human condition." Theirs is more of a long-range cognitive and intellectual examination of the human predicament involving the relationship with the Deity and with justice, with goals and the life course. Job suffers a crisis of faith; he is unable to understand why he, a righteous man who lived the God-fearing life, is punished by a vengeful YHWH. His notion of punishment as a consequence of sin has received a severe blow. He is barely able to maintain faith in his life-long image of a just Deity. The resulting discrepancy between his beliefs and the facts of life which he had to face causes a great deal of "cognitive dissonance" and constant defensive reaction to the inconsistency of the arguments of his disputatious interlocutors. Job's faith is shaken, but he maintains it in the face of the doubts that may have plagued him. However, his "dissidence" (Saffire, 1992) may be questionable. Overall, there is an obsessive preoccupation with the cracks in the edifice of his personal *Weltanschaung.*

Throughout the book of Ecclesiastes (Koheleth), the pessimism, nay, even the cynicism, is rampant ("All is vanity," Eccl. 2). The writer does not see any purpose in life except for pleasure and outright hedonism. There is no transcendent idealism, only lonely, selfish gratification, and even that is not completely satisfactory. Enjoyment of life is short-lived. Koheleth often sings an ode to the present and looks with disdain at the future which brings "nothing new under the sun" (Eccl. 1.9). It is a sort of intellectual pessimism and nihilism with little projection into the future, or a future time perspective. In a sense, his pessimism is more cerebral, but profound nevertheless. Yet, the bottom line is a sort of practical option: "A live dog is preferable to a dead lion." (Eccl. 9.4).

The so-called "cognitive revolution" in psychology has, among other things, also wrought some alterations in viewing the phenomenon and experience of depression. Traditionally, severe depression has been considered as the example *par excellence* of the so-called "affective" disorder. However, more recently, the cognitive aspects of the depressive process have come to light. In her book on *Positive Illusions: Creative Self-Deception and the Healthy Mind,* S. E. Taylor (1989) stresses the illusory aspects of mental health involving optimism and positive self-regard. On the other hand, there is the "depressive realism" of the relatively pessimistic orientation. We can readily see that much "affective expression" in the books of Jonah, Job and the Psalms point to a generous manifestation of elements of *"negative cognitive illusions"* that go far beyond the "depressive realism."

There is a group of disorders classified by modern psychiatry (DSM IV) that encompass a wide range of depressed states that go beyond the largely cognitive depressive realism. The major depressions, which include such symptoms as anxiety, tearfulness, and fear, as well as the "dysthymic disorders" and depressive personalities, demonstrate the affective as well as the cognitive dimension. There seems to be an interaction and feedback process between the affective and the cognitive.

Yet another dimension in our understanding of the emotional reaction to the perceived dangers of external or internal origins, such as guilt, is considered by traditional psychology as well as by the authors of the several biblical works. My reference is to the physiological or somatic involvement in the process. One of the three greatest progenitors of modern psychology Charles Darwin (Boring, 1929), more than a hundred years ago, in his volume on "The expression of emotion in men and animals" (1965/1872) quoted from the book of Job as follows: "In thoughts from the visions of the night, when deep sleep falls on men, fear came upon men and trembling, which made my bones to shake. Then a spirit passed before me; the hair of my flesh stood up" (Job. 4.13). Here, the physical components of the emotional reaction are also expressed ("trembling," "hair stood up") as is the perception of danger and the awareness and consciousness of one's affective state. It is reminiscent of some of the descriptions in the classic *The Wisdom of the Body,* by Walter B. Cannon (1932). We quoted passage from Job is very much akin to the quotation from the Psalms presented above.

Thus, the symptomatology of anxiety and depressive states have their roots in the biblical literature of Job, Psalms, and others. The experience of fear, anxiety or guilt, and the emotional and mood equivalents are readily noted, forming the bridge between ancient literature and modern day psychology and psychiatry.

OF DREAMS AND DREAMERS

HISTORICAL INTRODUCTION

Since the dawn of history, people have been intrigued by dreams, their origins, and, especially, their meaning. For the most part, dreams were considered as direct communications of the gods— conversation, commands and injunctions concerning behavior, as well as the prediction of the future. Since much of the dream experience involved strange, unusual, and unrealistic content and images, a special skill in the interpretation of dreams became the function attributed to various seers, magicians, priests, and soothsayers. The interpretation of dreams has a long and fascinating history in the religion, mythology, and folklore of many nations and cultures. Popular theories of dreams and dreaming concerned their divine origins and their prophetic value. Persons with special abilities to decode the divine messages the dreams were thought to contain have appeared in ancient societies and are even part of the scene in modern society as well. Biblical history, as we shall see, gives accounts of dreams and dreamers, of various seers, priests, and prophets, and of especially gifted persons who were able to decode and interpret the often strange and frequently bizarre visions and images which constitute the dreaming experience. For the most part, the meaning behind the dream content was revealed.

It was not until the latter part of the 19th century that attempts commenced to examine the dream phenomena systematically, critically, and scientifically. Some early work concentrated on the effects of external stimuli and recent life experiences upon the dream content. The impact of various brain conditions, such as injury and toxicity, also became of interest to investigators of the dream experience. However, it was not until the turn of the century that the most influential and seminal study of dreams ever appeared in print. First published in 1900, it was the pioneering and epoch-making work by one of the most original thinkers of the 20th century—Sigmund Freud. It is not possible to discuss the subject without reference to some of the basic principles of the origins of dreams and their meaning as set forth in "*The Interpretation of Dreams*" (Freud, 1900/1953).

Approach to Dream Analysis

In "*The Interpretation of Dreams,*" Freud starts his analysis, understandably, with the *manifest content:* the dream itself, as it is recalled or as it is told by the dreamer. Then, by breaking down the dream into elements or components, associations to them are solicited from the dreamer. By using these associations, it is possible to reconstruct the *latent content* of the dream. The latent content is the repressed material that was driven out (repressed) from consciousness into the unconscious.

Basically, according to Freud's conceptualization, the dream consists of experiences and related ideas that are repressed from consciousness because awareness of them is painful. Under conditions of sleep and lower alertness, the *censor,* or the repressive agent, relaxes his control and permits the forbidden, wishes and all, to become expressed in the form of a dream. This expression is, ordinarily, not direct or blatant in content, but is disguised by means of several operations subsumed under the title of "dream work." What is actually recalled is somewhat different from the dream experience itself. For one thing, the dream that is recalled is shorter than what was experienced in the original repressed ideation. The part of the dreamwork involved is that of *condensation.* Repressed wishes, persons, and activities are replaced by harmless symbols that slip by the censor. Thus, the *latent* content of the dream is disguised via the process of *symbolization.* Finally, when the dream is recalled and related, the *manifest* content includes some additions to and elaborations of the originally illogical and incomprehensible material, in order to make this material more logical and coherent.

Not only are the repressed wishes the building blocks of the dream, but the day's mental content and preoccupations also contribute to its formation and construction. Much unfinished business appears in the dream content. This has been labeled as the "day residue"—issues and ideas that have been mulled over during the day, that presented problems, but did not come to any resolution. Much of the recent work with dreams shows an increasing stress on the influence of current material upon the dream process. The unconscious is given its due, but is not considered the exclusive source of dream material. There has been an increasing emphasis in psychiatry on the continuity between waking life and night dreaming.

OLD TESTAMENT DREAMS

By examining biblical dreams and their interpretation, one can detect the similarity to some of the principles of analysis detailed in the previous sections. It is obvious that fairly clear statements of the manifest content are given in the biblical narratives. The origins and motivations underlying the dreams are barely spelled out and must be left to inference and speculation. However, the path that leads from the manifest content back to the latent content, to the *meaning* of the dreams, is demonstrated in the text. The principles by means of which the manifest content is decoded are apparent from the interpretations of imaginative, intuitive, and gifted persons. Joseph, as we shall see below, was one of these gifted and perceptive interpreters. Of course, the Bible does not tell us how these interpreters come to their conclusions. As is true of so much in the Old Testament, human behavior and understanding are attributed to divine direction and inspiration. Yet a careful dissection of the dream content may guide us a bit further along the less exalted path of human reasoning and cognition.

BIBLICAL DREAMERS AND THEIR DREAMS

Numerous accounts of dreams and visions are scattered throughout the biblical texts. Various kinds of dreams, interpretation of dreams, and dreamlike experiences are reported.

I shall concern myself first with the straightforward dream experience, such as dreams during sleep reported in detail and the meaning and representation of which are interpreted readily. Second, attention will be given to the interpretation of dreams by especially gifted and trusted interpreters. Third, a sampling of the dream-vision process as utilized by the prophets concerned with the religious, moral, and political health of the nation will be presented.

Joseph the Dreamer

Perhaps the foremost dreamer and interpreter of dreams in the Bible was Joseph, the second-to-youngest son of Israel's (Jacob's) large, multigynous family. The following excerpt presents the dreams of young Joseph, the interpretation of the dreams, the reaction to them by his father and hostile brothers, and their effects upon the life and career of this unusually gifted person.

> Now Israel loved Joseph more than al his children, because he was the son of his old age ... and when his brother saw that their father loved him more than all his brothers, they hated him and could not speak peaceably to him. And Joseph dreamed a dream and they hated him yet more. And he said to them, "Hear please, the dream which I have dreamed. For behold we were binding sheaves in the field, and lo, my sheaf arose, and stood upright, and behold your sheaves stood around and made obeisance to my sheaf." And his brothers said to him: "Shall you reign over us? Shall you dominate us?" And they hated him even more for his dreams and for his words. And he dreamed still another dream ... "the sun and the moon and the eleven stars are making obeisance to me." And he told it to his father and brothers, and his father rebuked him, and said— "What is this dream that you dreamed? Shall I and your mother and your brothers bow down to you, to the earth?" (Gen. 37.3–11).

The most obvious comment that needs to be made concerning Joseph's dreams is that their meaning was so transparent to the ordinary people that no special expertise, or assistance in their interpretation was required. Israel (Jacob) and his sons readily perceived the symbolism of the elements of the content and made the appropriate interpretation.

Nearly a hundred years ago, Sigmund Freud, in "*The Interpretation of Dreams*" (Standard Edition, IV, V) discussed extensively and analyzed the dream process, the "dream work" and the *manifest* and the *latent* content of the dream. In this instance of Joseph's dreams, the "manifest content" (the sheaves and the stars doing obeisance) was so transparent that lay people, the members of Joseph's family, quite readily understood the thinly disguised "latent content."

What is important about this episode is to the ready use of symbol and metaphor in human communication. It is quite possible that this broadly shared story, over the centuries, became part of Western Culture, and contributed to later, more sophisticated, theories concerning dreamers and their dreams.

The language of the dreams was apparently easily understood in ancient times. Erich Fromm, however, notes that "modern man" of the enlightened and scientific era has abandoned the "forgotten language" (Fromm, 1951). Our modern generation is so concerned with scientific "realism" and with the manipulation of the world about them that they are no longer attuned to the language of yore—the language of the symbols—the "pictorial images as words standing for an idea, feeling or thought ... for inner experience" (Fromm, 1951, p. 241–242). People nowadays are open to the communication of the symbolism of dreams under special circumstances and give "meaningful interpretation of the symbolic language employed" under hypnosis or free association as in psychoanalysis. Otherwise, they construe the dreams as meaningless. It seems that without the suspension of the critical conscious awareness, the meaningful associations do not occur. Modern folks, according to Fromm, seem to have lost the capacity of interpreting myth and dream, because the "forgotten language" has been in disuse for the past two millennia. Jung's *Man and His Symbols* (1964) echoes a similar criticism of the effect of modern rationalism upon the communication in symbols which is relegated to the dream world.

Mention should also be made, in the present context, of the belief in the prophetic aspect of dreams considered in ancient times. Unlike the predominant psychoanalytic use of dreams in modern times as the "royal road to the unconscious" in an attempt to explain and understand covert aspects of the personality in relation to the past and present, the ancients employed dreams and their interpretation as a form of prescience—as a glimpse into the future. C. G. Jung (1964) alone among the moderns is probably the exception, for he too preserved the future-oriented principle of prediction in his explanation of dreams.

In Joseph's dreams detailed above, the expectation of the obeisance of his family is not merely an expression of an attitude, hope, or desire. The Bible tells us that the state of affairs and aspiration expressed in his dreams actually came true after Joseph rose in station and came to power in Egypt. Some of the brothers, and then the entire Israelite family who fled the famine in Canaan, came to Egypt and placed themselves at the mercy of Pharaoh's powerful administrator, Joseph, their temporarily exiled and unrecognized kin. The dreams did come true.

Joseph the Interpreter of Dreams

Next, in the same book of Genesis, we encounter Joseph, not as dreamer, but as interpreter of the dreams of his master—Pharaoh, the king of Egypt—and of those of two of his functionaries.

While imprisoned on false charges made by the wife of his employer Potifar, Joseph met two of Pharaoh's servants who had also been imprisoned; one was chief of the butlers and another, chief of the bakers. They were very sad one morning, for they dreamed the night before and had no interpreter of the dreams. "Joseph said to them: 'Do not interpretations belong to God? Please tell me the dreams.'" And the chief butler told his dream to Joseph ... 'Behold a vine was before me; and in the vine were three branches; and it was as though it budded ... and the clusters brought forth ripe grapes; and Pharaoh's cup was in my hand; and I took the grapes and pressed them into Pharaoh's cup, and gave the cup into Pharaoh's hand. 'And Joseph said to him: 'This is the interpretation: the three branches are three days, within three days Pharaoh shall lift up your head and restore you to your position. ...' (Gen. 40.1–15).

When the baker heard the favorable interpretation received by the butler, he too related his dream to Joseph. The baker dreamt that he had three baskets of baked goods on his head, the uppermost basket contained baked goods that were eaten by the birds. In this case, Joseph predicted that in 3 days the bakers head would be "lifted" from his body and the birds will eat his flesh.

The Bible tells us that both predictions came true, but the protagonist of the story, Joseph, remained to languish in the Egyptian prison. However, some time later his services were sought by Pharaoh himself.

The Butler and the Baker

Before we move on to the dreams related by the king himself, a few comments are in order about the two dreams just quoted. It would seem that the interpreter based his predictions on two elements. First, the magical number 3 appeared in both instances (three baskets and three branches) and is similarly interpreted in temporal terms (3 days). Second, the contrasting conditions of the two dreams seem to be the basis for the highly different predictions in the interpretation. In the first instance, the grapes blossomed (signifying hope) and ripened, and were pressed into the monarch's cup. But in the second instance, the birds ate the food intended for Pharaoh (signifying negligence)—a rather frustrating, rather than a gratifying, state of affairs. The subsequent results suit the conditions presented by the two servants. It seems that the dreams of success and failure are used as predictors of the future in Joseph's "dream book."

It should be added that Joseph did not view himself as a professional interpreter of dreams, but instead as possessed of a gift from God. He claimed to receive the message from God, a special privilege of exceptional status and ability which he had claimed earlier in describing his own dreams, and that catapulted him into slavery and exile to the land of Egypt and subsequent rise to an exalted status.

Pharaoh's Dreams

Joseph's next venture as an interpreter of dreams took place several years later, when he was still in prison. This time he was brought to the attention of Pharaoh himself, who dreamt two dreams in succession, and for which his own wise men and magicians were at a loss to offer a satisfactory interpretation. "Pharaoh dreamed that he was standing by the river when out of the river came up seven cows, handsome and sturdy, and they grazed in the meadow. Then, seven other cows came up after them from the river; they were ugly and skinny and stood by the other cows on the bank of the river; and the ugly, skinny cows ate up the handsome sturdy cows. And Pharaoh awoke" (Gen. 41.1–4). Immediately after that, the king fell asleep again and dreamed another parallel dream which was almost identical with the first one, except that in this instance there were seven healthy and good ears of grain that were swallowed up by seven thinner scorched ears. It may be observed that the parallelism here is similar to that noted in Joseph's own dreams.

Joseph said to the king "Pharaoh's dream are one and the same; God (Elohim) has told Pharaoh what he is about to do, and the seven healthy ears are seven years. . . . The seven lean and ugly cows that followed are seven years, as are also the seven empty ears. . . . They are seven years of famine. It is as I told Pharaoh. Elohim revealed to Pharaoh what he is to do" (Gen. 41.25–8). Then Joseph went on to explain that the 7 years of abundance and prosperity in the country would be followed by 7 years of famine, and that preparation for that eventuality was necessary, even imperative.

The early dreams of Joseph himself were rather personal and expressed an undisguised, or rather, thinly disguised, wish for dominance and an attitude of superiority. Somewhat more disguised are the dreams of the butler and the baker, Joseph's prison mates. Least personal, and more socioeconomic and political in nature, are the concerns involved in the dreams related by Pharaoh himself. All of the dreams, of course, show the continuity of concern from waking life to the dream state. Issues that are problematic and of concern during the day, and that are unresolved and a source of anxiety, may be carried over into the dream state. Both Freud and Jung, as well as other analysts, have stressed this principle.

As to the prophetic aspects of dreams, in a sense the magical aspect in their interpretation, modern rational and scientific psychology finds it unacceptable. Joseph attributes his ability to predict the future from dreams to God. Supernatural explanations of this kind do not find a home in the precincts of modern science.

Freud questions the alleged prophetic aspects of the dream, both in *The Interpretation of Dreams* (Freud, Vol. V, Standard Ed.) and *The Psychopathology of Everyday Life* (Freud, Vol. VI, Standard Ed.). Freud points out that "The belief in prophetic dreams numbers many adherents because it can be supported by the fact that some things really happen in the future as they were previously foretold by the wish of the dream. But in this, there is little to be wondered at, as many far-reaching deviations may be regularly demonstrated between a dream and the

fulfillment which the credulity of the dreamer prefers to neglect" (Freud, 1938, p. 166). He states, however, that foretelling
the future on the basis of dreams "must depend on a clever idea
of direct intuition" (Freud, IV, 97): Thus the notion that prediction is possible, is not entirely rejected, but attributed to luck
and special gifts of the interpreter. Joseph must have been one
of those gifted, intuitive individuals who was lucky and succeeded more often than is ordinarily expected.

Erich Fromm, in his treatise on *The Forgotten Language* (1951),
classifies Pharaoh's dreams as nonpsychological, for they were
looked upon as visions coming directly from the Deity. However, he also sees some psychological features. It is possible to
look at Pharaoh's dream from a psychological viewpoint. He
could have known certain factors which would influence the
fertility of the soil in the coming 14 years, but this intuitive
knowledge might only have been available to him under the
condition of sleep. Whether the dream is to be understood in
this way is a matter of speculation; at any rate, the biblical
report, like many other reports of old Oriental sources, shows
that the dream was understood not as something coming from
man, but as a "divine message" (Fromm, 1951, p. 113). This
conclusion may actually be questioned, for Joseph's narration
of his own original dreams does not make any reference to their
divine origin. Joseph attributed to God his ability to *interpret*
dreams, but does not make reference to the divine inspiration
of his own dreams.

Kelman (1975) introduced a new concept in the vocabulary of
dream interpretation, that of the "day precipitate." It is Kelman's
contention, based on supportive clinical case material, that "the
dream is anchored in reality at both ends. They day residue
provides images and ideas for the construction of the manifest
dream. The compromise formation is then often acted out in
the subsequent psychoanalytic session and/or in the following
day, almost as if the manifest dream had served as a blueprint
for new action. We call this actualization of the manifest content
of dreams as their 'day precipitate' " (Kelman, 1975, p. 209). We
can quite readily see the elements of the predictive or "prophetic" in the subsequent behavior of the dreamer—stemming
from, and connected with, the manifest content of the dream
itself.

Some years later, the same author (Kelman, 1986) reported on the application of the concept of the "day precipitate" to the analysis of Pharaoh's dreams, especially to the relative success of the young slave, Joseph, in their interpretation. The author observes that Joseph's success depended upon his understanding (intuitive) of the day precipitate phenomenon. Since he was aware of the manifest dream content as it was told to him, he knew of the likelihood that the manifest dream content would be acted out, and therefore could be utilized in his interpretation. Kelman (1986) concludes that "The prophetic dreams of Pharaoh were manifestly dreams of replacement. That the prophecy was accurate can be viewed as an example of the day precipitate phenomenon: the dreamer in this case, with the assistance of the dream interpreter, acted out the manifest content of his dreams. According to this view, what was prophetic about Pharaoh's dreams was not that he predicted harvests correctly, but that he harvested prediction correctly; in Joseph's new preeminence over the magicians ... of the court ... the fat and sleek were replaced by the emaciated and lowly ... emaciated and lowly convict had an intuitive grasp of the change in the air often presaged by a dream" (Kelman, 1986, p. 309). We might be able to see the present discussion as complementary to Fromm's speculations concerning the Pharaohnic dreams already discussed.

OTHER DREAMERS AND VISIONARIES

Biblical literature abounds with accounts of dreams in many different situations and circumstances. In many occasions, YHWH communicates directly with his followers, his chosen emissaries such as Abraham, Jacob, and Moses, and with many of the prophets. Another mode of communication is less direct. This mode occurs when the individual concerned is asleep, and is not in direct communication with the Deity. The dream seemed to have been one of the ways in which people extended the range of their perceptions and comprehension of the intricacies of the world about them. People expected to receive advice and guidance via dreams as well as by means of more direct command and communication. Thus, we read in the book of 1 Samuel: "And when Saul saw the host of the Philistines, he was afraid and his heart greatly trembled. And when Saul inquired of the Lord, the Lord did not answer him, neither by dreams, nor by Urim, nor by prophets" (1 Sam. 28.5–6). We note three modes of possible divine communication: the magical priestly objects ("Urim"); theophany (appearance of the deity) involving direct communication via the dream, and the messages from God relayed by the prophets. The comments of one of Job's friends is appropriate in this connection: "For God speaks once or twice, yet man does not perceive it; in a dream, in a vision of the night, when deep sleep falls upon men in slumbers upon the bed. . . . Then he opens the ears of men and seals their instruction" (Job. 33.14–16).

We are told that "God came to Abimelech in a dream by night and said to him—you are to die for the woman you have taken, for she is a man's wife (Sarah)" (Gen. 20.3). Here, Abimelech returned the woman he abducted, for she was the wife of Abraham. Another example: "And an angel of God spoke to me in a dream, saying—'Jacob,' and I said here I am, and he said, lift up your eyes and see all the land" (Gen. 31.10).

In the second quotation regarding Jacob, an angel, a representative of YHWH, was the interlocutor. Throughout the text, an angel (Mal'ach) or angels are the visitors and the messengers of the deity. The same word in the Hebrew language is used for "angel" and for "messenger."

In this last quotation, there is a clear indication of the belief in divine communication via the dream. During wakefulness, divine communication is apparently ineffective ("God speaks once or twice, yet man does not perceive it"). During sleep, there is a certain openness or receptiveness to the instructions that are communicated. In a sense, this parallels the statement that might be made concerning the unconscious as a substitute for the deity. When man is asleep, he is open to the communication of the unconscious, and acts accordingly.

"Lucid Dreaming": Extending and Directing the Dream Life

During the 20th century, and especially since the publication of Freud's seminal work on *"The Interpretation of Dreams,"* considerable progress has been made in understanding and deciphering this human experience that has been reported in the annals of civilization for millennia. In the previous sections of this chapter, reference was made to the fundamental contribution of the unconscious to the formation of dreams and in motivating the consequent amnesia for them. The so-called "primary process" reigns supreme in the dream world and, according to psychoanalytic theory, consciousness, or using Freud's term, "secondary process," is kept out of it. In recent years, however, there has been a good deal of interest in the accounts reported over the centuries of dream experiences that are accompanied by conscious awareness of those experiences during sleep. To use the terms employed above, somehow the secondary process seems to encroach upon the domain of the dream world and of the primary process. There seems to be a clarity of observation of the dream on the part of the dreamer—a certain lucidity in the observation. Thus, the term "lucid dreaming" was coined.

A recent historical review of the experience of lucid dreaming, consisting mainly of anecdotal accounts may be found in *Lucid Dreaming,* by Stephen LaBerge (1985). This volume offers a systematic approach to the study of this phenomenon. The author, who is affiliated with Stanford University Sleep Center, subtitles his work "The Power of Being Awake and Aware in Your Dreams." In his foreword, Ornstein asserts that LaBerge "has proven scientifically that people can be fully conscious while remaining asleep and dreaming at the same time" (LaBerge, 1985, p. ix). On the surface, based on conventional wisdom, this statement appears quite paradoxical. How can one be fully conscious under the spell of sleep and dreaming, which are, by traditional definition unconscious states?

LaBerge argues that there are dreamers, whom he calls "lucid dreamers," who are able to combine the observational functions of the secondary process with the primary process of dreaming. Moreover, some lucid dreamers, as a result of their awareness during dreaming, are able to guide and direct the dreams themselves. Furthermore, LaBerge sets forth a procedure for *training* people in lucid dreaming.

The implication is also that what Fromm referred to as the "Forgotten Language" was alive and well in biblical times. The ability to shift and move from states of awareness (secondary process) to dreams and unconscious processes and back (primary process) was apparently much more widespread than in later millennia. A certain fluidity and ease of transition between lucidity and primary process characterized the experience and the mode of thought of many in the ancient times. The possible connection with prophecy and visions reported in the Bible will be considered in a later section.

THE POST-ANALYTIC ERA

Recent years have witnessed a marked erosion of the reigning psychoanalytic theory of dreams and dreaming. With expanded interest and research in cognitive psychology, there have developed a number of different approaches to the phenomenon of dreaming. The volume summarizing this trend, "*The Multiplicity of Dreams,*" (Hunt, 1989) gives us a fairly detailed account of the research that supports the theoretical expansion.

Dreams are viewed as part of the cognitive system which processes incoming information via our perception from the external environment. But, additionally, besides duplicating the imagery of the external world, the cognitive system also utilizes material and information from long-term memory. Basically, this is the old Jamesian stream of consciousness, including daydreams and fantasies which are not "unconscious," like night dreams, and are characterized by varying levels of awareness. Consciousness is a part of lucid dreaming as well as of fantasy and daydreaming. Even night dreams, according to modern views, reflect "conscious daytime worries, fears and hopes of people as well as their underlying psychodynamic tendencies" (Singer, 1984, p. 245).

The ancients, especially the prophets, have used the term *Halom* (dream) quite broadly and loosely. Many of the so-called dreams were conscious musings on the part of imaginative people, prophets especially, who frequently elaborated on them and "metaphorized" them to express worldly, not other-worldly, dicta to their audiences. To quote singer (1984): Daydreams can have adaptive value. they are a resource for planning the future and for considering possible courses of action (p. 245).

ON PROPHETS AND PROPHESYING

Fantasy, the sensory and perceptual experience without the presence of relevant stimuli to evoke it, is a universal aspect of human life. Members of the human species have reported, from time immemorial, such events as visions~voices, especially attributed to divine origin; and tactile experiences which seemed real, but had no corporeal existence. Such hallucinatory-like happenings are not confined to ancient times and to legend and folkloristic narrative, but are part of the developmental process of many individuals and of a great many adults' experience in modern society. Such unusual events are not to be relegated to the distant past, but are part of the present-day picture on the eve of the 21st century.

The phenomenon of the "imaginary companion" is well-known to students of child life and child development. It is variously estimated that one in every three or four children has at various periods in their childhood interacted with another person, usually another child, who did not in fact exist; such are figments of the child's imagination—the imaginary companion. It is not an abnormal phenomenon at all, as many have thought in the past, but a frequent experience which may even have salutary effects upon the child's development. These hallucinatory-like phenomena are apparently not pathological at all; they fulfill a certain need in the child's life and have a definite function in bringing children through critical times.

Early in the history of Israel as a united nation, a unique class of leaders emerged; they were called *neviim* or prophets. They were divinely inspired leaders, not secular, but spiritual, although at times their activities impinged on the social and political realms as well. They were viewed as the mediators between the Deity and the people; they spoke by divine inspiration. By this definition, Moses may be designated as the first prophet, for he was communicating the word of God to the people of Israel.

F. G. Bratton, in his *History of the Bible* (1967), writes that "The first Hebrew form of prophecy was that of ecstatics or dervishes, a type of religious-political leadership ... (they) roamed about in groups like troubadours and worked themselves into a frenzy by means of music (pp. 85–86)." Throughout the Bible we note references to "groups," "sons" and "schools" of prophets. Apparently, over time, and especially during the millennium before the Christian era, a relatively standardized professional group developed which operated and perpetuated itself in Israeli society. Two major features characterized these bands of prophets: Ecstasy and prediction. Many a royal family had their favorite "court prophets" who were consulted on numerous occasions, dealing with affairs of state as well as with personal matters; the major function of these "seers" or "men of God" prediction of the outcome of certain courses of action.

Shortly after he was anointed king by the prophet Samuel, Saul was sent on his way with a number of specific instructions regarding persons he would meet and places he would visit. He was also told by Samuel that "When you come to town, you will meet a group of prophets descending from a high place, and before them there is a harp, tambourine, flute and lyre, and they will be prophesying. The Spirit of YHWH will come upon you and you will prophesy with them, and you will turn into another man (1 Sam. 10.5–6)." It appears that "prophesying" was an activity, a state, and an experience that was not restricted to professional prophets; others may be exposed to such ecstatic experiences, even if they do not belong to the guild. What is most interesting is the comment that King Saul was to "turn into another man." It seems that this inspiration and unusual rapturous experience was instrumental in transforming a person—making him "another man."

Some chapters later, in the book of Samuel, we encounter additional accounts of prophesying. In one instance, Saul sent some messengers after David, but they came upon a group of prophets prophesying, and the Spirit of God also descended upon them, "they too prophesied" and did not return (1 Sam. 19.23). Finally, when two groups of messengers did not return, Saul himself went to look for David. But he too encountered the prophets and also "prophesied." This description of prophesying goes beyond the one quoted above: "And he took off his clothes also and prophesied ... and he lay down naked all that day and night (1 Sam. 19.24)." Thus, we note that nudity is occasionally an element of the prophetic ecstasy. The excitement experienced seems to have involved rather extraordinary behavior, beyond that found in everyday life. Isaiah too spent some time in a state of nudity in the desert (Isa. 20.2–3).

Two observations can be made in connection with these descriptions of prophesying. First, that prophesying is characterized by a hypnotic quality. The men who were sent by Saul seemed to have been dissuaded from their mission upon encountering the prophesying experience. They too joined the mass orgy, or hysteria, to which they were exposed, and surrendered to its overpowering and hypnotic effects. Even Saul, the king, became a victim of the persuasive and suggestive ecstasies of the group of prophets.

Second, we learn to some extent, what the state of prophesying entails. It seems to involve an entire disregard for conventionality (as evidenced by Saul's nakedness) and a period of semiconsciousness and intoxication. It is a state in which the controls of the ego ("secondary process" thinking and behavior) are relaxed, and free imagery and fantasy take sway. It is, presumably, in these states of freedom of the imagination, in dreamlike states, that inspiration and insight may become far-reaching and permit the prophet to rise above conventional wisdom to provide the charismatic leadership which is so vividly related in much of the biblical literature.

Reference was made above to King Saul turning into "another man." Although there are no explicit details regarding the nature of his transformation, it is reasonable to speculate that the reference is to the profound change in personality. It may refer to the greater freedom gained in thought, imagination, and behavior when compared to the prior status of the individual.

A multiplicity of functions were attributed to the prophetic class throughout the Bible. Prophets are described as seers, soothsayers, healers, poets, advisers to royalty, negotiators, guardians of morality, predictors and prognosticators of the future, and dreamers of the utopian destiny. All of these functions, although not within the scope of any one particular prophet, were based upon the extraordinary experience of the favored and inspired who communed with God, heard His voice either directly or in a dream, and felt compelled to communicate the message to the people. From a psychological point of view, the profession of being a prophet is not as interesting as is the experience and process of prophesying, which may have its parallels and equivalents in the experiences of modern persons.

In an earlier discussion of dreams, we concerned ourselves with the two distinctly different processes of mental functioning described by Freud, early in his career, in the volume on "The Interpretation of Dreams." Primary process thinking is described as primitive, image-oriented, unconcerned with reality constraints, and primarily stimulated by the unconscious. On the other hand, "secondary process" thinking is governed by the reality principle, is logical in nature, and is controlled by the conscious mind. As we noted, many dreams are governed by primary process thinking, in which the unconscious conjures a variety of bizarre and unrealistic images and situations (Freud, 1953, Vol. V, 599–611).

It is quite possible that the act of prophesying involved a frenzy and intoxication that led to self-hypnosis. The induction process in the group of prophets may have involved two factors. First was the musical, seen in the musical inspiration which was induced by several different instruments; second was the group effect itself, the influence and suggestion of the crowd. It implies a certain suggestibility on the part of the members of the group or gaggle of the sons of the prophets. The messengers of Saul, as well as Saul himself, succumbed to the hypnotic effects exercised by the group and "also prophesied" (1 Sam. 19.23). Psychologically speaking, the group effect apparently induced a state of regression to the primary process; it brought about either a state of inspiration, or a dreamlike state which was characterized by uncontrolled fantasy and behavior. These images and behavior transcended reality (as in the secondary process) and were associated with aspects of reality, as is the case with dreams as well. Certain insights deriving from unconventional thinking may have been achieved and acted upon when a return to "normality" took place.

Reports of the prophesies of the individual prophets which make up a number of the books of the Hebrew Bible generally do not stem from group seances and group inspiration. As far as we know, the several Isaiahs, Jeremiah, Ezekiel and the minor recorded prophets all based their prophesies on their personal dreams, visions, and conversations with the Deity. Some of them had apprentices who became charismatic figures in their own right (for example, Elisha, the pupil of Elijah), but most of them were inspired individuals who responded to their "call." Nevertheless, there were also many who pursued prophesy as a career and vocation which was part of the established institutional society (2 Kings 2.1–9).

By far the most detailed and elaborate description of visions are reported by the prophet Ezekiel. The visions are not part of a dream, but were a direct sighting of celestial creatures. In the very beginning of the book, the prophet tells us:

> the heavens opened and I saw the visions of Elohim (God)....
> And I looked and behold a whirlwind came out of the north,
> a great cloud and a flashing of fire and a radiance surround-
> ing it, and inside like amber in the fire and inside the image
> of four creatures, and this is their appearance. They had the
> appearance of humans. Each had four faces and four wings
> and their legs were a single straight leg, and the feet of each
> like a single calf's hoof, shining like burnished bronze; and
> they had human hands under their wings on their four sides
> and they had faces and wings on their four sides ... they
> had the face of a man, the face of a lion ... the face of an ox
> and the face of an eagle.... From above the expanse above
> their heads came a voice.... This was the appearance of the
> likeness of YHWH. When I saw it I fell down on my face and
> I heard a voice speaking (Ez. 1.2–25).

This unusual experience represents a somewhat more extreme instance in the prophetic literature. Such elaboration required considerable literary skill and imagination. Yet, it is the report of a "vision" which is not part of ordinary experience. This extraordinary visual imagery is probably an elaborated report following, or made as a part of, the ecstatic state. It is not a dream, but may be closer to the experience of daydreaming. It seems to be a sort of cognitive construction of numerous symbolic elements that were to be used by the prophet for his purposes. The ideas of "repression" and "unconscious" are not particularly relevant in this context, the concepts of imagery and daydreaming may hold some explanatory clues.

Although Milgrom (1990), writing in his commentary on the Torah, does not believe that a precise definition of the word "*hitnabe*" (prophesy) can be given, he stresses the two elements of ecstasy and possession. The former has already been discussed; but possession is an element not only in the experience of the prophet Ezekiel: "The hand of the Lord God fell upon me" (Ezek. 8.1) "And a spirit entered into me" (Ezek. 2.2), but in the experience of others who felt *compelled* to prophesy. Yet, the behavior of the prophets was both controlled (since there were "schools" of prophets) and not incapacitating. Heschel (1962) questions the diagnosis of psychosis which some latter-day specialists are willing to pin on the prophetic profession (e.g., Zilboorg, 1941).

In his erudite and thorough study, Abraham Heschel (1962) described the multifaceted characteristic of the prophets: "The prophet is a man who feels fiercely. God has thrust a burden upon his soul and he is bowed and stunned at man's fierce greed. Frightful is the agony of man; no human voice can convey its full terror. Prophecy is the voice that God has lent to the silent agony, a voice to the plundered poor, the profaned riches of the world. It is a form of living, a crossing point of God and man. God is raging in the prophet's words" (p. 8). Yet Heschel also points out that the prophet is not confined to prophecy, but is also a poet, preacher, statesman, patriot, social critic and moralist (1962/1975). It is this diversity of activity and concern in the real world that compel the author to oppose the diagnosis of psychopathology. To be sure, their behavior was often bizarre and certainly unconventional, but they always returned to their worldly roles. Heschel points out that the mind of the prophet is similar to the mind of the psychotic, insofar as they live in a non-normative world. Yet there is a significant difference between the two: "me prophet seems to sense, to hear, to see in a way totally removed from a normal perception, to pass from the actual world into a mysterious realm, and will be *able to return properly oriented to reality* and to apply the content of his perception to it" (Heschel, 1962, p. 188). The description of the prophetic experience is quite consonant with the psychodynamic formulations of the creative and artistic process. In both instances, there is a withdrawal of acute awareness of the external reality and the subsequent expression of an internal perception and experience. Overholt (1985), on the basis of his cross-cultural comparisons of the process of prophecy, has evolved the following model. First, there is revelation, followed by proclamation, then by feedback, and concluded by "explanation of confirmation."

The prophetic experience seems to have some commonalities with the mystical experience as described by William James (1902/1987). He lists four characteristics of the experience: Ineffability, noetic (intuitive) quality, transiency and passivity. Perhaps the noetic aspects are the most common element; the insights are central. But, generally, the experience of mysticism does not get translated into the sort of activism that characterized the prophets. The vision, dreams, and messages received by the prophets as well as their description as "possessed" as transmitters of YHWH's words and the religious experiences that were of interest to James are largely "supernatural" experiences, and not part of the ordinary, conscious cognitive awareness which seems to be primarily of concern to modern psychology. Yet, contemporary American society, and likely most other societies across the world, is not devoid of the sorts of experience that the prophets and others have had in biblical times. Results of a recent examination of *"Unusual Personal Experiences"* in the population at large were published in 1992. A poll conducted by the Roper organization revealed some fascinating, if not astounding, findings that surprise and even astonish the scientific secular mind. Fully 15% of the nearly 6,000 respondents to the poll questions reported that they had seen, at least once, a terrifying mythical figure such as a witch, monster, or devil. Eleven percent had seen a ghost; 14% had had the experience of leaving their body; and 10% had the feeling of actually having flown through the air. Thus, it seems that such unnatural or supernatural events are alive and well, and fairly common in the experience of ordinary people of the 20th century United States (c.f., "The Search of the Sacred," 1994). These experiences do not with the "reality testing" of the majority, but seem to be part of the existence of a sizable minority. Some of the criteria which modern rational people apply to the phenomena deported by men and women of ancient times are also applicable to the poll data detailed above. The rational judgments of our scientific age are relevant to these reported experiences. Strictly speaking, we would arrive at the same conclusions regarding the current (poll data) widespread irrationality of the human species and note the failure to place a clear line of demarcation between fantasy and reality. It also brings raises the issue of the possible continuity between the two domains of perception and imagination, or between the Freudian dichotomy of primary and secondary process akin to "lucid dreaming" referred to above.

In his discussion of the cognitive system, Singer (1984) comments that it "is designed to process information coming through the senses from the external environment. The imagery function of the system duplicates the external material but it also draws on material from long term memory. Daydreams or fantasies derive chiefly from this inner environment" (p. 239). Armed with a sense of mission, using metaphor and allegory, the prophet reports the outlandish and "illogical" in support of his aims, be they moral, political, or theological. In night dreams, external cues and stimuli are practically excluded, and the long-term memories occupy center stage; but in daydreaming, the combined content is frequently utilized. Both are the substance of what William James (1890) called the "stream of consciousness."

The following points may be justified:

First, the term "prophet" defines many roles in the Bible; all these persons are concerned with "real issues" such as ethics and morality, social justice, especially for the downtrodden, politics, and many other issues that were fundamental to the existence and the future of the Israeli nation and of the world of nations.

Second, "prophesying" involved a sort of transitional hypnotic state, often encouraged and generated in a group setting, and enhanced by charismatic figures, music, and other environmental factors. This state was evocative of rich fantasy and insight subsequently combined with environmentally determined cognition.

Third, the experience was apparently akin to the "noetic quality" ascribed to mysticism by James in his *Varieties of Religious Experience* (1902/1987). Also, in addition to the "transiency," there is a "passivity" in the sense of being compelled and being "possessed." The experience however, is far from "ineffability," since communication to and guiding the people was the prophet's major function.

Fourth, the unusual experience and imagery that was utilized by the prophets in their communication to the people is not extremely deviant, even in contemporary society. Our empirical rationalism has not completely banished or eliminated supernatural experience in the life of modern folks. Perhaps herein lies one of the effects of the Bible upon modern readers.

Finally, the relevance of daydreaming and lucid dreaming to the understanding of prophesying psychology has been hypothesized.

SUMMARY

In this chapter, I have included discussions of a number of psychological states that are in some ways exceptional and in some respects different from the quotidian and the commonplace. Some of the states described are "pathological" in nature, while others are definitely within the range of normality.

Several aspects of the state of madness are discernable in the biblical texts. First, it is deviant behavior, non-normative, that is not understood by ordinary people; it is irrational, for the motivation for the behavior observed cannot be identified with. David understood this principle when he feigned his madness.

Second, the person labeled as "mad" or "crazy" is not regarded as particularly dangerous; the group attitude towards them is benign, although somewhat pejorative.

Third, in some contexts, madness is identified with loss of control ("drives madly").

Fourth, the particular state is viewed as a "disease," similar to other diseases that the Deity visits upon people as punishment for their iniquities. This fact may be related to seeing the mad as rather harmless, more to be pitied than feared.

Finally, although he is not specifically labeled as "mad," King Saul's experience of periodic depression and hostile paranoia is another description of what we may today call severe psychopathology. It should be noted that these biblical data are descriptive of symptomatology, but do not go beyond the supernatural causality of the period.

Depressive states of varying degrees of severity are described in painful detail throughout the Hebrew Bible. The common element in all of these symptoms is the feeling of worthlessness, accompanied by guilt and states of helplessness, suicidal thoughts, or more precisely the wish to die. These emotions are often referred to, as is the radical solution and escape from anxiety and psychological pain that is represented by suicide.

First, the "wish to die" as expressed by Moses (Nu. 11), Elijah (1 Kings 19), Job (Job 3), and Jonah (Jonah 4), follows the narrator's feeling of extreme frustration and perception of self-inadequacy. These men do not plan to kill themselves, perhaps because it would be a violation of the Sixth Commandment; rather, they want YHWH to take their life, because they feel so inadequate to their task and cannot bear the guilt resulting from that recognition.

Second, the examples of the ultimate depressive solution, such as Zimri's self-immolation or Ahitofel's strangling himself, follow the "reactive depression" to the failure of their plans. The pain of failure and the narcissistic injury are unbearable, the state of non-being is then preferable.

Third, the experience of severe anxiety and the cry for help are clearly demonstrated, especially in many of the psalms. Some of the symptomatology described is akin to that seen in panic disorders and other anxiety states. The muscle spasms and autonomic nervous system activity are quite consonant with modern descriptions of the disorders in the standard manual (DSM IV, 1994).

All in all, it would seem that the biblical heritage concerned with the sensitivity to guilt and the pain of low self-esteem, and the affective reactions to these cognitions, has been passed on over the centuries, and is traceable in views of modern psychopathology.

In addition to the primarily psychogenic states of abnormality, the effects of wine and hard drink are detailed in numerous biblical texts and established a precedent for future generations. Noah, the first imbiber, planted his own vineyards and seemed to enjoy the fruits of his labors (Gen. 9.21–23). He became drunk and "uncovered his nakedness." Thus, improper and unconventional behavior appears to follow alcohol ingestion. Generally, the results of excessive drinking were viewed negatively. First, the Bible stresses the psychological effects. As we've seen in the case of Noah, or Lot, who drank wine and committed incest, the release of inhibition and the inability to maintain control, especially in the area of sexuality, are highlighted. Secondly, the impairment of the cognitive functions as a result of imbibing is also stressed ("forget the law"). Third, there is clear reference to the physical manifestations following the taking of wine and strong drink. Finally, there is the recognition of alcohol's addictive properties and the syndrome of addiction. Despite the ill effects enumerated by the biblical writers, and the poverty resulting from chronic abuse, the drinker says to himself: "I shall look for it again" (Prov. 23.33–35).

The charm and attractive aspects of alcohol are also recognized; the anesthetic qualities that help one "forget poverty and trouble" give us a hint of the possible motivation and dynamics behind alcohol consumption and alcoholism (Prov. 31.1–7).

It is of interest to note that craziness ("psychosis" ?), anxieties, depression and suicides, and alcoholic intoxication and chronic alcoholism are well described in the Bible; but the modern generalizations regarding psychological commonalities and generalizations of a conceptual nature were to await future generations.

The two final sections of this chapter are concerned with phenomena that are common within the experience of people in general and that are especially connected with a certain period in Hebrew history. Dreaming is the universal experience, prophesying is rather uniquely characteristic of the biblical literature. However, there is a strong connection between the two processes, for they both involve the imagination—perceptual experience without immediate environmental stimulation. They both belong to an era which enforced no strict separation between fantasy or dream and reality. This is not unlike the observations of James G. Frazer, who reported that the Indians he studied "are firmly convinced of the truth of what they relate; for these wonderful adventures are simply their dreams, which they do not distinguish from waking realities" (1960, p. 211). One qualification is in order regarding the process of dreaming and prophesying. In dreaming, the conditions are those of passive surrender with minimal external stimulation, while in prophesying, there is a great deal of stimulation, such as music, and group reinforcement, in creating the excited, ecstatic, and frenzied state (Frazer, 1975).

Consonant with the extensive use of metaphor and parable in the Hebrew Bible, dreams were used extensively to influence real-life decisions. This heritage was passed on, and the use of symbolism in the interpretation of dreams was adopted by modern psychodynamic theories. Also, consonant with the notion of the wide range of the functions in the cognitive system, including daydreaming and lucid dreaming, much of the concern with reality problems is reflected in the reported dreams. Paradoxically, the dream processes may also be accentuated under the special and extreme conditions of stimulation in the prophesying experience.

The Bible has influenced our culture and has called attention to a wide range of supernatural phenomena. They entered our belief system and seem to exert an influence on sizable groups in modern society. The modern investigation of the underlying mediators and maintainers of these beliefs and perceptions is one of the future tasks of modern psychology.

CHAPTER 8

Biblical-Psychological Themes

The title for this concluding chapter was deliberately selected to indicate the relatively modest and limited score of the present enterprise. I did rot strive to produce the sort of commentary represented by the massive Asimov's "Guide to the Bible" (1981), for I did not intend to address the vast number of issues covered in that work. Nor was it my purpose to offer insights based on speculative exegesis or hermeneutics, such as that characterize numerous works hitherto published by various religious and theological scholars over the centuries. My path does not lead me through the labyrinths of metaphysics and theology, but through the avenues connecting biblical descriptions and narratives regarding the early Hebrew civilization, and how it may have impinged upon the systematic attempts of modern psychology to understand the human mind and human behavior, both as an individual and in society. A reviewer of a recent book on poetry related to the Bible expresses himself as follows: "The legends, stories, and the very language ... of the Bible are the psychic DNA of Western civilization. Like our genetic inheritance which determines color and form, the Bible gives us the code by which we can explain ourselves to ourselves. We find in the stories the paradigm of our own behavior" (Bernstein, 1995, pp. 44–45). This quote is consonant with some of the notions presented in chapter 1 of this work. How does this psychic "DNA" pass on into some issues of 20th century psychology?

The biblical literature, like all literature, is concerned with the individual, with what is sometimes dubbed as the *idiographic* approach. This focus upon the individual concerns the behavior, thought, emotions, traits, and characteristics that are relevant to *that* individual. Scientific psychology, however, generally studies groups of individuals in an attempt to arrive at general laws concerning human thought and behavior. This *nomothetic* approach strives for generalizations about specific parameters and characteristics and how they appear in the person in general. As I hinted in chapter 1, follow a path from the specific in the Bible to the general in psychology; from the "little stories," to the scientific enterprise of the modern psychological quest for understanding the human condition.

What essentially is the "human condition?" As reflected in the Bible, it is the constant tension between the ideal and the real; between the laws stipulated by YHWH via his messengers and the actual behavior of an obstreperous people. The unvarnished portraits presented in the Bible side by side with the decalogue (Ten Commandments) clearly demonstrate subversion and a tension between the desirable and the actual or possible. Thus, the behavior of Lot or Reuben in the presence of prohibitions of incest, the adulterous behavior of David, and many other infractions that go unpunished are witnesses to the ubiquity of the conflict and tension that existed and was tolerated in ancient Israel.

Another aspect of this human condition lies in the Yawistic theology. On the one hand, YHWH was viewed as the master of the universe and the determiner of all behavior. Everything that happened to people was directed and controlled by the Deity. For example, that such mundane events as pregnancy occurred because the Lord opened the womb, and barrenness occurred because he closed it. Solomon's wisdom was granted to him in a dream by the Deity; and YHWH won many a war for his people Israel. At the very same time, many responsibilities are placed upon human shoulders. Principles of ethics and morality abound, for humans, from the days of Adam and Eve, were supposed to be able to distinguish between right and wrong. There is determinism on the one hand, and human obligations and responsibility for their behaviors and even thoughts on the other.

Perhaps the most important document of the Bible, the decalogue, the ten "words" or the Ten Commandments, is entirely concerned with the person's responsibility to other humans as well as to the monotheistic Deity. Only the first three commandments (regarding the worship of one God, no images, and not using the name in vain) are concerned with matters relating to YHWH. Five of the remaining six commandments, the exception being the one concerned with the Sabbath, involve human, interpersonal relationships. The prohibitions against murder, adultery, stealing, bearing false witness and coveting other peoples spouses and property, as well as the command to honor parents, all involve human interaction.

All these laws, rules, proscriptions, and prescriptions of behavior clearly highlight the responsibility laid upon the shoulders of the human species. They seem to be essential in maintaining a viable social and community existence. They also indicate the aspect of the conflict and strain between human nature and the demands of society and the consequent need for socialization of the upcoming generations. Here, the need for modes of teaching and learning becomes paramount.

In chapter 2 we discussed the issue of upbringing the younger generation and the biblical Guidelines to accomplish this task. We noted a rather strict mode of teaching, even involving corporal punishment. This method has been tested over the centuries and is still viable in many cultural settings. Only in the last few decades has this system been discarded by modern psychology and generally by most of Western society. However, during the first half of the present century the dominant behavioristic theories advocated the principle of *negative reinforcement,* which is nothing but the old fashioned principle of punishment for undesirable behavior. Scientific psychology has produced a variety of technologies that embody this principle. For example, "aversive stimulation," mainly in the form of electric shock, is an attempt to modify such diverse disorders as enuresis, autism, and (sic.) homosexuality.

Most of the themes from the Bible that penetrated western society and psychology concern issues of family and interaction between family members. It is interesting to note that the two European countries, in which psychology was originally rooted, England and Germany, gave a great deal of attention to the Old Testament or the Hebrew Bible in the course of their religious and cultural development. The themes of this work are consonant with those already discussed regarding control of children's behavior.

In examining issues of the family, let us start with the problem of barrenness or infertility which loomed large in the lives of many of biblical women (Sarah, Rachel, Hannah, etc.). It may be speculated that a good deal of the problem was due to the immaturity of the younger married women. There was no transitional period between childhood and adolescence (see chapter 2) there was no adolescence. Most of these newly married women were not yet mature enough biologically to bear children; hence, the temporary infertility that was attributed to the all-powerful YHWH. Clearly, the main *motivation for having children* was to fulfill their destiny (a response often found women even in contemporary Western countries) or to obey the command to "be fruitful and multiply." Having children, especially sons, was a way to satisfy both the needs of the male and the needs of the economy. It was also a means of maintaining status in the multigynous family.

The persistence of the women in the attempt to be cured of their barrenness, including accusations directed at the husband ("Give me a child, or I die," Gen. 30.1) maybe indicative of even more complex motivations, such of the need for self-fulfillment and altruistic needs (see chapter 5).

The *"cure" for infertility via surrogacy or adoption* is a related issue that has its parallels in current biopsychological science. Although statistics are not consistently supportive of the validity of this "cure," there are some data and credible theorizing arguing against the complete dismissal of the cure hypothesis.

Following the discussion of the construction a family, the motivation for having children, we must examine those parameters of the biblical family that are relevant to modern psychology. First is the question of *individual differences.* Human beings were not viewed as a group of identical organisms. However, the portrayal of members of the same family and children of the same parents is of some interest. Cain and Abel had markedly different occupational interests, as did Esau and Jacob. Moreover, Esau is described as an outdoorsman, favored by his father, while Jacob was a stay-at-home mama's boy. These two sons of Jacob are described as quite different from each other, and especially as characterized by their father on his deathbed. Reuben was seen as impulsive, Simon as violent, Judah as a leader, etc. (Gen. 49). There is a clear stress on individual differences in terms of behavior and life-course trajectory. Another contrast between brothers is represented in the story of Aaron and Moses—the latter, the charismatic leader, while the older brother is the staid priestly figure.

An important and related issue is that of *sibling rivalry*. It is shown to be the source of a great deal of strife within the biblical as well as the modern family. Much of psychodynamic psychology as well as developmental psychology has shown concern with this issue. There seems to be a struggle between siblings for the limited resources (psychological, affection, and others within the family. Most obvious in the Bible is the struggle between the two sons of the first family, described in the book of Genesis. Cain's jealousy of his brother Abel leads him to the murder of his brother—the first murder recorded in the Bible, Jacob's deception of his brother Esau, instigated by their mother, also arouses a good deal of animosity. Jacob's sons were especially jealous of their younger brother Joseph. The implied emotional component involved in all these relationships should not be overlooked. We note here the emotions of jealousy, envy, and hostility that result in *aggressive behavior.*

The relationship between *birth order and personality* is reflected in the biblical literature as well as in the interests of modern psychology. The special and privileged position of the oldest son in the family has a long history in the Bible, but we noted in Chapter Four, this tradition was often subverted. The life trajectories of the siblings show a subversion of the primogeniture principle. The younger, or even the youngest sibling turn out to be the more successful and privileged (ultimogeniture). Some even referred to this trend as the success of the underdog. This is noted in the stories of Cain and Abel, Esau and Jacob, Moses and Aaron, and Gideon and David.

The Bible shows a distinct subversion of primogeniture showing the unmitigated superiority and ultimate success of the younger or youngest son. In chapter 4 I have shown how psychology has come to similar conclusions, after systematic study, detailed historical examination of the matter (Sulloway, 1996) shows consistency with the biblical pattern.

One theme of prime concern in recent years, in modern popular culture as well as in contemporary psychology, is an aspect of individual differences, namely *sex and gender differences.* In chapter 6, male-female differences are taken up in some detail. Although the Bible reflects a dominant androcentric orientation, the limited treatment of females is more complex than what had been assessed by earlier evaluators of biblical texts.

In some instances, women are regarded as morally in a negative light. They are described as deceivers, lacking in compassion, and as temptresses (e./g., Eve; Potifar's wife; Rebekkah and Yael). However other women are illustrative of heroism, courage, loyalty, and good sense (c.f., Deborah, Michal, and Abigail). Although the women mentioned by name in the Bible are few in number in comparison with men, there are some who serve in important roles such as prophets, judges, and independent members of royalty.

Men are similarly characterized in both negative and positive terms. They are heroes in battle, are charismatic and trusted leaders, and save the guardians of morality. On the other hand, they can be ruthless, cruel, violent, and untrustworthy. In keeping with the patriarchal nature of the society, their roles as warriors, judges, prophets, rulers, and elders are particularly salient. It should be stated, however, that with the exception of the priesthood, there were no important roles that were never performed by women. Overall, men were more "agentic" and women more involved in "communion"—patterns which are described in modern psychology involving different distributions of roles and traits, but not a radical dichotomy by gender. Only in recent decades has psychology directed its attention to the systematic study of sex and gender differences. Some of the early findings, e.g., boys' superiority in mathematics, reflected mainly cultural differences, rather than substantive contrasts of intelligence.

Sex and sexuality, the concerns of chapter 3, are significant topics in the biblical literature. However, over the centuries, the strong influence of the movement of asceticism has kept this topic in the shadows of obscurity and denial. This influence may have extended into the early development of the new field of psychology in the 19th century. If we look at the index of the unabridged edition of William James' "Principles of Psychology"

(1890/1950) we find only one reference to sexuality, and that is concerned with the cerebral effects on sexual functions in birds and other animals. Early psychology adopted the attitude toward sexuality that dominated the cultures in which the field originated, and the medieval traditions which they have perpetuated. Denial of sexuality seems to nave gone along with the prevalence of ascetic self-denial.

The Hebrew Bible abounds in sexual episodes, along with specifications of the code designed to control sexuality. It was not until the turn of the century that sexuality began to penetrate academic psychology via its relation to psychiatry. Some of the age-old attitudes detailed in the Bible were then taken over by modern culture and psychology. *Sex and sexuality* have become legitimate areas of investigation, especially in the study of human motivation, as well as deviations from the "normal" patterns of sexual behavior and identification.

Infractions of the biblical code that were designated as "sins" became "disease" the psychiatric and psychological nomenclature. For example, homosexuality was only recently removed from the roster of mental disorders. Other modes of "sexual deviance" were also adopted as disorders, after a long career in the catalog of sins. The *positive aspects of sexuality* (understood as heterosexuality) were discovered by modern dynamic psychology. *Love and eroticism,* such as we note in the Song of Songs—despite the attempts to see it as a metaphor of the love of God for his people Israel—figure importantly in the mental health precinct of the discipline.

The issue of *masturbation* is an interesting footnote to the overall subject of sexuality. Based on the episode of Onan (who let his seed drop to the ground, Gen. 38.9)—an action that would have been classified as "coitus interruptus" in modern terminology—the traditional asceticism generalized the religious prohibition to incorporate all self-stimulation. Thus, masturbation became a "sin," and by the last century had become understood as a symptom of mental disease. This is another instance of a sin being converted to a disease, representing a sort of compromise between religion and 20th century scientism.

Onan's sin was not so much in the actual sexual act, as it was in his depriving his dead brother of an heir. The current, more permissive and liberal attitude of modern psychology toward masturbation is more consonant with the biblical story than with extremely negative views concerning this practice that developed in the subsequent asceticism of the Christian era. The Bible does not make any pronouncements on this subject.

The topics of rape and prostitution are not of direct concern to modern psychology; they are hardly mentioned, if at all, in the standard modern textbooks of general psychology. Prostitution was in some ways institutionalized in the society of ancient Israel; there were male and female prostitutes connected with religious ritual. Although fathers were admonished not to put their daughters into prostitution, most of the biblical references are suggestive of the tolerance of the profession. It apparently filled a need in the society. Considering the viability of this profession to date, a similar conjecture may be made even at the present time.

Much recent psychological speculation attempts to explain the phenomenon of prostitution and its continuing popularity as the result of the separation between the emotions of tenderness and sensuality. Tenderness is reserved for the spouse, whereas the downgraded sensuality needs to be expressed elsewhere. However, the Bible does not offer any such explanations. We have presented the facts, but modern psychology has not fully addressed them in a systematic manner.

Like prostitution, rape is also relegated to the field of criminology, for both modes of behavior violate society's rules and standards. The loss of *control of the sex drive and of aggression* involved in rape remain incompletely addressed psychological issues as well as social problems.

Finally, in the last chapter, chapter 7, a miscellany of "special states" are described which with the exception of prophecy are familiar in our contemporary world. The experience of King Saul and some of the psalmists is quite indicative of *depression* and *depressive moods,* often accompanied by *paranoid ideation.* The authors of the Psalms tell about enemies and beseech the Lord to save them from their foes; Saul had a specific enemy, David, whom he feared was plotting against him. Many psalms make reference to nonspecific fears as well to specific enemies that are plotting the poet's demise. Clearly, the experiences of *guilt* and *anxiety,* often accompanied by *psychosomatic* symptomatology and sleep disturbance, are painfully detailed. In contrast with Saul, whose condition was due to an "evil spirit from the Lord," the psalmist often blames his own behavior and his iniquities for the misfortune that has befallen him.

An interesting difference in the treatment may also be noted. In the case of Saul, *musical therapy* seems to have been the treatment mode. In the psalms, however, where the intimate relationship of the supplicant to his Lord is described, catharsis, forgiveness for sins, and relief from guilt are the means by which recovery is achieved. This is a sort of *psychotherapy* of which prayer and pleas, and confession of sins, and release from guilt are the possible components. Faith in God and spirituality are the underlying principles.

In this connection, a 1997 statement in a brochure published by the Harvard Medical School may be of relevance:

> For more than 25 years laboratories at Harvard Medical School have systematically studied the benefits of mind/body interactions. The research established that when a person engages in a repetitive prayer, word, sound, or phrase, and when intrusive thoughts are passively disregarded, a specific set of physiological changes ensue. There is decreased metabolism, heart rate, rate of breathing and distinctive slower brain waves. These changes are the opposite of those induced by stress and are an effective therapy in a number of diseases that include hypertension, cardiac rhythm irregularities, many forms of chronic pain, insomnia, infertility. This work led to a consideration of the healing effects of spirituality, since research later established that people experienced increased spirituality as a result of eliciting this state regardless of whether or not they used a religious repetitive focus. Spirituality was expressed as experiencing the presence of a power, a force, an energy, or what was perceived of as God and this presence was close to the person (Harvard Medical School, 1997).

Spirituality, although not a term used in modern psychology, is operationally defined in the above quotation which is akin to the experiences of the psalmists, discussed earlier. Most of the physiological components of stress and anxiety are alleviated by psychological means. It is also interesting to note that even infertility may be affected by this treatment—a notion quite consistent with our earlier discussion of this subject.

Following the conditions of psychosomatics, it would be well to mention the instance involving somatopsychics (the effects of the soma on the psyche) referring to the *effects of alcohol,* both upon the psyche and the soma. Also, the resulting *chronic alcoholism* remains of considerable interest to modern psychology and psychopathology.

Biblical *dreams* and visions of the prophets have been subjects of intensive study and speculation. The *symbolism* of the dreams and of the visionary literature of the prophets helped to point the way to our understanding of these phenomena in modern times. The "visions," although often presented as "dreams," are actually imaginary scenes and portrayals of unusual symbolic and metaphoric figures produced by the creative dreamer to communicate semiconsciously formulated messages. The complexity of many of these "visions" would require such greater participation of the cognitive system's rational guidance and conscious control. The similarity to the *daydreaming* process is considered.

We do not have sufficient details about the detailed conditions that facilitate the prophesying process. We know that it involves *musical induction* and *group effects* in the production of the frenzied and excited state. There is also a *creative process* involving temporary suspension of attention to the external environment and its stimulation—as well as one's critical attitude—and a surrender to the imagery that is subsequently utilized in the mundane world.

In this final chapter I attempted to review these topics and emphasize some key areas in the Bible which have exerted a more direct influence upon modern psychology. The word "direct" may not be quite accurate, for the effects have actually filtered through Western culture over the centuries. These are but a limited selection of issues that reflect the author's interests; some gleanings that are relevant to psychology. For the most part these are the phenomena and a few of the conditions of psychology in the Bible. I have not dealt with some of the big issues: the soul, traits, and the psychology of personality. These would take us too far afield, and are better left for future enterprises.

References

Adler, A. (1927). *Understanding human nature.* New York: Garden City Publishing Co.

Adler, A. (1969). *The science of living.* New York: Anchor. Original work published 1929.

Alcalay, R. (1965). *The complete Hebrew-English dictionary.* Tel Aviv, Israel: Massadeh Publishing Co.

Alter, R. (1992). *The world of Biblical literature.* New York: Basic Books.

American Psychiatric Association. (1952). *Diagnostic and statistical manual of mental disorders* (2nd ed.). Washington, DC: Author.

American Psychiatric Association. (1994). *Diagnostic and statistical manual of mental disorders* (4th ed.). Washington, DC: Author.

American Psychological Association, Science Directorate. (1993). *Vitality for life: Psychological Research for Productive Aging.* Washington, DC: Author.

Archives of the New Hampshire Asylum for the Insane (March 5, 1839). *New Hampshire Sentinel.*

Aries, P. (1962). *Centuries of childhood.* New York: Vintage.

Asimov, I. (1981). *Asimov's guide to the Bible.* New York: Wings.

Bakan, D. (1966). *The duality of human existence: Isolation and community in Western man.* Boston: Beacon.

Bernstein, M. (1995). The Bible as code and yoke: Review of modern poems in the Bible, D. Curzon (Ed.). *Midstream, 51,* 44–45.

Biale, D. (1992). *Eros and the Jews.* New York: Basic.

Birren, J. E. and Fisher, L. M. (1990). Integration of approaches and viewpoints. In R. J. Sternberg (Ed.) *Wisdom: Its nature, origins, and development.* Cambridge, MA: Cambridge University Press.

Bloom, H., & Rosenberg, D. (1990). *The book of J.* New York: Random House.

Boring, E. G. (1929). *A history of experimental psychology.* New York: Century.

Bratton, F. G. (1967). *A history of the Bible.* Boston: Beacon Press.

Bruner, J. (1979). *On knowing: Essays for the left hand.* Cambridge, MA: Harvard University Press.

Bruner, J. (1986). *Actual minds, possible worlds.* Cambridge, MA: Harvard University Press.

Bruner, J. (1990). *Acts of meaning.* Cambridge, MA: Harvard University Press.

Bultmann, R. (1965). *Life and death.* London: Adams & Charles Black.

Butler, R. H. (1963). The life review. *Psychiatry, 26,* 65–76.

Butler, R. N. (1975). *Why survive?* New York: Harper & Row.

Cannon, W. B. (1932). *The wisdom of the body.* New York: Norton.

Clausen, J. A. (1966). Family structure, socialization and personality. In L. W. Hoffman & M. L. Hoffman (Eds.), *Review of Child Development Research.* New York: Russell Sage Foundation.

Counte, M. A., Garron, D. C., & Branda, H. C. (1979). Factor structure of Rabin's Child Study Inventory. *Journal of Personality Assessment, 43,* 59–63.

D'Andrade, J. (1966). Sex differences and childhood institutions. In E. Maccoby (Ed.), *The development of sex differences* (pp. 173–203). Stanford, CA: Stanford University Press.

Darwin, C. (1965). *The expression of the emotions in man and animals.* Chicago: The University of Chicago Press. Original work published 1872.

DeMausse, L. (1982). *Foundations of psychohistory.* New York: Creative Roots.

Dunn, J., & Plomin, R. (1990). *Separate lives: Why Siblings are so Different.* New York: Basic Books.

Eagly, A. H. (1996). Differences between women and men: Their magnitude, practical importance and political meaning. *American Psychologist, 51,* 159–159.

Eagly, A. H. (1995). The science and politics of comparing women and men. *American Psychologist, 50,* 145–158.

Edelman, R. J., & Connolly, K. J. (1986). Psychological aspects of infertility. *British Journal of Medical Psychology, 59,* 209–219.

Eisdorfer, C., & Lawton, M. P. (Eds.) (1973). *The psychology of adult development and aging.* Washington, DC: American Psychological Association.

Erikson, E. H. (1963). *Childhood and society* (2nd ed.). New York: W. W. Norton. Original work published 1950.

Ernst, C., & Angst, J. (1983). *Birth order: Its influence on personality.* New York: Springer-Verlag.

Fenichel, O. (1945). *The psychoanalytic theory of neurosis.* New York: W. W. Norton.

Forward, S., & Buck, C. (1978). *Betrayal of innocence: Incest and its devastation.* New York: Penguin.

Fox, E. (1995). *The five books of Moses.* New York: Schocken.

Fox, G. L. (1982). *The childbearing decision.* Beverly Hills, CA: Sage.

Frazer, J. G. (1960). *The golden bough: A study of magic and religion.* New York: Macmillan. Originally published 1922.

Frazer, J. G. (1975). *Folklore in the Old Testament.* New York: Hart.

Freud, S. (1938). *The basic writings of Sigmund Freud* (Trans. A. A. Brill). New York: The Modern Library.

Freud, S. (1933–1974). *The standard edition of the complete psychological works of Sigmund Freud.* (Vols. I-XXIV). London: The Hogarth Press.

Freud, S. (1972). *A general introduction to psychoanalysis.* New York: Pocket. Original work published 1924.

Fromm, E. (1947). *Man for himself.* New York: Rinehart.

Fromm, E. (1951). *The forgotten language.* New York: Rinehart.

Gilligan, C. (1982). *In a different voice: Psychological theory and women's development.* Cambridge, MA: Harvard University Press.

Gilligan, C., Brown, L. M., & Rogers, A. G. (1990). Psyche embedded: a place for body relationships and culture in personality theory (pp. 96–147). In A. I. Rabin, R. A. Zucker, R. A. Emmons, and S. Frank (Eds.) *Studying persons and lives.* New York: Springer.

Golb, N. (1995). *Who wrote the Dead Sea Scrolls?* New York: Scribner.

Guttmann, D. (1987). *Reclaimed powers.* New York: Basic Books.

Halpern, B. (1995). Erasing history: The minimalist assault on ancient Israel. *Bible Review* (Dec.).

Harvard Medical School, Dept. of Continuing Education. (1997). *Course catalog* [Brochure]. Cambridge, MA: Author.

Heschel, A. J. (1962). *The prophets.* New York: The Burning Bush Press.

Hirsch, E. (1991, February 21). Review of H. Bloom & D. Rosenberg, D., *The Book of J. The New Yorker.*

Hirsch, E. D. (1987). *Cultural literacy: What every American needs to know.* Boston: Houghton Mifflin.

James, W. (1987). *The principles of psychology* (Vols. I & II). New York: Dover. Original work published 1890.

James, W. (1987). *The varieties of religious experience in: Writings 1902–1910.* New York: The Library of American.

Jung, C. G. (1964). *Man and his symbols.* New York: Doubleday.

Kardimons, S. (1958). Adoption as a remedy for infertility in the period of the patriarchs. *Journal of Semitic Studies, 3,* 123–126.

Kassuto, V. (1983). *The documentary hypothesis and the comparison of the Pentateuch.* Jerusalem: Magnes Press, The Hebrew University.

Kastenbaum, R. (1975). Is death a life crisis? On the confrontation with death in theory and practice. In N. Datan & L. H. Ginsberg (Eds.), *Life span developmental psychology* (pp. xxx). New York: Academic Press.

Kelman, H. (1975). The "day precipitate" of dreams: The Morris hypothesis. *International Journal of Psychoanalysis, 56,* 209–218.

Kelman, H. (1986). The day precipitate of Pharaoh's dreams. *Psychoanalytic Quarterly, 55,* 307–309.

Kolb, L. C., & Brodie, H. K. H. (1982). *Modern clinical psychiatry* (10th ed.). Philadelphia: W. B. Saunders.

Korzybsky, A. (1949). *Time-binding: the general theory.* New York: Dutton. Original work published 1926.

Kubler-Ross, E. (1969). *On death and dying.* Toronto: Macmillan.

LaBerge, S. (1985). *Lucid dreaming: The power of being awake and aware in your dreams.* Los Angeles: Jeremy P. Tarcher.

Levinson, D. (1978). *The seasons of a man's life.* New York: Knopf.

Levinson, D. (1981). Explorations in biography: Evolution of the individual life structure in adulthood. In A. I. Rabin (Eds.) *Further explorations in personality* (pp. 44–85). New York: John Wiley.

Lindsey, G. (1991). *Saudi Arabia.* New York: Hippocreme.

Maas, H. S., & Kuypers, J. A. (1974). *From thirty to seventy.* San Francisco: Jossey-Bass.

Mandelkern, S. (1955). *Concordance on the Bible* (Hebrew) (Vol.s I & II). New York: Shrolsinger Brothers. Original work published in 1896.

McCary, J. H. (1973). *Human sexuality.* New York: Van Nostrand. Originally published 1967.

Meyers, C. L. (1992). Everyday life in the period of the Hebrew Bible. In C. A. Newsom & S. H. Ringe (Eds.), *The women's Bible commentary* (pp. 244–251). Louisville, KY: Wesmeister/John Knox Press.

Michaels, G. Y. (1988). Motivational factors in the decisions and timing of pregnancy. In G. Y. Michaels & Q. A. Goldberg (Eds.) *The transition to parenthood* (pp. 23–61). New York: Cambridge University Press.

Milgrom, J. (1990). *The JPS Torah Commentary: Numbers.* Philadelphia: The Jewish Publications Society.

Minois, G. (1989). *History of old age.* Chicago: The University of Chicago Press.

Mowrer, O. H. (1950). *Learning theory and personality dynamics.* New York: The Roland Press.

Muuss, R. E. (1988). *Theories of adolescence* (5th ed.). New York: Random House.

Myrdal, A. (1968). *Nation and family.* Cambridge, MA: The MIT Press. Original work published 1941.

Niditch, S. (1987). *Underdogs and tricksters: A prelude to Biblical folklore.* San Francisco, CA: Harper & Row.

Overholt, T. W. (1985). Prophecy: The problem of cross-cultural comparison. In B. Lang (Ed.) *Anthropological approaches to the Old Testament.* Philadelphia: Fortress Press.

Patai, R. (1960). *Family, love and the Bible.* London: Maccibon & Kee.

Pohlman, E. H. (1969). *The psychology of birth planning.* Cambridge, MA: Shenkman Publishing.

Poon, L. (Ed.) (1980). *Aging in the 1980s: Psychological issues.* Washington, DC: American Psychological Association.

Pritchard, J. B. (1955) (Ed.). *Ancient Near Eastern texts: Relating to the Old Testament.* Princeton, NJ: Princeton University Press.

Rabin, A. I., & Greene, R. J. (1968). Assessing motivation for parenthood. *Journal of Psychology, 69,* 39–46.

Rainwater, L. (1965). *Family design: Marital sexuality, family size, and contraception.* Chicago: Aldine.

Saffire, W. (1992). *The first dissident: The Book of Job in today's politics.* New York: Random House.

Sarna, N. M. (1966). *Understanding Genesis.* New York: McGraw-Hill Book.

Schulberg, C. (1981). *The music therapy sourcebook.* New York: Human Science Press.

The search of the sacred. (1994, November 25). *Newsweek.*

Seibel, M. M., & Taymor, M. L. (1982). Emotional aspects of infertility. *Fertility and Sterility, 37,* 137–145.

Shanks, H. (1997). *The Biblical mini-malists. Bible Review, 13,* 32–52.

Shneidman, E. S. (1985). *Definition of suicide.* New York: Wiley.

Singer, J. L. (1984). *The human personality.* New York: Harcourt Brace Jovanovich.

Sivan, G. (1973). *The Bible and civilization.* Jerusalem, Israel: Keter Publishing House Jerusalem Ltd.

Skinner, D. B. (1938). *The behavior of organisms: An experimental analysis.* New York: Appleton-Century-Crofts.

Smith, J. C. (1990). *Psychoanalytic roots of patriarchy: The neurotic foundations of social orders.* New York: New York University Press.

Speiser, E. A. (1960). Three thousand years of biblical study. *Centennial Review, 4,* 206–222.

Stanton, A. L., & Dunkel-Schetter, C. (Eds.) (1993). *Infertility: Perspectives from stress and coping research.* New York: Plenum.

Sternberg, R. J. (Ed.) (1990). *Wisdom: Its nature, origins and development.* Cambridge, MA: Cambridge University Press.

Storandt, M., & Vandenboss, G. R. (Eds.) (1989). *The adult years: Continuity and change.* Washington, DC: American Psychological Association.

Sullivan, H. S. (1953). *The interpersonal theory of psychiatry.* New York: Norton.

Sulloway, F. J. (1996). *Born to rebel: Birth order, family dynamics and creative lives.* New York: Pantheon.

Sutton-Smith, B., & Rosenberg, B. G. (1970). *The sibling.* New York: Holt, Rinehart & Winston.

Szasz, T. S. (1961). *The myth of mental illness.* New York: Harper & Row.

Tavris, C. (1992). *The mismeasure of woman.* New York: Simon & Schuster.

Viehe, V. R. (1991). *Perilous rivalry: When siblings become abusive.* Lexington, MA: D. C. Heath.

Weinberg, S. R. (1963). *Incest behavior.* New York: Citadel.

Zilboorg, G. (1941). *A history of medical psychology.* New York: Norton.

Appendix A

Biblical Texts Consulted

The Holy Bible (Authorized King James Version) (1943). New York: Random House.

The Jerusalem Bible. (1971). Garden City, NY: Doubleday.

Kasuto, A. D. (Ed.) (1964). *Torah, Neviim Kethuvim* (Hebrew) (16 vols). Tel Aviv: Yavne.

The New English Bible: Oxford Study Edition. (1976). New York: Oxford University Press.

TANAKH—The Holy Scriptures. (1988). Philadelphia: The Jewish Publication Society.

Torah, Neviim and Kethuvin (Hebrew) (1928). (Under strict supervision of Meir Halevi Letteris). London.

Appendix B

The Books of the Hebrew Bible

TORAH (PENTATEUCH)

Genesis (Gen.)
Exodus (Ex.)
Leviticus (Lev.)
Numbers (Nu.)
Deuteronomy (Deut.)

NEVIIM (PROPHETS)

Joshua (Josh.)
Judges (Jud.)
1 Samuel (1 Sam.)
2 Samuel (2 Sam.)
1 Kings (1 Kings)
2 Kings (2 Kings)
Isaiah (Isa.)
Jeremiah (Jer.)
Ezekiel (Ezek.)

TWELVE MINOR PROPHETS

Hosea (Hos.)
Joel (Joel)

Amos (Amos)
Obadiah (Obad.)
Jonah (Jon.)
Micah (Mic.)
Nahum (Na.)
Habakkuk (Hab.)
Zephaniah (Zeph.)
Haggai (Hag.)
Zechariah (Zech.)
Malachi (Mall)

KETHUVIM (WRITINGS)

Psalms (Psa.)
Proverbs (Pro.)
Job (Job)
Song of Songs (SS)
Ruth (Ruth)
Lamentations (Lam.)
Ecclesiastes-Kobelet (Eccl.)
Esther (Esth.)
Daniel (Dan)
Ezra (Ezra)
Nehemiah (Nehem.)
1 Chronicles (1 Chron.)
2 Chronicles (2 Chron.)

Appendix C

Names and Common Biblical Expressions and Metaphors in English

---

The sign of Cain
David-and-Goliath encounter
False prophets
Sacrificial lamb
Scapegoat
The Tower of Babel
The Garden of Eden
Tohu Va' vohu (formless and void)
Wisdom of Solomon
Jeremiad
The fleshpots of Egypt
Manna from heaven
The patience of Job
A Jezebel
Received on Mt. Sinai
Exodus
A mess of pottage
Tree of knowledge
Sold his birthright
Uriah the Hittite
Joseph sold for 20 pieces of silver
The Lord is my shepherd
Vanity of vanities
Sodom and Gomorrah
The plagues of Egypt
Daniel in the lion's den

Index

Aaron, 90–91, 197
Abel, brother of Cain, 78, 196, 197
Abigail, 123, 131–132, 140, 198
Abnormality, 144
Abraham, 13, 16, 17
    death of, 38, 39
    family of, 77, 88–89
    son's marriage, 46
    wife Sarah, 36, 42, 62, 98, 105
    YHWH communication with, 177
Absalom, 15, 43, 52–53, 62, 158
Absolute parental authority, 18, 21
Abstinence, 43, 75
"Acting Crazy," 145–146, 189
Actors, 4, 15
Adam, 79–80, 82, 86, 87, 88, 94, 124, 128, 194
Addiction, 162, 163
Adler, Alfred, 85, 86, 87, 88, 94
Adolescence, 10, 19–20, 44, 196
Adonijah, 121
Adoption, cure infertility, 104–111, 196
Adultery, 49–50, 56–57, 75
Adults, adulthood, 10, 11, 12, 13, 16, 18, 19, 23, 24, 25, 26, 44
Affect-negative, 166–167
Agency, vs. communion, 140, 142, 198
Agentic behavior, 140, 142
Aging, 27–30, 32, 35
Agony-unhappiness, 152–153, 164–166
Ahab, 121–122, 127–128, 138, 153
Ahasuerus, 136–137, 160
Ahera (Goddess), Astarte, 55, 111, 138
Ahitophel, 158–160, 190
Altruism, 48, 97, 196
American Psychiatric Association, 151, 159
American society, 65
Amnesia, 179

Amnon and Tamar, 52–54, 61
Androcentric society, 71, 77, 116, 139–140, 198
Anecdotal material, 112
Anhedonia, 28–29
Anxiety, 149–150, 151, 152–160, 161, 163–167, 190, 191, 200
Aphorism, 21, 23
Aramaic, 2
Aries, P., 12, 13
Asceticism, 75, 198
Athalia, the queen, 118, 119, 120–122, 140
Autonomous female, 118
Avishag, the Shunamite, 29

Baal, 138
Babylonian Exile, 55
Bakan, D., 8, 140
Barrenness, 19, 46, 47, 97, 135, 194, 196
Barzialai, 28
Bathsheba, 118, 121
"Be fruitful and multiply," 46, 67, 70–71, 94, 97, 98, 103, 104, 196
Beauty, good looks, 123
Bereavement, 43
Bestiality, 70, 76
Betrayal, 128
Birth order, 78–85, 86, 87–96, 111, 197
Bisexuality, 73
Blessing, 8–82, 89, 94, 124
Bloom, H., 5, 8
Boring, E., 6
Brain condition, 168
Brattor, F. G., 181
Bruner, J., 4, 6, 7
Butler, R. H., 35

Cain, brother of Abel, 79–80, 82, 86, 87, 88, 89, 91, 94, 113, 196, 197

Canaan, Canaanite, 14, 23, 55, 81, 91, 129–130, 173
Cannibalism, 65
Caretaking, 143
Censor, 169
Census, 23–24
Chaotic impression, 7
Charismatic leaders, judges, 23, 27, 42, 153, 183, 188
Chastise, 50
Child development, 85
Child rearing, 16, 18, 194
Child sacrifice, 16–17, 18
Childhood, 10, 12, 196
Childless women, 19, 46, 47, 97, 104–111, 135
Christian era, 3
Christianity, 18, 41, 69, 71, 73
Chronicles, book of, 78, 112, 120
Clinical observations, 144
"Closed womb," 20, 70, 98–99, 104, 105, 108
Cognition, 30
    deficit, 39
    and love, 48, 160–161, 190
    and wine, 160, 162
Cognitive, 166–167
    assessment, 163
    deficit, 28–29, 168
    psychology, 180
    system, 180, 187, 188, 192
Coitus interruptus compulsion, 199
Communion, vs. agency, 140, 142, 198
Competition for status, 79, 94
Concubines, 60, 73, 77
"Conditions" (James), 7
Confusion, 146, 161
Contextualism, 23
Continuity–past, future, 35, 39–40
Cultural anthropology, 2
Curses, 135, 146
Cynicism, 166

Dagon, 156
Daniel, 113
Darwin, Charles, 94, 167
Daughters, 63

David, King, 15, 17, 21, 24
    adultery of, 49–50
    adulthood, 27, 194
    aging, 28, 29
    Ahitophel, 158–160
    ancestry, 61
    anointing of, 92
    Bakan and, 140
    Bathsheba, 121
    birth order, 197
    choice of as king, 116
    feigning madness, 145–146, 189
    good looks, 123
    house of, 31
    mourning, 42–43
    polygynous family, 62
    rape, incest, 62
    Saul, 157
    Saul and, 200
    soul, 149–152
    virtues of, 149–150
Day precipitate, 176–177
Day residue, 169
Daydreams, daydreaming, 185, 188, 189, 192, 202
Death, dying, 35, 37–41, 44, 80–82
    mourning, 41–43
    suicide, 155–160, 190
    wish to die, 152–160
Deborah, the prophetess, 114, 117, 119, 130–131, 140, 198
Decalogue (ten commandments), 2, 75, 194
Deception, deceit, 128, 129–133, 146
Deity, 92, 97, 114, 131, 135, 146, 149, 154, 155, 166, 176, 177, 181, 184, 189, 194
Delilah, 126–127, 128, 155
Denial, 40, 41
Dependency, 43
Depression, 40, 144, 149–150, 151, 152–160, 163–167, 189–190, 191, 200
Determinism, 194
Dethronement of firstborn, 87, 90, 94–95
Deuteronomy, book of, 62, 66, 91, 104, 146

Development psychology, 20, 78
Development trajectories, 78, 85, 197
Dichotomizing traits, 23, 26
Dimmed vision, 29, 37
Dinah, 51–52
Discipline by adults, 16, 21–22
Discrepancy between law and behavior, 74, 96
Dissidence, 166
Diversity, 85
Dominance, female, 128
Draconian measures, 49, 50–51, 76
Dreams, dreaming, 202
   daydreams, 185, 188, 189, 192, 202
   dream analysis, 169–170
   dream work, 169, 171
   dreamers, 169, 170, 171–173, 176–178, 179
   historical perspective on, 168
   interpretation, 168, 170, 171, 172, 173–177
   Joseph, 171–73
   lucid dreaming, 178–180
   Old Testament dreams, 170–175
   prophetic, 172, 175–178
   psychoanalytic theory of, 180
Drunkards, 160–163
DSM-IV, 74, 151
Dynamic psychology, 146
Dysphoric affect, 43
Dysthymic disorder, 167

Eagly, A., 142
Ecclesiastes. *See* Koheleth
Ecstasy, ecstatic, 148, 151, 181, 182, 183, 186, 191
Ego development, generativity and integrity, 40
Ego insufficiency-break, 146
Ego, integrity vs. despair, 11, 25, 35
Egypt, 90–91, 152–153, 173, 174
Elders, 31, 37, 115, 128
Eli, the priest, 30
Elifaz, 108
Elihu, Job's interlocutor, 32, 33, 34

Elijah, the prophet, 117, 122, 128, 153, 185, 190
Elisha, the prophet, 117, 147, 185
Elkanah, husband of Hannah, 13, 47, 78, 103, 105, 144
Elohim, 175
Emerson, Ralph Waldo, 5
Emotions, 34, 53, 149–150
Envy, competition, 77, 80–82, 98
Ephraim, 90, 124, 160, 162
Erikson, E., 11, 25, 35, 40, 44
Esau, 39, 80–81, 82–83, 86, 89–90, 94, 113, 124, 140, 196, 197
Eve, 82, 124, 128, 194
Evil spirit, 149–152
Exodus, book of, 17, 23, 54, 90–91
Expansion of self, 101, 103
Experience, 83
Ezekiel, 56, 115, 120, 144, 184, 185, 186

Family
   extended, nuclear, patriarchal, 18, 72, 77, 78, 79, 116, 129, 139–140
   multigynous, 98, 104, 105, 111, 196
Fantasy, 180, 181, 183, 184, 188, 191
Fear, 18
Feeling of abandonment, 164–165
Feelings, 34, 53, 149–150
Feigning madness, 146–146, 189
Female, 67
   aggressiveness, 142, 198
   independence, 140
   passivity, 140
   violence, 140
Feminism, 123, 143
Fleshpots of Egypt, 152
Folklore, 168, 181
Forensic, legal code, 70
Frazer, J. G., 88, 191
Freud, S., Freudian, 10, 23, 43, 143
   dream analysis, 168–169, 171, 175, 178, 184, 188
   ego functions, 23
   genital stage, 11
   masturbation, 69
   oedipal events, 64

Freud, S., Freudian *(continued)*
  sibling rivalry, 85–86
  women, 137
Fromm, Eric, 38, 48, 172, 176, 179
Future generations, 35
Future time perspective, 152–153,
  159, 166

Galton, Sir Francis, 87
Gaza, 127, 156
Gender, 5, 9, 112, 113, 117, 198
Gendered language, 113
Generativity, 11, 25–26, 40
Generosity, 129
Genesis, book of VIII, 27, 29, 45, 59,
  75, 88, 94, 98, 117, 123, 173, 197
Gerontology, 28, 30, 37
Gibeah episode, 53, 54, 73–75
Gideon, 91–92, 197
Golden calf, 91
Goliath, 116, 131
Guilt, 152, 164, 166, 167, 190, 200

Hagar, 16, 88, 89, 98
Hall, G. Stanley, 20
Hallucinations, visual, 161
Hallucinatory-like, 181
Hannah, wife of Elkanah, 13, 47, 78,
  103, 105, 144
Harlots, 54–57
Harmlessness, 145–146
Harp playing, 149–150, 151
Hebrew Bible VII, 5, 6, 17, 18, 27,
  38, 41, 42, 75, 76, 106, 112, 115,
  116, 120, 184, 193, 199
Hebrew(s), 18, 113, 129–130
Helpless, hopeless, 146
Heterosexuality, 45–48
Hirsch, E., 5
Historical period, 53
Hivite tribe, 51
Holy Ark, 134
Homosexuality, 53–54, 70, 73, 76, 199
Hulda, the prophetess, 114, 117
Hushai, 158–159
Hypnosis, 183, 184, 188
Hypocrisy, 57

Idolatry, 56–57, 75
Imagery, 168, 181, 183, 184, 185,
  188, 202
Imaginary companions, 181
Imagination, 185, 188, 191
Impulsive behavior, 147
Impulsivity, 22–23, 44, 89, 91, 93–94
Incest, 184, 190
  taboos of, 58–64
  in Western society, 64–66
Indaism, Law, 68
Independence, 142
Individual differences, 34, 37, 196–
  197, 198
Individualism, 103
Infancy, 10
Infertility, functional, organic, 108–109
Insecurity, 150, 164–165
Insight, 187
Instinct for motherhood, 110
Instrumental motivation, 101, 102,
  103
Integrity, 11, 25, 35, 40
Intelligence, 33, 34
Intermarriage, 81
Intimacy, vs. self-absorption, 11, 25,
  26
Isaac, 13, 16, 17, 29, 35, 38, 39, 46,
  80–81, 88–89, 124, 129, 128
Isaiah, 115, 120, 162, 183, 184
Ishmael, 16, 77, 88–89
Israel, Kingdom of, 31, 78, 91–92,
  156–157, 158, 188

Jabin, King of Canaan, 124, 130
Jacob (Israel), 46
  barren wife, 98, 105
  Dinah, daughter of, 51–52
  dream interpretation, 113, 171,
    173–175, 177, 178
  family of, 78
  incest behavior, 62
  male roles, 140
  marriage of, 46
  sibling rivalry, 80–84, 86, 89–90,
    94, 124–125, 196, 197
  sons of, 35, 38–39, 42, 60, 91

James, William, 6, 7, 187, 188, 198
Jealousy, 78, 94, 104, 105, 111, 125, 151, 157
Jeremiah, 115, 120, 137–139, 184
Jeremiah, book of, 148
Jeroboam, 31
Jezebel, 118, 121–122, 127–128, 138, 140, 153
Job, 153–154, 165–166, 167, 190
Job, book of, 32, 33, 96, 153
Jonah, 154, 190
Jonah, book of, 167
Jonathan, 42, 151
Joseph, 78, 81–82, 86, 95, 123, 125–26, 142, 170, 171–173, 197
Joshua, book of, 27, 112
Juda, 60–61, 66, 82, 84, 120, 142, 197
Juda, Kingdom of, 31, 36, 55, 78
Judaism, law, 68, 73, 75
Judges, 25, 26, 32, 73, 91–92, 114, 126, 129–130, 156
Judges, book of, 27, 46, 56, 130
Jung, C. G., 172, 175

Kadesh, male ritual prostitute, 55
Kadesha, female ritual prostitute, 55
Kelman, H., Pharaoh's dreams, 176–177
Kethuvim, "Written" books of Bible, 1
King James' translation, of Bible VIII, 14, 17, 106, 165
Kings, books of, 27, 29, 78, 112, 117, 118, 120, 127, 147
"Know" (biblical euphemism for sexual intercourse), 53, 72, 73
Koheleth (Ecclesiastes) "Wisdom" born, 1, 165–166

Laban, 46
LaBerge, S., 179
Lapidoth, 131
Leah, wife of Jacob, 46, 62, 78, 83–84, 95, 105
Learning, 20–21, 33, 34
    theory, 163
Lebidocentric, theory, 11
Lesbianism, 70, 71, 72

Levi, tribe of, 24, 25
Levinson, D., 23
Levirate, law of, 56, 66, 76
Leviticus, book of, 17, 49, 54, 58, 62, 63, 70, 71, 91
Life course, 23
Long-term memory, 188
Lot, Abraham's nephew, 53, 59–60, 72, 190, 194
Love, 75, 199
    altruistic, 48
    heterosexual, 45–48
    romantic, 45–48
Lucid dreaming, 188, 189, 192
Lunatic, 148

Madness, 189
    clinical observations, 148–149
    as a disease, 146
    prophets and, 147–148
    Saul's evil spirit, 149–152
Male authority, 140
Male, vs. female, 112
Marxist orientation, 162
Masculine
    activities of, 112–116, 139–140
    behavior, 68
    dominance, 136–137
    male roles, 116–122, 198
Masturbation, 66–69, 76, 199–200
Menashe, 90, 124
Menopause, 36–37
Mental disorder, 68, 69
Mental health, 167
Mesha, king of Maabites, 17
Meshuga (crazy), 144–145, 148, 189
Methuselah, 27
Michal, 133–136, 151, 198
Midianites, 91–92
Minois, G., 27
Miram, 117
Modern society, 57, 75, 76, 181, 187, 192
Monotheism (Hebrew), 2, 60, 91, 139
Moral judgement, 160
Mosaic law, code of, 8, 50, 53, 54, 59, 71, 73, 90–91

Moses, 25, 56, 90–91, 155
  abstinence, 162
  adulthood, 27
  birth family of, 90–91
  death, 42
  incest, 58
  as infant, 16
  infertility, 104
  as leader, 197
  masturbation, 66
  old age, 30, 34
  as prophet, 117, 181
  wish to die, 152–153, 190
  YHWH communication with, 177
Motherhood, 98–100, 110–111
Motivation for parenthood, 97, 100, 110–111
Mount Sinai, 155
Mourning, 39, 41–43, 44, 81
Mowrer, H. O., 164
Multidimensionality of women, 33, 133
Multigynous family, 98, 104, 105, 111, 196
Murder, 155
Musical therapy, 149–152, 201
Musicians, 25
Mystical experience, 187
Mythology, 168

Naar (youth m.), 20
Naara (youth m.), 20
Nabal, 131–132
Naboth, 121–122, 127–128
Nakedness, 58–64, 182, 190
Naomi, 36
Narcissistic motivation, 101, 102, 103, 104
Nathan, the prophet, 49, 117, 121
Nation building, 70, 71, 76, 97
Natural selection, 96
Nazirite, 13, 162
Negative reinforcement, 22
Neviim (prophets), 181
New Testament, 69
Noah, 28, 190
Nonconformity, 148

Nubile girls, 16, 19
Nudity, 58–64, 182, 190
Numbers, book of, 17, 23, 90–91

Oedipus formula, 46, 60, 64
Old age, 10, 11
Old Testament, 18, 40, 67, 106, 164, 170
Onan, 54, 66–67, 68, 76, 111, 199
Onanism, 67, 68, 76
Optimism, 167
Orgasm, 68

Palti, 134, 135
Panic disorders, 168
Paranoia, 131, 150, 151–152, 189, 200
Patai, R., 55, 57, 73
Patriarchal society, family, 18, 72, 78, 79, 116, 129, 139–140
Patriarchs, 39, 42, 97
Patrilineal family, 116
Pentatench (Torah), 1, 5
Pentateuch, 58, 63
Personality development, 78, 85, 87–96
Pharaoh, 16, 18, 90–91, 116, 125, 173, 174–177
Philistines, 46, 116, 126–127, 133–134, 155–157, 159, 177
Polygamous society, 52, 77
Polygynous family, 23, 52, 77, 82, 95
Polytheistic practice, 137–139
Potifar, 116, 125, 142, 173
Prediction, 172, 182
Pregnancy, 70, 98–100
Prehistory of Israel, 60, 61
Priests and soothsayers, 168, 183
Primogeniture, 78, 88, 90, 95, 197
Prophecy, prophesying, 26, 27, 120, 147–148, 150–152, 153, 176–177, 181–189, 191–192, 202
Prophets, major and minor, 2, 4
Prostitution, 54–57, 75, 200
Proverbs, book of, 21, 22, 32, 160
Psalms, book of VIII, 1, 155, 160, 163, 164, 167, 190, 200, 201

Psychiatry, 71, 74
Psychoanalysis, theory of, 10, 23, 57, 64, 65, 68, 69, 85, 163, 172, 180
Psychodynamics, 86, 144, 192
Psychogenics, 108–109
Psychology VII, 4, 7, 30, 33, 50, 57, 103, 110–111, 146, 163, 164, 167, 175
Psychopathology, 69, 144–145, 148, 149–150, 163, 186, 189, 190
Psychosis, 186
Psychosomatics, 202
Puberty, 16
Punishment, 99, 146–147, 166, 189

Queen of Heaven, 138, 139
Queen of Sheba, 117, 118–120

Rachel, 46, 60, 62, 70, 95, 98, 103, 105, 106, 107, 110
Rape, 50–54, 61–62, 72, 73, 200
Rationalism, 172
Reactive depression, 159, 190
Reality testing, 187
Rebekkah, 45–46, 80–81, 83–89, 124–125, 126, 128, 129, 198
Rebellious female, 136–137
Rehoboam, 31–32, 115
Religion, 168
Renaissance, 12
Repression, 66, 169, 185
Reuben, 14, 81–82, 84, 91, 94, 98, 194, 197
Revenge, 156
Rivalry of siblings, 78–82, 85–87, 93–94, 96, 103, 197
Roles
  female, assertive, 133–139
  female, negative, 123–133, 198
  male and female, 116–122, 198
Ruth, book of, 36
Ruth, the Maobite, 36, 61, 142

Samson, 46, 113, 126, 128, 155–156, 162
Samuel, book of, 28, 47, 98, 115, 120, 149, 151, 177–178, 182

Samuel, the prophet, 13, 17, 42, 92, 115–116, 120, 131, 144, 162, 182
Sarah (Sarai), 16
  birth of child, 13, 28, 36
  childlessness, 89, 98, 103, 105, 106, 108, 110
  death of, 42, 46, 62
  male and female roles, 123
  wife of Abraham, 62, 77, 78, 178
Saul, king, 42, 92, 115–116, 120, 131, 133–136, 144, 145, 149–152, 156–157, 159, 177–178, 182–183, 184, 189, 200, 201
Schechem and Dinah, 51–52
Seers, 168, 183
Self-control, 22–23, 90, 160, 161
  denial, 163
  destruction, 154
  expansion, 140
  observation, 29
  protection, 140
Senescence, 10, 13, 24, 25, 27–28, 44
Sensory activity, 36
  deficit, 28–29
Sex differences, 142–143
Sexuality, 75, 199
  gratification, 68, 69
  subversion, 142
Shame, 152
Sheol (underworld), 41
Sibling rivalry, 78–82, 85–87, 93–94, 96, 103, 197
Simon, 197
Sisera, 124, 128, 130
Social science, 19
Socialization, 22, 86
Sodom and Gommorah, 53, 59, 72, 73
Solomon, king, 21, 31–32, 50, 56, 115–116, 118–119, 121, 138, 194
Song of Songs, book of, 1, 48, 75, 123, 142, 199
Stream of consciousness, 180, 188
Stress reduction, 109
Suicide, 152–160, 191
Supernaturalism, 20, 187, 189, 192
Surrogate wives, 104–110

Symbolism, 4, 169, 171, 172, 192, 202
Syncretism, 55

Talmud, 69
Tamar, 52–54, 55–56, 60–62, 142
Tanakh (Hebrew Bible), 47, 78
Ten Commandments, 5, 8, 10, 91, 113, 155
Theophany, 178
Thought, 145
    primary process, 179–180, 184
    secondary process, 179–180, 183, 184
Tillich, 48
Time binding, 38
Tolerance of deviance, 64
Torah VII, 1, 47, 185
Traits, diversity, 85
Trajectories, 78, 85, 197
Transformation, 183
Traumatic events, 146, 159–160

Ubiquity of subversion, 194
Ultimogeniture, 88–89, 90, 92, 95, 197
Unconscious, 169, 184, 185
Unconventionality, 186
Underdogs, 94, 96
Uriah the Hittite, 49–50

Values of children, for parents, 101–102
Vashiti, the queen, 136–137, 160
Vision(s), 148, 178, 180, 181

Weaning, 12–13, 15–16
Weltanshuang, 166
Western society, 62–63, 64–66, 74, 99–100, 103, 137, 163, 172
Wine, 53, 59, 160–163, 190–191
Wisdom, 1, 20–21, 23, 30–35, 37, 44, 115, 118–119, 165–166
Withdrawal, schizophrenic, 69

Women
    adulthood, 23–24
    aging of, 36–37
    arranged marriages, 45
    child bearing, 20, 70
    childlessness, 19, 46, 47, 97, 98–99, 104–111, 135
    incest, 58–66
    lesbianism, 70, 71, 72
    masturbation, 67
    Menopause, 36–37
    multidimensionality of, 33, 133
    prostitution, 54–57, 75
    rape, 50–54, 61–62, 72, 73
    roles of, 116–122, 123–139, 198
    surrogate wives, 104–110
Work of mourning, 42

Yael, 124, 126, 128, 140, 198
Yalda (child f.), 14, 20
Yeled (child m.), 14, 20
YHWH, Jehova VIII, 138
    children, 96, 103, 111
    communication from, 177
    death, 35, 41
    evil spirits, 149
    faith in the order of life, 40
    Garden of Eden, 124
    Holy Ark, 134
    idol worship, 56, 57, 75, 91–92, 146, 153
    incest, 63
    Levatribe, 24
    male vs. female prophets, 117
    Moses, 91
    prophets, 131
    punishment, 41, 146, 166, 189
    Sarah giving birth, 36

Zacharia, 160
Zilboorg, Gregory, 144
Zimri's rebellion, 158, 159, 190
"Zona" (harlot), 54